nick nairn
cook school

Over 120 delicious recipes and 40 professional techniques
from the Nick Nairn Cook School

photography by
Francesca Yorke

CASSELL
ILLUSTRATED

nick nairn
cook school

Over 120 delicious recipes and 40 professional techniques
from the Nick Nairn Cook School

This book is dedicated to the staff
and most importantly the customers
at the Nick Nairn Cook School.

All photography by © Octopus Publishing Group Limited/
Francesca Yorke, except for the following:

Pages 10, 69, 80-81, 82 (left), 84-85, 90, 96-97, 112-113, 114,
116, 288 (left) © Nick Nairn Cook School/ Stephen Kearney

First published in Great Britain in 2008 by Cassell,
a division of Octopus Publishing Group Ltd,
2–4 Heron Quays, London E14 4JP

A CIP catalogue record for this book is available
from the British Library.

ISBN-13: 978-1-844-03581-6

Designer: Grade Design Consultants Ltd
Photographer: Francesca Yorke
Commissioning Editor: Laura Price
Editor: Joanne Wilson
Production: Caroline Alberti
Publisher: Iain MacGregor

Printed and bound in China

10 9 8 7 6 5 4 3 2

contents

contents

introduction

I set up the Nick Nairn Cook School in April 2000 with one very simple aim: to give ordinary people the skills necessary to be able to turn raw ingredients into great food.

The idea had been in my head for about 15 years, ever since I began teaching classes in the small, sweaty kitchen of my first restaurant, Braeval. But having a good idea and turning it into a reality are two very different things, and what I needed was a catalyst to turn my vision into something solid. In the end, I got two: the availability of premises – an old piggery on my family's estate – and the opportunity to work with wonder-chef John Webber.

John and I come from vastly different culinary backgrounds, but what we had in common was a real passion for food and a desire to share that passion with the wider world. Neither of us knew exactly how to set about it and when the school first opened, everything was done on a very small scale. But even with only a few hundred customers, the results were astounding and we soon learnt that even the most unpromising toast-burners nurtured a hidden foodie passion.

That fact was a great comfort, as for many years I'd been noting with concern our society's shift away from the experiences offered by 'real food'. Issues of seasonality, regionality and freshness all seemed to have been subsumed by a desire instead for 365-day availability, and an ever-advancing tide of ready meals and convenience foods. To me it seemed we no longer had knowledge of where our food was coming from, nor the requisite skills to prepare it.

It's a far cry from the days when cooking skills were passed on from generation to generation, and the result, I think, has been disempowerment. Our lack of culinary ability means that big food and drink companies now take care of how our meals are prepared, and unlike our parents and grandparents, they don't always have our best interests at heart. Relying heavily on this processed food means that not only does our diet suffer and obesity rates soar – with all the associated illnesses you might expect – but we also start to lose the huge benefits that come with communal cooking and social eating. People also become so tied into the 'fast food', non-cook lifestyle that they actually believe themselves incapable of creating meals from scratch. It's something we hear time and time again at the School: I'm sorry, I can't cook.

You know what, you can cook! All budding chefs really need is encouragement, a few skills, and some basic knowledge, and at the Nick Nairn Cook School, this was something we could offer. We created a warm, friendly environment where like-minded people could come together and share a fantastic experience of food, a little wine, and a lot of fun and start to re-awaken their inner cook. The same toast burners who came in believing they couldn't cook were soon walking out the kitchen with a plate piled

high with their delicious creations, and grinning from ear to ear at their achievement.

The question was: once we had these people fired up to cook, how could we physically teach them? We couldn't treat them like chefs. Chefs learn to cook by repetition; a combination of constant observation and trial and error. They quickly develop an instinctive style of cooking that necessitates making continual small changes to the elements affecting the outcome of the dish. It becomes second nature, as does using their senses to help deliver perfect results. For example, when cooking a piece of meat, a chef will listen to the sizzle in a pan, smell the degree of caramelisation, see the colour developing and feel tension in the meat grow as it cooks and go as it relaxes. We had to tell people about this.

Learning how to get that instinctive, sensory, years-of-knowledge thing across was daunting. We had to adopt a non-intimidating, non-threatening approach and develop a language that would allow people to understand the complex nature of good cooking without being terrified by what was involved!

As we grappled with these big questions, the school continued to grow. Soon, our few hundred customers became a few thousand and John and I were joined in the kitchen by the omniscient Alan Mathieson. Together, we continued to gather a unique insight into what the cooking public needs to know in order to make cooking at home a success, and we also began to find a teaching style that really seemed to work.

A pinch of this and a handful of that was no longer sufficiently accurate. We learned to weigh, measure, time and check the temperatures of every single one of our dishes in order to explain exactly how to recreate them. After all, if we didn't totally understand a dish, how could we possibly teach anybody to prepare it? So, out came the scales, the measuring jug and the thermometer. We started a logbook to record the critical stages in every dish, and as we taught, we allowed our pupils to teach us what they really needed to know.

That in-depth, seven-year process has brought us here: the *Nick Nairn Cook School Book*. It's been a joy teaching the 20,000-plus eager students who've passed through our doors since 2000, a real pleasure watching as individuals experience those dawning moments of culinary realisation and clarity. But now it's time to write it all down and pass it on to an even wider audience.

We hope that what we're offering you is an insight into our combined knowledge, an easily accessible, and hopefully enjoyable learning tool that will help you to prepare the type of food you've always wanted to know how to cook. We'll show you how to avoid mistakes, steer you through the critical points of each recipe, advise you on produce, and give you an understanding of the basic techniques that you need to know when you step into a kitchen.

For us, this has been a long, difficult but rewarding journey. For you, the journey towards culinary empowerment may be just beginning.

Nick Nairn

the cook school chefs

Nick Nairn

Nick says: *'Good cooking comes from knowledge, experience and confidence. But everybody has to start somewhere, so just go for it, and I promise that you'll surprise yourself. Once you've mastered the basics, it's vital to move out of your comfort zone of familiar dishes if you're going to continue to improve. We can all cook – it's not rocket science – and yes, that means you!'*

Nick first discovered a love of food while travelling the world with the Merchant Navy, but it wasn't until his student days that he taught himself how to cook. In 1986, he opened his first restaurant, Braeval, through which he won his first Michelin Star, and in 1997, he opened Nairns restaurant in Glasgow. By this time he'd also begun a successful television career with appearances on the BBC's *Ready Steady Cook*, and his own series, *Wild Harvest*, *Wild Harvest 2* and *Island Harvest*. Further shows included *Nick Nairn and the Dinner Ladies*, and a winning appearance on *Great British Menu*, which resulted in him cooking lunch for The Queen on her 80th birthday. He also presents the rural affairs programme, *Landward*, for BBC Scotland. Nick part-owns his own catering company, Nairns Anywhere, and is the author of 11 books (including this one!). In 2007, he was awarded an honorary doctorate in recognition of his outstanding contribution to Scottish cuisine and his work in promoting healthy eating. He's married to Holly and has two children.

John Webber

John says: *'There is a saying that luck is when preparation meets opportunity. That's also a perfect description of cooking. Good cooking is 50% preparation and 50% taking advantage of the opportunities presented while you cook.'*

As the school's head tutor, John Webber is much loved by fellow chefs and pupils alike. Trained at the Dorchester in London under Anton Mosimann, John's four decades in the catering industry mean his culinary knowledge is second to none. His career has taken him from Gidleigh Park in Devon, where he won his first Michelin Star, to Perthshire's Kinnaird Country House, where he won a second. He's taught at the Cook School since it opened in 2000, and his eternal patience, amiable personality and great sense of humour have all helped to keep the wheels turning smoothly. John is married to Caroline, who also works at the school, and has three children.

Alan Mathieson

Alan says: *'Cook with passion and don't be afraid to experiment. Some of the best dishes are ones that have come from mistakes.'*

Alan, our senior tutor, is a dynamic chef who's worked in some of the finest kitchens in Britain. His distinguished career has included the position of head chef at Edinburgh's Atrium and on the Royal Scotsman train, as well as sous chef at Greywalls. He's also spent time in the States working for Charlie Trotter's, Wolfgang Puck and Michael Mina. Alan worked under John for almost 3 years at Kinnaird House, and this kick-started the unique relationship that's still very much evident in the classroom today. He also worked previously for Nick at Nairns Executive Dining. Alan joined the school early in 2004 and is a hugely popular tutor with visitors. He set up and developed our smoked salmon business, which he continues to run, and works extensively on recipe and menu development. Alan lives with his partner, Joanne, and has two children.

opposite, from left to right Alan, John and Nick

produce, technique and harmony

Here at the Nick Nairn Cook School our philosophy for creating great food is based on three fundamental elements: produce, technique and harmony, or as we refer to them, PTH. Whether you're making a five-course gourmet meal or a cheese sandwich, these are the areas you need to focus on, as each will dramatically affect the outcome of your cooking.

P (produce)

Let's start with the most important of the three, and unsurprisingly it's produce. I know what you're thinking: yawn, yawn, another chef piping on about 'fresh seasonal produce'! But for me, produce really is king, and the single most important part of the journey towards creating great food. If you start out with fabulous raw materials then there is a real chance that you'll be able to create something tasty and memorable. Try to cook with produce that's sub-standard, and the results are never going to be spectacular.

The first step is allowing yourself to be inspired. This might happen in your fishmongers, it might happen at the butchers, it might even happen on your weekly trip to the supermarket. But wherever you're shopping, look for the best produce and allow this to influence what you're going to cook. It might be tempting to choose your recipes after looking at the enticingly glossy pictures in magazines and cook books. But when you do that, it's easy get a fixed idea in your head of what

you're going to create, say turbot with shrimp cream, and become blinkered to all the other produce available. That beautiful image of the finished dish leads you to walk past fantastic herring and spanking-fresh mackerel, because for you, only turbot will do, even if it's been hanging around the fishmonger's slab for a few days.

Try to turn things around in your head: buy first then decide what dish you're going to make. There are hundreds of fish recipes in the world, and if you can get something really fresh like mackerel, bake it, roast it or fry it, and it'll be head and fins above that old bit of turbot. Adapt to what's available and seasonal rather than shopping with fixed ideas, and if you can put 25% of your effort for a dish into finding the right produce first, then you won't go far wrong.

When we talk about quality produce, what should you be looking for? We'll take you through the important pointers in subsequent pages so I'm not going to generalise too much here. But there are a few basics to watch out for and the first is seasonality. Most fresh produce has a season, a

time when, due to growing conditions or weather conditions or breeding conditions, it's at its best. Take asparagus, for example. In Britain, it's in season in June and July and when you get it fresh at this time of the year all you need to do is boil it, partner it with some good butter and it will taste incredible. In other months it's going to be imported from somewhere like Peru and will lack that elusive fine flavour that makes it so prized. Or look at mussels, available all year round, but really only at their best in the colder winter months when they're not spawning; they're often flabby and tasteless in the summer.

Another basic thing to consider is where your food has come from. Good quality produce will be selected, handled and cared for with skill. That skill takes effort, time and expense, all of which usually translates into a higher price for the consumer. So yes, expect to pay a bit more for great food. But we should be paying more for our food! In the 1950s, the average UK household was spending about a third of its income on food. Now it's closer to 10%. Be prepared to spend a bit more on better produce, and you should find it's well worth it.

T (technique)

Now we understand the importance of good produce, let's look at technique, because it's not enough to buy fabulous raw materials, you also have to cook them properly to get the best results. After all, there's no point in buying a really fresh piece of fish and then baking it to death. The fibres will shrink and squeeze out the juice so the fish ends up dry and tasteless. Likewise, you don't buy a piece of Aberdeen Angus beef fillet and then poach it or steam it for an hour or two, as you're not going to get the best flavour out of it. What you need to do is fry it or roast it, get a hot pan and caramelise it on the outside, get a nice crust on it, that's where the flavour is. Then you need to go through the process of relaxing the meat, as during the hot cooking process the fibres shrink and force all the juices to the centre. The meat has to be left in a warm place to allow the fibres to relax and the juices to re-distribute throughout until it's tender and succulent and flavoursome.

Important cooking techniques like this aren't complicated, and in fact, the simplest things in the kitchen, like adjusting the heat of a pan, can make a huge difference to the outcome of every dish. For example, how do you chop an onion so that all the pieces are the same size? Should you allow your vegetables to sweat or caramelise? How do you stir a risotto? What's the best and quickest way to whisk egg whites? These are the basics that will revolutionise the way you cook, but which most cook books won't teach you. We will. These techniques may slow you down at first, but once you've mastered them you'll cook with more confidence and achieve far better results.

H (harmony)

The third thing to consider is harmony. Take any plate of food, either in a restaurant, or on your own dinner table and ask yourself why everything is there. Does it all have a purpose and bring something to the party? Can it put its hand up and say: I'm here because I provide the protein; I'm here because I provide the balancing carbohydrate; I'm here because I provide some nice vegetable flavour and texture; I'm here because I provide the sauce that gives the dish succulence, and surrounds it with interest and subtlety and complexity. What you don't want is something that's there because it looks pretty; like a physalis dipped in caramel that's expensive and time-consuming to produce; or trendy, like a foam that's badly made and adds nothing to the dish. Everything on a plate should be justified and there for a reason, and if that can happen, then the whole becomes greater than the sum of its parts and a little bit of magic creeps into the dish.

Some ingredients have a natural harmony and want to be together on a plate, like tomato and basil, lime and coriander, vanilla and cream or lamb and rosemary. On the other hand, there are some combinations you should always stay clear of, like chocolate and red wine, or fish and mint. There is an absolute elegance in simplicity and some of the best dishes I've ever eaten have definitely been the simplest. I once tasted a mango that had fallen from its tree just at the perfect point of ripeness, and was still hot from the sun. Eaten there and then, the intense, musky flavour was a revelation, and a million miles away from something picked under-ripe and shipped halfway across the world. I've been lucky enough to eat a piece of three-and-a-half-year-old parmesan broken off a wheel of cheese in a cellar in Bologna. At its peak of perfection, it had an incredible intensity of flavour and wonderfully gritty texture

that needed nothing to accompany it. These are the foods that stay in my head, not the complex 2 and 3 star Michelin dishes that I've eaten in some of the word's best restaurants. However elegant the ambience, it is the elegance of simple food that sizzles my bacon.

So challenge yourself: find great produce, cook it properly, and combine it with what it gets on with so that the flavours and textures compliment and enhance each other. I can't lie, doing all this will take more effort than a weekly supermarket shop but I know that this book can provide you with all the basics you need to make creating great food much easier. We'll talk you through sourcing the best ingredients and then advise you all the best ways to cook them, as well as providing you with some great recipes to try out.

Give this philosophy of produce, technique and harmony a go, even just for one meal, and your culinary world will begin to change forever. A bit of an audacious statement, but I know the 20,000 plus who've spent time at the school can't be wrong.

produce

meat

I love good meat, and I mean really love! For me, a great piece of barbecued beef gets me pretty close to my culinary Nirvana. And I'm not the only one with this passion. Demand for meat has shot up around the world since the 1950s, an appetite influenced by our growing affluence and the ready-availability of a product that provides us with a wonderfully tasty source of protein.

The big issue with all this demand, however, is that it increases pressure on farmers to up their supply. As they cut costs, so the process becomes intensified, and more animals end up on that unfortunate conveyor belt of factory farming, producing meat that's certainly cheap, but also tough and, let's face it, pretty tasteless. The good news is that there's still top-quality meat to be had – though you'll find that, as with all sectors of the food industry, the market has been split in three. At the top end, the prime motivator of production is quality, and you'll find happy, healthy beasts living a full life, facing a calm slaughter and undergoing a proper hanging and butchering process. In the middle, quality is balanced with cost, and the animals will undergo some sort of intensive process, living shorter lives, eating high-energy feeds and moving more quickly through the slaughter process. At the bottom end, cost is the only motivator, and you get into dark and rather disturbing areas of mechanically recovered meat, and imports from countries with potentially dodgy practices.

The vast majority of the meat we eat will have come from the middle sector, which can still produce something rather wonderful. But having said that, I'm going to assume that since you're reading this book, you're looking for quality, so let's concentrate on the best!

Beef

The best beef tends to come from native beasts, breeds like Highland, Luing, Aberdeen Angus, Shorthorn, Shetland and Galloway. Ideally, they'll be farmed 'extensively': eating grass and toughing it out through the winter months, with minimal time spent indoors on intensive, cereal-based diets, and enjoying the good husbandry of a decent and caring farmer. Maturing later than continental breeds, they'll go to slaughter at around 25–30 months, in a local small abattoir where they're not subject to stress (something that induces the release of adrenaline and spoils the meat). They'll be expertly butchered and hung for up to 28 days, allowing the meat to tenderise and develop a proper intense flavour.

It's a different shed of cows when cost comes into play and the process becomes more intensive. Intensive farming tends to use breeds like Belgian Blue, animals that are bred to be lean and have less of the marbling of fat that can be vital for proper flavour and succulence. Their feed, often grain and silage, complements a life spent partly indoors, and at around 14 months, they're potentially faced with having a stressed slaughter and being hot boned and vacuum-packed in plastic. I'm generalising here of course, and meat from this process can actually be of a decent standard, but it can also be poor and disappointing. So what makes the difference?

The most important factor in producing great meat is simply a matter of good farming practice. If the farmer is cutting corners, the end product will never be something memorable. But factors such as the land, climate, feed, transport and herd size can all affect the quality. I used to judge steaks at the Royal Highland Show in Edinburgh, and generally you would expect the winning steak to have come from a native beast raised under all the best conditions. But at least one year, the winning steak came from a big Belgian Blue. So it's hard even for the experts to predict what will make a perfect piece of meat!

That's why it's so important to rely on the knowledge and skill of a really good butcher. A proper 'family' butcher should be able to tell you exactly what breed you're eating, where it's come from, where it was slaughtered and how long it was aged. But don't go in expecting to have this conversation on a Saturday lunchtime. If there are a dozen people behind you trying to buy sausages, your chances of

having a long and engaging discussion are slim. Go when it's quiet, introduce yourself and tell him or her why you are there and what you're wanting to buy. Also think about ordering your meat in advance, giving them time to get in what you're looking for. If they're a decent butcher, they'll be more than happy to help. If it helps, tell 'em I sent you! (Better still, if you get the chance, talk directly to a farmer selling his product at a farmer's market and hear it all straight from the horse's mouth.)

One of the contentious issues among butchers at the moment is that of vacuum packing and 'wet-ageing'. Butchers like to 'vac-pack' their meat because it's convenient. It makes the meat easier to transport and cuts down cross contamination and the need for expensive chillers. I prefer dry-aged meat, which has undergone proper evaporation and an enzymic reaction, allowing for the development of flavour and texture. Try both to see which you prefer.

Once you've sourced high quality beef, the next thing to consider is the cut. All meat is muscle, and in general, the less work it does, the more tender the meat. Lazy muscles are best for dry cooking; frying or stir frying: sirloin, fillet, rib eye, popes eye (or rump); or roasting: rib, sirloin, wing rib or the cheaper topside. Active muscles contain more connective tissue, fat and tough fibres, creating braising cuts: blade, brisket, flank (or round steak), shoulder, chuck and shin. These are more suitable for long, slow wet cooking, like stews and casseroles.

If you're forking out on top quality beef, the big advantage will be flavour. Well raised, properly hung meat will cost more, but the cheaper cuts from such an animal will knock the socks off a bog-standard sirloin or fillet and personally, I'd much rather have a cheaper cut from a good carcass than a pricey fillet from a three-legged donkey!

Lamb

In theory, you could let a flock of sheep out onto the hills and leave them to it. Cows need care and attention. Sheep can more or less take care of themselves. So the process by which lamb is produced is generally much less intensive and is, barring the odd dip and injection, practically organic.

Good lamb is a fabulous meat: sweet, tender and succulent, but as with cattle, traditional sheep breeds tend to produce the best results for flavour, and my favourites are the Scottish black face and black face crosses, which are hill sheep. Some people prefer bigger pastoral grazers like the Suffolk and Cheviot-Suffolk crosses, which are usually very tender, but I don't think it has the same depth of flavour. What I'm also not a big fan of is the large quantity of imports that make their way into this country, mostly from New Zealand. To me, it's just unnecessary food miles, though I do grudgingly admit that some of it provides good eating.

Spring lamb is an ever popular meat, but it's usually produced by a process that results in something very tender, but I often find it to be bland. For me, spring lamb should be a lamb born in the spring and eaten in the autumn. Even better is hogget, a lamb that's seen out a winter. Mutton, a sheep over two years but best at four, is tougher, but packed full of flavour. A long slow-cooked leg is particularly fine.

When choosing a cut, the sirloin, usually called loin, is sold on and off the bone as a chop, rack, crown or 'French-trimmed' which is the eye of the meat trimmed of all fat. But the leg is probably the finest cut, certainly it's the most popular. Individual muscles from the leg can also be boned out to make a prime roasting cut that chefs call chump. The shanks, shoulder and neck are all perfect for braising. With lamb and mutton, the older the animal at slaughter, the longer you hang the meat. Spring lamb usually hangs for up to 7 days, autumn lamb, hogget and mutton, anything up to 14 days.

Pork

I have to admit, my favourite pork eating comes from processed meat: bacon, pancetta, Parma ham and sausages. But a really good piece of roast pork and crackling also wows, and braised pork belly… now you're talking! (see page 154). In my experience really good pork comes from pigs that have had a bit of decent husbandry, access to nice pasture and good organic feed. Sadly, the majority of our pork comes from pigs that are intensively reared, and the quality of the meat isn't as good as it could be. Again, rely on your butcher to advise you on what's best to buy. Pork belly is packed full of proper, porky flavour. It's a fatty cut so needs proper, long, slow cooking. Other fatty, but flavoursome cuts include neck-end and shoulder, while the leaner (more expensive) cuts are loin, leg, chump, chops and ribs.

For bacon lovers, there are mouth-watering varieties to be found at the top end of the market, the best are dry-cured or traditionally cured, like Ayrshire. Farmers who go to the trouble of rearing traditional and rare breed pigs, like Gloucester Old Spots and Tamworth, also produce very tasty bacon. However, at the lower end of the market, the cheap mass-market stuff is injected with a brine solution that plumps it out and contains preservatives and flavour enhancers. Stick it in a hot pan and all the water oozes out as a milky muck, reducing the pan temperature and causing the meat to braise rather than fry, making it impossible to caramelise properly.

Italian bacon, or pancetta, which is salt-cured and air-dried, is great stuff, and you should be able to find it as lardons or cubetti di pancetta in the supermarket. These 'wee bits of bacon' are a fridge essential and also freeze particularly well.

As for sausages, I don't think there's anything else in the food world that exists in such polarity. At one end they're a perfect balance of hand cut meat and fat, stuffed in natural casings. At the other they're little better than meat slurry. I love good, high quality sausages, though I'll always check the salt content, it shouldn't really be over 1%. My favourite banger has a bit of bacon in it and Tesco do a good one in their Finest range. Puddledub farm in Fife also do a wonderful selection of tasty sausages, as does Peelham Farm in the Borders. See the suppliers list on p288 for more details.

fish

There are few things as brilliant as a well cooked piece of spanking fresh fish. Really fresh fish has a wonderful pronounced flavour, which unfortunately starts to recede very quickly. So the most important thing to look for with fish is that it's fresh, fresh, fresh! A fish caught less than 48 hours before you buy it will offer great eating potential regardless of what species it is. Fish that's been lingering in ice and polystyrene for several days will simply have lost the potential to deliver a memorable eating experience. But how do you tell what's fresh and what's fit for the cat?

Buying whole fish makes this easier – get your fishmonger to fillet it for you, or learn to fillet it at home (see page 72) – and look for the following signs:

Smell The definitive sign of freshness! Don't be embarrassed to stick your hooter in and give the fish a really good sniff. It's the best way of judging quality. What you're looking for is a clean, iodine smell, like the sea or a fresh sea breeze. If the fish actually smells fishy, then it's on its way out.

Eyes They should be bright and pronounced.

Gills As a fish ages, the blood in the gills begins to oxidize and go brown. Fresh fish will have nice, pink or red gills. However, if the gills are nice and pink, but the eyes are shrunken and look burst, then the fish may have been frozen.

Slime A slimy fish is a really fresh fish, as the slime only clings to the body for a couple of days.

Firmness Firm fish is a good thing. Avoid anything soggy or soft.

However, finding fish this fresh isn't always easy. Good fishmongers are few and far between these days, and the quality of supermarket fish tends to be patchy – unless you're shopping for farmed salmon, smoked fish or bags of mussels – although they can surprise you (Waitrose is your best bet, and I recently had some fab fresh tuna from Sainsbury's). Try figuring out your supermarket's delivery days for fresh fish, or another option is to look on the internet for good mail order companies (see suppliers p288) that will deliver direct to your door. Otherwise be prepared to put a bit of effort into finding a fishmonger who really knows his

stuff. Give them regular custom, talk to them about their fish, and like your butcher, give them a bit of notice if you're looking for something special. They should be happy to tell you what's in every day, and walking out with something you know is really fresh is always more satisfying, and ultimately more rewarding, than coming out with something expensive that's of questionable age.

While freshness should always be your number one consideration when shopping for fish, you might also spare a thought for conservation. Several of our most popular species are already on the slippery slope to oblivion and protecting the surviving stocks is the best way to ensure continued supplies for the future. Lists of what we should be avoiding seem to change weekly, but some reports suggest that the following may be in danger: Atlantic cod, dogfish, some haddock, halibut, ling, monkfish, wild salmon, wild turbot, bluefin tuna and tusk.

Again, talk to your fishmonger about the issue and see what they suggest, but remember there are always plenty more species of fish in the sea! Try out less common species not on the endangered list or look into buying farmed and line-caught fish.

Farmed fish

In the face of depleted stocks, fish farming could be a great solution for long-term sustainability. The most commonly farmed fish in Scotland is salmon, and at its best, it's a fantastic product with an excellent global reputation. As with all produce, however, the best quality tends to be at the higher end of the market and at its worst, the quality of farmed salmon can suffer from problems caused by poor husbandry, particularly over-stocking and high-energy diets. The issue for consumers is that there are few marks of quality to point you in the right direction so it can be hard to know what to buy. The good news is that farmed salmon is something that even supermarkets do well, so with a few pointers, you should be able to pick up something quite delicious.

Look for a nice pale pink fillet that's not too glow-in-the-dark. Don't be put off by the very pale flesh of some organic salmon – which don't have chemical dyes added to their food – though the very best will have a natural pinky hue due to a high percentage of shellfish meal in their feed. Look also for a texture that's quite tight and not gaping. The white lines you'll see are fat lines, and you don't want these to be too thick or prominent as it makes the fish taste fatty. In general, organic methods tend to produce salmon with a superior flavour and texture and importantly, do it in a sustainable manner, so organic salmon would always be my first choice.

Other farmed species to look for are cod, turbot and halibut, which are all relative newcomers to the market but have seen some early success. Aquaculture is still a science in its infancy, but I personally believe it has great potential so long as its driving force is quality rather than the cost of production.

Smoked fish

Salmon is the ultimate fish for smoking, and you'll find both hot-smoked and cold-smoked salmon on the market. Cold smoking preserves the fish and the resulting texture is firm and slightly chewy. Hot smoking preserves and cooks it through, resulting in a flaky texture, and both varieties can be utterly delicious. Alan prepares our own smoked salmon at the Cook School, cold-smoking it at a low temperature using smoke generated by wood chips from whisky barrels for a result that is quite unlike anything you'll find in the shops (though it is available online, see p286 for details). Smoked salmon is a great example of what once was a great delicacy, but has now been commercialised and industrialised into little more than a sandwich filling. When you source impeccable raw materials and subject them to proper artisan craft skills, you've got a product fit for a king or queen, or even an indulgent foodie!

Another chap who's pursuing the time-honoured skill of smoking is Iain Spink, and you might be lucky enough to run across him and his barrel at an agricultural show. He hot smokes haddock to produce a classic Arbroath smokie, and serves them warm and fresh. One of life's great treats! Also look out for cold-smoked haddock, the best being the fabled Finnan haddie, but avoid the dyed glow-in-the-dark stuff; it's a mystery to me why this is still being sold, or indeed why anyone would choose to buy it over un-dyed.

Storing fish

Try to eat fish as soon as possible after purchase, as there's no point in buying it fresh and then leaving it to linger in the fridge for two days! If you have to store it, place in a covered container in the coldest part of your fridge, usually the bottom shelf.

I don't recommend freezing fish at home, as the freezing process damages the delicate flesh and makes the fish soggy (for more, see page 42). If you have to freeze fish, go for the IQF (individually quick frozen) method. Have the fish whole or in thick fillets, wrap individually in cling film, and freeze, preferably in the quick freeze drawer if you have one. Defrost overnight in the fridge on a piece of kitchen towel to absorb any liquid.

shellfish

Shellfish are one of nature's greatest gifts to us, and I love just about anything that comes in a shell. We have a great range of inspiring shellfish recipes on our classes at the school: from Alan's lobster Thermidor, to my scallops served with pancetta and butter sauce. Preparing shellfish is a great thing to teach as it forces people to get their hands messy, and when our budding cooks face up to the challenge of dealing with something like a lobster, they really begin to connect with what they're eating. Some do feel squeamish at the idea of dispatching their own dinner, but my advice is: stay focused on the mouth-watering rewards that await!

The key to sweet, succulent shellfish is ensuring that what you're going to prepare is alive right up to the moment you cook it. All shellfish will deteriorate rapidly once dead, and crustaceans in particular, like lobsters and langoustine, contain digestive enzymes that quickly leak out into their bodies after they're killed, breaking down the flesh until it becomes soft and inedible.

Luckily, your nose should keep you right, and as with finfish, don't be afraid to stick your hooter in and give your shellfish a really good sniff. When fresh they'll smell of a sea breeze and seaweed. Any whiff of ammonia or fishiness, don't touch them with a barge poll.

Shellfish are seasonal, and although most are available all year round you'll find lobsters to be at their very best in the summer and scallops and mussels in the colder winter months, while langoustines reach a peak in the spring.

Lobster

The most famous crustacean is without doubt the lobster. You'll find two types on the market: the greeny-coloured American and the dark blue European. Both will turn that classic red/pink colour only after cooking. I'd always go for European over American, and in my opinion, they have to be Scottish. They can be expensive, but are definitely well worth it. When choosing a lobster, try to avoid anything that's been sitting around in a tank for a long time. You want it as fresh out the sea as possible, and lively. Also be suspicious of a lobster that's shiny and lacking barnacles, as it may have recently shed its shell

and will be light on meat. Pick it up, it should feel heavy. Females tend to have more meat for their size, and can usually be identified by their broader backs. Optimum size is around 600g, with anything over that tending to be a bit stringy and best suited for making a mousseline.

Brown crab

I'd be hard pressed to choose between crab and lobster, as crab is every bit as sweet and tasty, and has the added advantage of being kinder on the wallet. If you can get it, Scottish brown crabs are superb, though I have to confess that the Cornish variety is often bigger and therefore yields more meat. Big is beautiful here and you particularly want one with good-sized claws, though 2.5 kg/5 lb 8 oz is the maximum overall weight I'd go for. There are two types of meat in a crab, white and brown and while some people only eat the white, mainly from the claws, I find the brown meat to be delicious and often mix it in with the white for a more intense crabby flavour. Although fresh is best, crabs can be tricky customers to deal with at home so you can substitute picked crabmeat from a reliable fishmonger instead. If you ever happen to be on the Isle of Skye, look up Rick Simons at Loch Bracadale Crabs for some of the finest crabmeat around. And if you're catching a ferry to Portavadie in Tarbert, pop into Prentice Seafoods which sits right beside the port. They sell a big selection of fresh seafood as well as their fabulous crab (see also p286).

Langoustine

My favourite crustacean of them all is the langoustine, or Dublin Bay prawn. Look for creel-caught langoustines which tend to be better handled than trawled langoustines, and are more likely to reach you in good condition. Langoustine are very susceptible to temperature changes, and are often aggressive as they're being transported, so they should really come in tubes or have their claws banded to prevent them killing each other. They also need to be kept in a stable cold and humid environment, but even under ideal conditions, they'll only remain alive for about 24 hours out the water, after which time that old digestive enzyme thing kicks in, and the flesh starts to break down. You should be able to tell if they're on their way out, as they change colour from a lovely translucent orange to a dull yellow. The secret is to buy them lively and get them into the kitchen and cooked as fast as possible. To enjoy the meat at its best, try to cook and eat without any refrigeration in the middle, (this goes for lobster as well). Possibly the best way to do this is to blanch them in boiling water for 1½ minutes, cool at room temperature, serve with a big bowl of mayonnaise, and let people get stuck in. This is a personal favourite of mine as a starter for dinner parties; it's a great way to break the ice! You should also remember to try the wonderfully sweet claw meat, fiddly to get at, but well worth the effort.

Shrimps

I'm not a massive fan of farmed hot-water prawns; but the North Atlantic ones are best if you must. I would recommend buying brown shrimps instead; essential for a good shrimp cocktail. The best come from Morecambe Bay where they're traditionally netted before being cooked and peeled – often by hand. They're a fantastic, old-fashioned product available all year round with an intense, shellfish flavour. They store well in the fridge. They also freeze extremely well. We get ours from Griggs of Hythe (see suppliers p288).

Mussels

Mussels are extremely good value for money, and easy to get hold of from any decent fishmonger, or even at the supermarket. Most of our mussels are now farmed in sea lochs, though to be honest the word 'farm' is a bit of misnomer, as they're really just given a place to live. There's very little human involvement in the process and the mussels seed and feed themselves naturally. Mussel farming delivers a consistently reliable, high-quality product, and has done a lot in recent years to break the connection between mussels and bad tums. My personal favourite at the moment are mussels from Loch Etive, though Shetland mussels are also very good. Collected estuary mussels are said to be superior in flavour, but the fattest specimens are often found near sewage outfalls, with the obvious health risks that suggests! Your nose will tell you whether your mussels are fresh (any fishy pong, chuck them out) but you should also tap any with open shells, either on the work top or with the back of a knife, and discard those that don't start to close up. A little-known fact is that the bright orange-fleshed mussels are female and actually taste better than their male counterparts, though sexing them before you buy isn't usually an option!

Scallops

Always look for hand-caught scallops, which will have been individually selected and picked off the sea bed by skilled divers. They're expensive because of the effort and risks involved, but well worth it. Other scallops will be dredged, a process that can force sand and debris into the scallop shells, damaging them and sometimes suffocating the scallop inside. It also tends to ruin the sea bed and does little for our marine ecosystems. Hand-caught scallops are usually shucked straight away and then soaked in water – which they absorb like little sponges – before being sold by weight. They may look nice and plump when you buy them, but when you try to cook them they fart and squeak the water out into the pan like cheap bacon, making it very difficult to caramelise them properly. Look for King rather than Queen scallops (which are much smaller) and try shucking them yourself at home. It's such a useful skill to learn and our high success rate in classes at the school has convinced me that everyone should give it a go (see page 80 for more details). When it comes to freshness, trust your nose, and if they're open, give them a tap to make sure they start to close. But watch your fingers, scallops are surprisingly strong!

poultry

It's hard to beat a roast chicken dinner, but only if you're eating a top quality chicken. This is actually an area where the supermarkets can do rather well and organic chicken, particularly from Tesco in Scotland, is of excellent quality.

Chicken

A roast chicken dinner is one of life's great treats, and it's something my family and I enjoy every single week, summer or winter. Chicken is one of our most versatile meats, with uses stretching from salads to stir-fries and curries to casseroles. It's also a fantastic vehicle for carrying flavours, like in John's Spanish chicken (see page 152) or my chicken with tarragon and mushrooms (see page 156). But in my opinion, there's very little that can beat the simplicity of that succulent roast chicken dinner. Out of it you get a great meal, but you also get great left-overs, and a pot of top-quality stock, and all that from something that's very easy to get your hands on.

You can actually buy excellent chicken in most supermarkets now, with organic chicken meeting particularly high standards. Organic specifications can differ (for vigorous standards, look for a Soil Association mark) but the word 'organic' should mean that the birds have been allowed to roam freely outside, had a diet of organically-produced feed, and importantly, no unnecessary veterinary or chemical intervention in their development. Free range (look specifically for the words 'Traditional free range') chickens have also been allowed space to roam and access to the fresh air, and both free range and organic birds are given 81 days or more to mature, something that's vitally important to the final flavour of the meat. Further down the quality stakes and you're into the murky realms of the intensive or 'barn reared' chickens from which around 98% of our chicken meat comes. With short lives of around 56 days, and an inactive lifestyle spent inside cramped conditions, the resulting flesh can be watery and bland.

As you'd guess, free range and organic chickens are more expensive to rear, and so are more expensive to buy. But for me, it's worth every penny. If, however, you still find yourself reaching for that bog standard chicken in the supermarket, do this simple calculation. That standard whole chicken will probably cost you around £3, and out of it you'll get four portions at 75p each. Upgrade to a free range bird, and you're looking at about £8, but that's still only £2 a portion. Surely that's not too much to spend on a good meal (plus leftovers and tasty stock)?

When buying chicken, you should always consider getting a whole bird rather than the individual cuts – with the carcass used for stock or soup it's a more cost-effective way to purchase your meat.

produce

You can roast it whole – my personal favourite with its crisp skin and succulent meat – or learn how to remove the breasts, drumsticks, thighs and wings (see page 70). The boneless breasts remain the most popular cut, but don't overlook the possibilities of slow-cooked thighs and drumsticks, or the wings, roasted to perfection in a gloriously sticky sauce, and then served up to hungry guests at parties. The ultimate finger food!

Always be careful when handling chicken as the raw and undercooked meat does pose a risk of food poisoning from bacteria such as salmonella and campylobacter. Wash your hands well after touching the raw meat, and whatever you're preparing, make sure it's cooked all the way through (measure the core temperature with a thermometer – it needs to get to 80°C/175°F). Also be careful not to cross contaminate between the cooked and raw meat. If you're using frozen chicken, defrost thoroughly before cooking and don't re-freeze it without cooking it first.

Duck

You'll notice a big difference between wild duck like mallard or teal and the cultivated duck for sale, usually as breasts or legs, and most commonly from the large French Barbary duck. We'll look at cultivated here, look in the game section for our wild feathered friends. The breasts are very good for pan frying and roasting, once you've trimmed off the fat, and the legs are excellent for confit or slow braising. Another breed I seek out is the Gressingham, a hybrid of a wild and farmed duck.

It's leaner than the Barbary and smaller, and the meat is slightly chewier, though I think it has a better flavour. Again look for organic birds, which will have been given access to a lake or stream to swim in, something that isn't obligatory even for free-range ducks.

To joint a whole duck, follow the instructions for jointing a chicken on page 70, and make sure you keep the fat. Rendered down (see page 247) it'll take your roast potatoes into a whole new league!

game

If you're looking for top quality meat that's about as organic as it comes, then go for game. You just can't beat the tender texture and rich gamey flavours of a simply roasted pigeon breast, or the supremely flavoursome saddle of a roe deer that's lived out its days running wild in the woods.

These animals haven't been stressed or kept in concrete containers, and the only selective breeding they've endured is the natural process of survival of the fittest. Despite this, there is still resistance when it comes to eating game. Mention venison, and somebody is bound to mutter something about 'slaughtering Bambi'. But responsible deer management calls for regular culls. They're incredibly prolific animals, and if left unchecked the population would grow to unsustainable levels, destroying vegetation and leaving the deer starving and weak. Similarly, pigeons and rabbits are shot as pests, and there seems little point in all this wonderful, free-range meat going to waste.

However, farmed game is available, for those who prefer it; mainly venison. It's usually cheaper than the wild alternative and is a great product, healthy and tender with a mild flavour that makes it excellent as an introduction to game eating. My kids love farmed venison, as they find wild a little overpowering. As with all farming, the quality of your game will be down to the individual farmer. Wild game is seasonal, though there is usually something available all year round. See below for more details.

Venison

Wild venison will always be more 'gamey' than its farmed cousin, and it's a wonderfully lean meat best cooked quickly and without fuss. If you're lucky, you might see fallow, Sika or Muntjac for sale, but more commonly it will be red or roe.

Red deer venison tends to be stronger than roe, and is best from young animals as the meat from deer that have seen out a few winters – particularly stags – can be strong and off-putting. Roes are smaller and the meat is sweeter, though both red and roe can be superb. Scottish roe venison was given top billing when I won the chance to cook a roast loin for the Queen's 80th birthday luncheon at Banqueting House in London. Afterwards Her Majesty told me that she'd thoroughly enjoyed it, and Prince Philip was even more enthusiastic!

Expect some variation with wild venison, as you might get a young roe that's super tender or a big old red stag that's been rutting for years and will have tough meat flooded with hormones. Also be wary of anything that might be poached, as it's usually handled badly and may have been dragged off the hill behind a Land Rover. I've been lucky enough to take part in several days of deer stalking, the most memorable on the Isle of Rum, where the deer are taken off the hill on the backs of ponies.

When choosing a cut look for haunch or shoulder for braising and stewing meat (though a roe haunch can be fabulous when roasted) and the loin, also known as saddle, for a tender roasting or frying cut. Ask your butcher or game dealer for advice.

Wild duck

For wild duck, you're most likely to see my personal favourite, the mallard, and for maximum flavour, roast it whole on the bone. If you're boning it (see page 70 for chicken) the legs will be too teeny to do much with, so use the breasts, which are packed full of gamey flavour. The carcasses also make a great stock for game soup. You might also see teal and wigeon, which are both fabulous to use, but are small so give smaller portions. Wigeon is about the size of a pigeon and will yield a starter-size portion. For me, duck should always be served pink to preserve the maximum flavour and succulence.

Pigeon

A vastly under-appreciated meat, pigeon has no closed season, but it's best around sowing and harvest time (spring and autumn) when there's an abundance of grain. It's a lean meat, full of gamey flavour and the carcasses make wonderful stock. Pigeon is also very cheap, though I have noticed that it's becoming difficult to buy oven-ready and life just seems too short for plucking. Always look for pigeons that haven't been frozen and check to see if they've been blootered with shot. A quick inspection of the skin should reveal too much bruising or an excess of bullet holes. A young pigeon should look dry, pale and matt, with the older birds becoming dark and shiny. Most of the pigeon we eat will be wild wood pigeons, but occasionally you might find the pricey, plump pigeonneau, a farmed French bird that's very tasty, with great flavour and texture and no lead pellets.

Pheasant

Pheasant can be delicious, especially the breasts from a young bird, and like pigeon and duck, the carcasses make excellent stock. It's a cheap meat that's easy to get hold of, particularly towards the end of the season when it's a good time to buy half a dozen and stick them in your freezer. Many birds come from big shoots and are peppered with shot at close range, so be selective. Because it's low in fat, pheasant can also be dry, particularly if overcooked, and I always find the legs a bit tough as they're packed full of hard to remove tendons. The solution is to use the breast meat and cook carefully. Pheasant is great cooked with bacon and cream, which keep the meat succulent and moist.

Partridge

Similar to pheasant, but smaller, you'll need one per person. Partridge is a delicious meat, and well worth seeking out. We often have it on Christmas day as an alternative to turkey. The native grey partridge is pretty thin on the ground these days, so you're far more likely to see the French red-legged which is reared specifically for shoots.

Grouse

Red grouse is a terrific game bird, unique to the UK. Most people are familiar with the 'Glorious Twelfth' (August 12th) when the grouse season officially starts, but in my book, they're better eaten later in the year when the distinctive flavour has had a chance to develop. Grouse are best cooked simply, preferably roasted whole until nice and pink, then served with game gravy and a dollop of bread sauce.

Game seasons

This is not a list of shooting seasons but rather a guide to game at its best. Farmed game is available all year round, as is pigeon, rabbit and hare.

January Pheasant, partridge, mallard, widgeon, teal

February Widgeon, mallard, teal

March Pigeon

May and June Roe deer (bucks)

July Pigeon, rabbit.

August Pigeon, rabbit, red deer (stags)

September Pigeon, rabbit, mallard, widgeon, teal, red deer (stags, early September only)

October Pigeon, rabbit, grouse, pheasant, partridge, mallard, widgeon, teal

November & December Pigeon, rabbit, grouse, pheasant, partridge, mallard, widgeon, teal, red deer (hinds), roe deer (does)

vegetables

Our organic garden at the Cook School always wows the visitors,
and people on a break from their class can often be seen going for
a relaxed wander between the raised beds. The garden is managed
by my wife, Holly, and it's a real oasis, as well as being a bountiful
source of fresh produce. In fact, in the summer, I tend to go almost
totally veggie, because at that time of the year, the selection and
quality of what's available is just so good. My kids have grown up
eating fresh vegetables, and they love 'em, especially eaten raw.
In the shorter days of winter, when the garden isn't so productive,
I still try to source my vegetables locally and prefer to buy from
Scottish or British producers, organic when possible.

Of course, I know that many of you reading this won't have the advantage of a vegetable plot outside your back door, but you should still try to source your veg as seasonally and locally as possible. Try signing up to a local organic box scheme, which will not only provide you with veg straight from the fields, but may also encourage you to start cooking with unfamiliar vegetables.

All vegetables are at their best in season, and whether you're preparing a fresh tomato salsa or chargrilled asparagus, shopping seasonally will go a long way towards helping you achieve fab results. Summer is glut time for fresh veg in the UK, and from June to September our garden is overflowing with peas, beans, spinach, beetroot, courgettes and salad leaves. In Autumn, British squashes and

pumpkins come into their own along with leeks, carrots and celeriac, while winter is a time for hardy root veg like turnips (swedes) and staple brassicas like Brussels sprouts and Savoy cabbage.

Sourcing seasonally is the most reliable way to locate fresher, tastier veg. In fact, it's such an important issue, that I'm not going to say much else about vegetables in general, except to give you a guide as to what's best when (see below). I do, however, have more to say about two of my personal favourites: potatoes and mushrooms.

Potatoes

I picked up my potato obsession from my father who's been growing spuds all my life. Over the years we've experimented with every kind under the sun,

harvesting around 20 varieties, from earlies to main crop, tiny new to floury lates, so for most of the year there's something available that's right for the table.

Choosing the right potato for the job is all about matching variety and cooking method. The two main varieties are floury and waxy, and while floury potatoes contain a starch that breaks down during cooking to give a fluffy result (great for mash), waxy potatoes tend to stay firm (perfect for boiling). The issue is further complicated by the existence of 'all-rounders' and also by the fact that people tend to have their own potato preferences. For instance, I like dry, fluffy chips, so make them using Golden Wonder or Kerr's Pink. Some people, however, prefer a chip that's a bit mushy inside and absorbs more oil so choose King Edward or Maris Piper.

You'll notice in the recipes that I've recommended my top varieties for each one and I've based this on 25 years of growing, selecting and cooking experience. But in general, if choosing a waxy potato my preferences are: Belle de Fontenay, Charlotte, Ratte and International Kidney (when grown on Jersey, these are sold as Jersey Royals). All-rounders are: Maris Piper, Wilja, King Edward's, Desiree and my personal favourite, the Red Rooster. Flouries are: Kerr's Pink, Golden Wonder and Red Duke of York.

Potatoes are available to buy all year round, but earlies and new potatoes are at their best in the spring and early summer, main crop in the late summer and autumn. All main crop potatoes still in the ground in October are harvested and stored at a constant temperature to preserve them through the winter. They'll keep well like this, but as soon as

they come out of store, they want to grow, and will start converting some of their starches into sugar. So once you've got your tatties home, keep them in the fridge and use within 7 days. If left in the light they'll go green and should go straight in the bin.

Mushrooms

I love mushrooms, and the finest are without a doubt the wild ones you pick yourself, my personal favourites being chanterelle and cep. However, if you're going to go picking, then you need to familiarise yourself thoroughly with the different varieties. Foraging is satisfying, but eat the wrong thing and it could land you in hospital! I'd recommend finding yourself a copy of Roger Philip's *Mushrooms and Other Fungi of Great Britain and Europe*, and never eat anything you're not sure about.

Wild mushrooms have big flavours that are fantastic for soups and sauces, but sadly, they're only available for a few months of the year. Fortunately there's a great selection of cultivated mushrooms now on the market. I can take or leave the ubiquitous white button mushroom – though I do like its bigger brother the open cap mushroom, which has much more flavour, and is fab stuffed with garlic! Flavoursome brown chestnut mushrooms are only a few pence more, or further up market, you'll find Shitake, Pleurotus (or oyster mushrooms) and sometimes Enoki. Personally, oyster mushrooms leave me a bit cold, and you need to treat Shitake with care, as the texture can be either silky or slimy depending on how you cook them. For an intense mushroomy flavour I'd recommend using

re-constituted dried cep or morel mushrooms mixed with oysters or open caps, and add in the soaking liquid for an extra flavour boost. I also like using dried morels mixed in with fresh chestnut mushrooms to make devilled mushrooms on toast. Sensational!

When it comes to preparing mushrooms, people seem terribly worried about a bit of dirt and start scrubbing and peeling, but that just takes away flavour. I never wash or peel my mushrooms, just brush them clean, though I might trim off a bit of the stem if it's dark. It's worth pointing out that cultivated mushrooms are grown in sterile soil.

My last comment on mushrooms has to be a favourite flavour combination of mine: mushrooms and soy sauce. If you're making a mushroom soup, there's nothing better than a good splash of soy.

Seasonal calendar of vegetables

New growing methods, particularly the use of poly-tunnels, mean that UK veg now has extended growing seasons. You'll also find that harvest dates differ in the north and south, so treat this list as a rough guide only as to when things are at their best.

January White, green and red cabbages, leeks, onions, turnip, Brussels sprouts, parsnips, kale, winter greens, forced rhubarb, shallots, sea kale and celery.

February Artichokes, Brussels sprouts, all cabbages, winter greens, kale, leeks, onions, potatoes, turnip, sea kale.

March Purple sprouting broccoli, green cabbages, spring greens, leeks, sea kale.

April Purple sprouting broccoli, green cabbages, cauliflower, spring greens, wild garlic, radishes, watercress, morels, Jersey Royals.

May Asparagus, green cabbages, carrots, cauliflower, lettuces, wild garlic, radishes, watercress, new potatoes, broad beans.

June Asparagus, broad beans, carrots, cauliflower, lettuce, peas and sugar snaps, new potatoes, radishes, watercress,

July Beetroot, broad beans, carrots, cauliflower, chard, courgettes, French beans, garlic, kohlrabi, all lettuces, onions, pac choy etc, peas and sugar snaps, new potatoes, radishes, samphire, spinach, early tomatoes, watercress.

August Aubergines, beetroot, broad beans, broccoli (calabrese) green cabbages, carrots, cauliflower, courgette, cucumbers, fennel, French beans, garlic, kohl rabi, lettuce, onions, pak choy, peas and sugar snaps, peppers and chillies, potatoes, radishes, runner beans, salsify, samphire, spinach, sweet corn, tomatoes and watercress, chard.

September Aubergines, beetroot, borlotti beans, calabrese, cabbages, broad beans, carrots and cauliflower, chard, courgettes, cucumber, fennel, garlic, kale, kohlrabi, onions, pak choy, peppers and chillies, potatoes, pumpkins and squashes, runner beans, salsify, spinach, tomatoes, watercress.

October Beetroot, borlotti beans, calibresse, cabbages, red cabbages, carrots, cauliflower, celeriac, celery, chard, courgettes, fennel, kale, kohlrabi, leeks, onions, peppers and chillies, last of the potatoes, squashes and pumpkins, radishes, salsify, spinach, tomatoes, turnips, swede.

November Artichokes, beetroot, white and red cabbages, carrots, celeriac, celery, chard, garlic, winter greens, kale, kohlrabi, leeks, winter lettuce, onions, parsnips, pumpkins, salsify, turnip, swede.

December Artichokes, sprouts, white and green and red cabbages, carrots, celeriac, celery, winter lettuces, winter greens, kale, leeks, onions, parsnips, turnip, swede.

dairy

In my early days of cooking, a lot of my dishes were reliant on the richness of dairy fats such as butter, cream and eggs. Age and an increasing interest in health and diet has caused me to reduce the amount that I use. I still love my butter, eggs and cream; I'm now just a lot more judicious in their use. A good diet is all about balance and dairy produce still has an important role. Just don't overdo it!

Milk

I think there's a bit of confusion when it comes to the fat content of dairy products, particularly milk, and people are often surprised to learn that there's not really much difference between the varieties. Whole milk (which we use at the school) is usually around 3.5% fat, semi-skimmed 1.6%, and skimmed 0.1% fat. Which type you keep in your fridge at home will be down to personal taste, and although all our recipes use whole milk, they'll work well with semi-skimmed, if that's what you keep in your fridge at home.

Apart from that, there's not much else useful we can tell you about milk. Modern production is mostly under the control of a few very large companies who pool their milk from farms and dairies all over the country. This means that what you're drinking is pretty anonymous and of virtually the same quality wherever you go. We're lucky at the school, as we get our milk from a local company, Graham's Dairy, just down the road in Bridge of Allan, and they also provide us with excellent quality butter and cream.

Cream

There's been a recent trend against using cream in cooking – presumably down to concerns over health and the high fat content. Personally I still like to use quite a bit, as I find it imparts a wonderful richness that nothing else can match. At around 48% fat, you'd be wise to use double cream judiciously, but let's be honest, sometimes only cream will do!

That high fat content makes double cream very stable, so it's perfect for cooking and won't split when boiled or added to acidic ingredients. Use in desserts or add to savoury dishes such as sauces and soups.

Whipping cream, at around 40% fat, is less stable. With care it can still be added to hot dishes, though it's most useful for whipping.

At 18% fat, single cream isn't an option for whipping or cooking, but it's perfect for potato Dauphinoise and some desserts. I keep double cream at home and mix it with milk when I need single.

Clotted cream, at 55% fat, isn't great for cooking with, but in my opinion, there's very little that can beat it piled thickly on a scone with

butter and jam: nice but oh so naughty. It's what we ply our customers with at morning coffee…

Crème fraîche, a soured cream made from double cream, can be whipped and served like ordinary cream, or used to add a luscious zing to hot sauces, soups, stews and cold desserts. When made originally in France, natural lactic acid fermentation created the distinctive acidic taste, but now a culture is added to aid the process. Half fat crème fraîche is also available and with care, can be used for cooking, but no-fat crème fraîche can't stand the heat, and is only suitable for cold preparations like dips and desserts. Sour cream is lighter and produced from single rather than double cream. It's useful for dressings and dips, but is likely to split if added to hot dishes.

Butter

There are loads of buttery spreads and margarines on the market, but my preference will always be for real butter. Vegetable spreads derived from blended oils are never going to have the same flavour, and although they may contain less saturated fat, they often contain trans fats from the process of hydrogenation, which increases shelf life. Our bodies have no way of dealing with trans fats, so you should try to avoid them whenever possible. Non-hydrogenated spreads are now available, but for me, butter is still the number one choice.

Butter is produced by churning cream and removing the liquid buttermilk so that only the yellow fat remains. The French and Danes add a culture to their cream before churning it, while in

the UK we just churn the cream as it is. These two distinct styles (sometimes called lactic and sweet) taste quite different and while I prefer the French-style, what you go for will be down to personal choice. You also have a choice between salted and unsalted, and my vote is always for unsalted. The salt was originally added as a preservative, but it's now used as a flavour enhancer and can mask the use of cheap ingredients as well as adding to your daily hidden sodium intake. All our recipes use unsalted butter.

Yoghurt

At the school we mainly use full fat natural bio yoghurt. If you're planning to cook with yoghurt, stabilize it first by adding a little cornflour or arrowroot so that it doesn't split. Better still, use Greek yoghurt which is more stable due to its higher fat content, but watch the calories! Greek yoghurt is also great for dips or add chopped fruit and honey for a fabulously simple dessert.

Cheese

We're extremely lucky in Scotland to have a cheese god in our midst in the form of Iain Mellis, and over the years, Iain has opened my eyes to all the wonderful cheeses we have available in the UK. Because of him, I could now fill ten books on the subject, so I'm not going to go into depth here.

Cheese is produced by adding rennet to milk causing it to separate into curds and whey. The curds can then be eaten as cottage cheese, or drained, pressed and matured. It's the maturing

process that creates all those wonderful different varieties, textures and flavours. Personally, I like a cheese where you can taste the cream, and given a choice, I'd go for smaller, artisan producers, though my fridge will usually have a stock of commercial varieties such as Parmigiano-Reggiano, buffalo mozzarella and a nice cheddar, like Isle of Mull or Mull of Kintyre. I love those little crunchy bits you get in good hard cheddar (or any hard cheese), something which, I am reliably informed by the cheese buffs at IJ Mellis cheesemongers, occurs when an amino acid called tyrosine forms into hard white crystals within the cheese. One thing I'm not a big fan of is orange cheddar, and why we feel the need to add these sorts of dyes to our food, I don't know.

It's safest to keep all cheeses in the fridge, but warm them to room temperature before using. I'd advise against wrapping cheese in cling film as it causes it to sweat. The FSA also warns of a risk of contamination by plasticisers when high fat foods are wrapped in cling film. Instead, wrap your cheese in greaseproof paper and place in an air-tight container.

Soft cheese

Cream cheeses, like mascarpone, are made with single or double cream rather than milk. I use cream cheese mainly for creating sumptuous cheese cakes, but you'll see it popping up in desserts like tiramisu and in certain pasta dishes. Fromage frais is a cheese made of skimmed milk, though it's often enriched with cream. If in doubt over the fat content, check the label of the pack.

Eggs

Where would we be without eggs? There really is nothing like a proper egg from a hen that's been grubbing around for natural insects and fattened up on kitchen scraps and organic pellets. You should be able to find fresh farm-bought eggs at farmer's markets and butchers shops and you'll really appreciate the brilliant yellow yolks and wonderful flavour. Soft boiled and eaten simply, an egg like this is one of life's great pleasures. If you can't get farm fresh, buy organic or failing that, free range. All the recipes in this book use large eggs, unless otherwise stated.

Intact and left in their shells, eggs should keep for several weeks, though they will start to deteriorate. A fresh egg should have a firm yolk and a white (albumen) that's thick and clings tightly to the yolk. Older eggs have yolks that are liable to burst, and clear, runny albumen. Eggshells are permeable and will collect more air as time passes so a good way of testing the age of an egg is to place it in a bowl of water. New eggs will sink and older eggs bob up to the surface. If you get an egg that floats, throw it out. See page 44 for more information on eggs.

Although the risk from the dreaded salmonella has gone down in recent years, you should still take precautions to protect vulnerable individuals from dishes that call for partially cooked or raw eggs, like homemade mayonnaise. For some recipes you can substitute pasteurised eggs, which have been heat treated.

store cupboard

Most of us have some level of guilt when it comes to our store cupboards. We know that they're full of long-forgotten ingredients and age-encrusted jars of who-knows-what, but we can't bring ourselves to clear them out and start again.

Absolve yourself! Take a wet Saturday afternoon and work your way to the back. Even the most fastidious of us will have something that's out of date, so check and chuck out anything that's past its best. You're bound to find all sorts of things you've bought or been given, but if you haven't used something in a year you probably never will so ditch it and claim back the space.

After all, if your cupboard is a jumbled mess, you'll never be able to find the things you need. So if you're re-stocking, try to put things in some sort of an order. I use a couple of shoe boxes at home to keep my herbs and spices tidy and it's such a simple solution as they just slide neatly out when I need something. Use your cooking habits as a rough guide to what you should have in store, but below I've listed a few basics that I wouldn't be without in my kitchen.

Salt and pepper
I'm not a big salt person but to the western palate, certain dishes improve with seasoning. Use sea salt rather than table salt, which has anti-caking chemicals like calcium silicate added, but it will need to be ground. At the school, we use Maldon sea salt which has big soft, flaky crystals that you can crush between your fingers. Maldon salt has a clean iodide-type flavour and the structure of the crystals also means that you get these little zingy crunches of salt while you're eating.

White pepper and black pepper come from the same plant, black being the dried, unripe berries and white being the seed. For the best black pepper, look out for the Indian varieties, Tellicherry and Malabar. They have a complexity of flavour that's a million miles away from the blander varieties more commonly for sale. Always buy whole peppercorns, the fresher the better, and get yourself a really good grinder. The mechanism is far more important than any flashing lights so look for Peugeot, Cole and Mason or the new kid on the block, CrushGrind.

Dried herbs
I use dried herbs for long slow cooking and dishes like John's Spanish chicken (see page 152), where the more intense flavours have a chance to mellow and absorb into the dish. They lose their potency within weeks of opening, so keep stored in air-tight containers. Seasoned Pioneers (see p286) do a great zip-lock container for this very purpose. I keep basil, oregano and thyme.

Ground spices

Like dried herbs, ground spices quickly lose their distinctive flavours, so if you can, buy whole seeds and grind them as needed in a spice mill, pestle and mortar or coffee grinder (but don't use it for grinding coffee afterwards!) If you toast them before grinding, it intensifies the flavour. I keep coriander, cumin and cardamom seed as well as cinnamon bark. Also ground Garam Masala, ginger, paprika and cayenne. Seasoned Pioneers also do a fab selection of spice blends.

Curry paste

Every curry paste varies wildly depending on the ingredients, and it's not within the scope of this book to go into too much detail. The advantage of a paste is that the spices are already cooked out, so you'll find it less harsh than a powder. At the school we use Patak's curry paste.

Garlic

The bulbs of garlic you buy at the supermarket or greengrocer are usually dried, and if stored properly (garlic gurus say whole in a dry place at room temperature and away from direct sunlight) they should keep for weeks, or even months. You can buy specially-designed 'garlic-keepers' but a paper bag makes a pretty good alternative. Fresh garlic has a milder flavour with a subtle perfume, but its British season is very short. If you're lucky enough to get your hands on some, treat it like fresh veg and keep in the fridge for a few days only. The flavour of garlic varies depending on how you prepare it: halved bulbs or whole cloves for a sweet, subtle flavour, finely diced or puréed for something with a bit more oompf!

Stock cubes

Your number one option for stock is making your own (see page 82). Your second option is to find a good liquid stock (many supermarkets now do ready-made fresh stocks – though they can be a bit salty – and Knorr do a great liquid bouillon that will keep in the fridge for up to three weeks). Your third is to buy stock cubes. Commercial cubes tend to be very strong and salty, so only use with dishes that can hold their own in terms of flavour, like minestrone soup, beef and red wine casserole. I'm a recent convert to Kallo organic stock cubes.

Flour

Once opened, flour must be kept in an air-tight container and should keep for a few months, processed white flours lasting longer than their wholemeal counterparts. Cornflour is a thickening agent used mainly for sauces and stews, though I prefer to use arrowroot, a bit of a wonder-starch that cooks out straight away without going opaque or leaving a trace of starchiness.

Raising agents

Shop-bought baking powder is the easiest raising agent to use. It contains an acid and an alkali that react and produce carbon dioxide on contact with liquid and then again with heat in the oven for an extra boost. You can make your own simple baking powder by mixing 1 tablespoon of bicarbonate of soda with 2 tablespoons of cream of tartar. 1 teaspoon of this will turn 200 g/7 oz of plain flour into self-raising flour.

Sugar

For me, unrefined sugar is the only choice; give it a sniff and you'll appreciate that whack of molasses character. In contrast, refined sugar has virtually no scent whatsoever. Billington's is the number one brand in unrefined sugar though Plantation Reserve also has a heavenly aroma. Keep golden brown granulated and caster. I also like to keep unrefined icing sugar in a duster; perfect for topping a creamy crème brûlée before blasting it with a blow torch.

Oats

I'm not keen on the texture or flavour of porridge made from rolled oats, though it is quick to make. It's better to use fine, medium or pinhead oatmeal, which will require a good 20–30 minutes of slow cooking. Use pinhead for skirlie, and rolled oats, toasted with sugar, for cranachan.

Rice

There are loads of different varieties of rice, but in my opinion you only need to keep basmati and risotto. All rice contains two different types of starch, and it's the relative amounts of each (as well as your cooking methods) that will affect its ultimate stickiness. Basmati rice contains a lot of stable starch molecules so tends not to clump together when cooked. Risotto rice contains a core of stable starch but is surrounded by more sticky starch, and when this layer is scraped off with continual stirring it gives risotto its characteristic creaminess. Common types of risotto rice are Arborio and Vialone Nano, but I prefer Carnaroli as it's the most forgiving to cook with, and is superior in flavour. You can also use risotto rice to make rice pudding.

Quinoa

A nutritious grain with a high protein content, quinoa has a pleasant texture and can be used as a substitute for grains such as rice or bulgar wheat.

Couscous

Not a grain, but a very fine pasta that was traditionally steamed over stews. Today's quick-cook varieties just need to be re-hydrated by soaking in about 1½ times as much boiling water. Place in a bowl covered with cling film and leave for 5 minutes before fluffing up with a fork. Then re-cover and leave for another 5 minutes. Rather bland on its own, couscous is a great vehicle for carrying flavours, so load it up with herbs, spices, chilli or citrus zest and juice.

Dried pasta

Everyone has their favourite pasta shapes, and mine are *strozzapreti* (translates as the 'priest choker'!), penne and spaghetti. The crucial thing with pasta is matching the shape to the sauce – you want something that picks up the maximum amount of sauce possible. Thinner shapes, like spaghetti are best for thinner, butter or oil-based sauces, whereas thicker shapes are better for heavy sauces. Choose a pasta shape with holes or ridges for sauces with chunks as they help to pick up the 'bits'. For the best sauce retention, look for pasta made from traditional bronze moulds, as they produce a rougher finish and a less slippery pasta. Most dried pastas are made from just durum wheat and water, though a few contain egg. The whole point of egg pasta, however, is that it should have a more delicate mouth feel and a subtle egg flavour, and this is hard to replicate successfully in a dried pasta. Wholemeal pastas are also widely available, and are both healthy and tasty.

Dried noodles

The pasta of the far east, noodles come in many forms. I find egg noodles are the best, and medium ones hold a decent amount of sauce, cooking in around 4 minutes. I'm not a fan of glass noodles – they tend to go a bit slimy when cooked – but fine rice noodles are fantastic deep fried. You always know you're onto a winner when you get these in your *Ready Steady Cook* bag as there's a great audience reaction at the sight of the noodles puffing out when they hit the hot oil.

Vinegar

Not just for acidity, vinegars can add a real depth of flavour. A good wine vinegar should cost about the same as a bottle of good wine (or sometimes even more), as that's how it started out in life. Keep a white wine vinegar, like Chardonnay, for general use and a Cabernet Sauvignon vinegar for dishes that can stand up to the strong, distinctive flavour. I used to be guilty of making balsamic reductions, as they had a great consistency and looked right good drizzled round the edge of a plate. I've since learned the error of my ways, and now only use decently aged balsamic, which is naturally thick and glossy, has a fab flavour, and is great for salad dressings or with strawberries. The gentle, less acidic rice wine vinegar (we use Mizkan at the school) is useful for more than just Asian cooking and I also like to keep a good mixed fruit vinegar, like Womersley for finishing sauces, soups and stews. See page 246 for our simple vinaigrette recipe.

Oils

Standard blended olive oils have a mild flavour and are suitable for both frying and dressing salads. Pay a bit more for extra virgin or the top single estate oils and you'll enter a world of big flavours, from the strong, green, peppery to the mellow, grassy style. Use these oils for dressings and sauces, never for frying as they break down under high temperatures. Judy Ridgway's *Best Olive Oil Buys Round The World* is my olive oil bible. For deep-frying use a refined vegetable oil; and sunflower oil is good for shallow frying. The relative newcomer, cold-pressed rapeseed oil, is a strong oil with a wonderful golden colour and nutty flavour and works well in mayonnaise. Its high flash point also means it's great for high-temperature roasting. I'm broadly in favour of UK rapeseed oil, and I'm a particular fan of Oleifera, which is produced in the Scottish Borders.

Honey

I mostly use Scottish heather honey for its depth and complexity of flavour. It's a million miles from the stuff you get in plastic containers for drizzling.

Tinned tomatoes

I have a thing about decent tins of tomatoes and always have plenty in store. Buy Italian, San Marzano if you can get them, and brands like Vitale and Mutti. I've found non-Italian brands can be watery and quite acidic and tins of chopped tomatoes in particular are often produced from inferior quality toms. When you make a sauce, believe me the difference is like night and day; richer, sweeter and thicker. A bottle of tomato ketchup (or sauce rouge!) is also essential for cocktail sauces or adding richness to soups and casseroles. Heinz organic is my personal favourite.

Tins of pre-cooked pulses

Very handy for bunging in casseroles and soups. Try to find unsalted and unsweetened chick peas, kidney beans, butter beans and mixed pulses.

Tabasco sauce

For quick chilli heat, it has a pronounced wood-aged, oaky flavour, though cayenne is better for a pure chilli hit.

Thai fish sauce

Essential in Asian fish cookery, it may smell of a Bombay sewer but used judiciously, it tastes heavenly. Very high in salt though.

Tinned anchovy fillets

The ones in oil are best, and the fillets are fat, pink and luscious. Ortiz is one of the top brands. Cheaper ones tend to come pickled in vinegar and are thin, brown and unappealing.

Soy sauce

A Japanese brand is best, like Kikkoman's, and I prefer light soy sauce. Also look out for Kecap Manis, a thick, sweet soy sauce from Indonesia, which is great for dips.

Worcestershire sauce

Anchovy-based, but not as powerful as Thai fish sauce, its more complex flavour is great in Bloody Marys, soups, casseroles and marinades.

Sweet chilli sauce

All good chilli sauces should contain only chilli, sugar, vinegar and salt, like Linghams, and look for ones that are still manufactured in Asia, as they tend to be better quality.

Dried mushrooms

A great store cupboard staple, dried mushrooms like ceps and morels keep for ages. Reconstituted by soaking in water, they provide an intense mushroomy flavour and are perfect on their own or mixed with fresh mushrooms and added to sauces, soups and casseroles. Morel, chicken and cream is an all time classic combo.

Powdered English mustard

I love these big, strong flavours.

Wasabi powder

The powder has a finer flavour than the luminous stuff in tubes and also keeps better. Wasabi is essential for sashimi and sushi, but also adds a fiery horseradish kick to any dish.

Pepperdew peppers

Pickled mild chillies that are great for pizzas, salads and salsas.

Olives

Always buy with the stone in for better flavour. I like Kalamata and Nicois. Buy them brined or in oil, and generally, you get what you pay for.

Capers

Get the best quality you can and go for the salted rather than brined variety. Give them a really good wash before using. They should have an intense, almost exotic perfume. Use capers sparingly.

Coconut milk

Go for the thick and unsweetened variety. It's great for curries and desserts. With top quality brands, John suggests leaving the can to settle for a couple of days in a cool place (or even the fridge) to let the fat rise to the surface. If you open the can carefully, you should be able to scrape the thick coconut cream off the top, leaving the thin water behind, great for enriching a curry.

Condensed milk

Many years ago I was a navigator in the Merchant Navy and this is the stuff we had in our coffee so it's an incredibly evocative flavour for me. Good for real banoffee pies and essential for proper Scottish tablet.

Leaf gelatine

I don't get on with powdered gelatine and find it tends to go lumpy. Leaf gelatine comes in different strengths (measured in 'blooms') but the stronger varieties are sold in smaller leaves, so they're all roughly equivalent to each other. Soak your sheets for 4 minutes in cold water, squeeze out the excess liquid, whisk into other hot ingredients, and you won't go far wrong.

Redcurrant jelly

Not only a condiment, it's an essential ingredient in many sauces and casseroles. The thing I use it for most is Cumberland sauce, though its sweetness is also perfect for finishing game gravies.

Water biscuits

I have a weakness for good cheese, and can think of no better place for it to rest itself before consumption than on a Carr's water biscuit. For some reason, I like the wee ones best.

Wine

If you've got any leftover wine, keep it corked for up to eight weeks and it will start to oxidise slightly and take on a vinegary flavour that's great for use in sauces, stews and risottos. Leftover wine can also be frozen in ice cube trays.

Chocolate

For me, chocolate starts to get interesting at around 50% cocoa solids, but anything over 70% and the flavour is lost on me. Around 60% is optimum, but don't get too hung up on cocoa solids. A lot of the flavour in chocolate is down to the selection of the beans, the cocoa butter and how it's cooked. If you're tasting chocolate, try not to taste one type in isolation (a great excuse to eat more!) Personally, I've always been a fan of Valrhona, though Lindt can be easier to source. Chocolate pistole (buttons) are good for melting, but be warned, they're terribly morish! White chocolate isn't technically chocolate at all, as it doesn't contain any cocoa solids, just cocoa butter. Buy good quality brands like Valrhona, as the cheaper kinds contain a high percentage of vegetable oils.

fridge and freezer

Get into the freezer habit!
Believe it or not, there are nights when even I go home and can't face cooking! That's when I rely on my freezer. To me, a freezer is like a convenience store and I keep mine well stocked with a good selection of home-made 'ready meals', like casseroles and soups, which can be zapped in the microwave and ready to eat within minutes. These dishes are easy to prepare in bulk then frozen in individual portions, and are 100% better than their shop-bought counterparts in terms of taste and nutritional value. They don't contain unnecessary salt and sugar, and I've got full control over every ingredient.

FREEZER

A freezer is also indispensable if you're going to go to the effort of making your own basics like stocks, as it's just as easy to make big quantities instead of smaller ones, and freeze what you don't need. Next time you need a few tablespoons of your stock to enrich a sauce, you can casually open your freezer and the stock will be conveniently to hand. But if you're going to do this, I'd recommend purchasing proper disposable containers and getting into the habit of writing directly onto them with indelible pen the name and date (including the year!) of every item you freeze.

If you're freezing protein (like meat or fish) the key to success is doing it quickly. Slow freezing causes large ice crystals to form in the food – these crystals are sharp, and damage the internal structure of delicate items as they form. When you defrost something that's been frozen slowly like this, liquid leeches out from the damaged areas, and the items become soggy and tasteless. Domestic freezers aren't designed to freeze things quickly; they can't get down to low enough temperatures. For this reason, I'd recommend against freezing delicate produce, like fish, at home (unless you're planning to use them in something like a pie). Scallops are the one exception here, as their low water content makes the formation of ice crystals less of an issue.

Freezing isn't complicated, but here are some simple guidelines to help you achieve the best results:

1 Make sure whatever you're freezing is completely cold before it goes in the freezer.

2 Individually wrap items like meat or scallops in cling film and freeze spaced out on a tray. Anything in a clump will take longer to freeze to the centre causing more damage to the tissues.

3 Freeze liquids, like stocks and sauces, in ice cube trays. When frozen, tip the cubes into zip-lock bags and label with indelible pen; handy portions that can be quickly zapped in the microwave and served within minutes.

4 Don't try to freeze milk, yoghurt or whole eggs, emulsions like mayonnaise or fruits with a high water content. Separated egg whites can be frozen successfully, however, and the process actually helps to de-nature the albumen and produce better meringues (see page 212).

5 Keep your freezer full, but never over-fill as it makes it inefficient and can be dangerous.

6 You can defrost sauces, soups and casseroles quickly in the microwave. With meat etc, it's better to defrost overnight in the fridge on some kitchen towel to absorb any liquid.

7 Never re-freeze defrosted produce without cooking it thoroughly first.

Once you get into the habit, you'll find your freezer filling up quickly, but here are some basics which you should consider leaving space for.

Sauces and gravies
Most home-made sauces can be frozen using the ice cube tray method (see above), and then stored until needed. Basics include tomato, pesto, green paste and tapenade, and you may be surprised to learn that cheese sauces will also freeze perfectly well. Gravies can also be frozen using this method.

Stocks and soups
Every time I roast a chicken, the carcass becomes the backbone of a fantastically simple stock, which will get frozen in tubs for later use (see page 228). Soups are most useful frozen in portions for 2 or 4, but don't add any cream or cheese before freezing.

Casseroles
Freeze portions in tubs, and again, don't add cream or cheese before freezing.

Fruit and vegetable purées
If you're weaning young children onto solids, bulk making purées and then freezing them in ice cube trays is a fantastically simple and healthy way to introduce them to fruit and vegetables. My kids ate no jars of food at all at that age; we even managed to feed them home-made purées on holiday!

Butter
Freezing butter will change its texture, but when defrosted, you can still use it to cook with. Grated frozen butter is useful for making certain types of flaky pastry.

Pancetta and spicy sausage
A lot of the supermarkets stock cubed pancetta in conveniently segmented packets. Bung them in the

freezer and they'll last for ages. Pancetta can be cooked from frozen and is great mixed through soups, stews, risotto and stir fries. Chorizo picante, a spicy Spanish sausage, is another thing my freezer wouldn't be without.

Lentils

I use a lot of puy lentils in my cooking, as they're fantastic mixed through salads, stews and soups. For convenience, I batch cook and freeze them, taking out small quantities as required.

Pastry

Make big batches and then freeze. I keep flaky (easy puff) and shortcrust. Don't freeze filo as it goes crumbly.

Ginger

You can freeze fresh ginger, though I find it's easier to freeze the juice. Grate a piece of unpeeled root and place in the centre of a clean tea towel or muslin. Gather the material up and hold with the ginger in the centre, then twist it round like a piping bag. As you twist, you'll be able to squeeze out a surprising amount of juice, which can be frozen using the ice cube tray method.

Raspberries

Out of season, I'd much rather have frozen Scottish rasps then fresh imports.

Peas

The great thing about frozen peas is that they preserve so much of that essential sweetness fresh peas lose within hours of picking. Birdseye petit pois are a particular favourite.

Shrimps

I'm not a big fan of farmed hot water prawns, but I adore real brown shrimps (see page 26), which freeze extremely well.

Pine nuts

I've found that all nuts are best kept in the freezer, as it stops them going rancid.

Vanilla pods

Freezing is by far the best way to keep them fresh. Individually wrap in cling film and keep in a zip-lock bag.

Bottle of vodka

For Bloody Marys. Only if you have any space left in your freezer!

FRIDGE

I like to think of my fridge as a staging area for food rather than somewhere for long-term storage. Some items do keep for a few weeks, but if your fridge is a cluttered mess of half-empty jars of olives and bits of mouldy cheddar cheese, you'll find you're chucking a lot of things out. We're a wasteful country when it comes to fresh produce, discarding around a third of the food we buy. This has a big environmental impact, as well as being a drain on the wallet. Why put effort into shopping for tasty, high-quality produce if it's only going to end up feeding your wheelie bin? It makes more sense to shop smarter, perhaps buy a little less, and most importantly, plan in advance what you're going to cook.

For safety, you need to keep your fridge below 5°C/40°F, and it's a good idea to stick in a decent fridge thermometer in a visible place so that you can check regularly. Also try not to overload your fridge or put in anything hot, as this will raise the temperature. For more information on dairy produce see page 34.

Butter

For most uses, butter needs to be at room temperature, so keep a little out of the fridge for immediate use. Keep the rest tightly wrapped in the paper it came in and refrigerate. I'd recommend President, Lurpak (who also do a great unsalted spreadable butter) and Wheelbarrow. Our local dairy Graham's produce an unsalted organic butter that's also up there with the best!

Eggs

It's said that a non-refrigerated egg deteriorates four times faster than one in the fridge, but if you are keeping your eggs in the fridge, bring them to

room temperature before using. Eggs will keep for around three weeks, but their uses are age specific. For more info see page 36.

Fresh herbs

For really fresh herbs, investigate the possibility of growing your own, like flat-leafed parsley, coriander and basil. Bought fresh herbs should be stored for short periods only. A good idea is to keep them in sealed plastic bags that have been puffed up with some air.

Fresh ginger

Unpeeled ginger root will keep for several weeks.

Onions

A culinary essential and an incredibly useful item to have in the fridge! Store them in their skins or they'll oxidize. They should keep for several weeks.

Lemons and limes

Stored in the fridge, they should keep for some time, but to maximise juice output, you'll need to warm them to room temperature before squeezing. Another trick is to heat them for a few seconds in the microwave and then roll the whole fruit firmly between your hand and the counter top. Don't overlook the zest, which is full of citrus character, but it's all contained in the oil in the top 1 mm of zest. When zesting lemons and limes (and oranges!) always do it over a plate or bowl so that you catch the fine mist of oil that's released at the same time.

Parmesan cheese

It can keep for months, but you have to store it properly to avoid mould and flavour contamination. Never wrap cheese in cling film, but keep it in its original wrapper or wrap in greaseproof paper and place in an air-tight container. For extended storage, hard cheeses can be kept in the freezer.

Fresh chillies

They'll keep for several weeks without losing their flavour. You can also buy chillies in oil, or dried, or better still keep a small bush and grow your own. Leave them to dry on the plant, then stick them in a jar and they should keep for weeks.

Mayonnaise

The fresh stuff is fab, and isn't nearly as hard to make as you'd think (see page 240). But I also keep a jar of Hellmann's for making super-quick sauces like Marie-Rose and for perking up sarnies.

Mustard

I'm not a huge fan of whole grain mustard, but I do like to have both smooth French and English in the fridge. French mustard is slightly more fragrant but isn't as punchy. Once open, mustard goes off quite quickly, so buy smaller jars. I don't bother with speciality mustards, good quality plain stuff is best – in my opinion there's nothing better as a dip for cold sausages.

your kitchen

kitchen equipment

When it comes to selecting kitchen equipment the best piece of advice I can give you is to ignore gadgets and gizmos and put your money into the essentials. A chef needs his knives, pans and chopping boards every bit as much as a doctor needs his stethoscope or a gardener needs a fork. At the School our students cook with a huge array of top-notch kit, but for the home cook, budget and space will require you to be more selective. These are my recommendations:

Knives

For any cook, knives are their most personal and valuable tool. Go for good quality, as although cheap knives save you a bob or two in the short term, they tend to be unbalanced, bendy and blunt quickly. A blunt knife means you use more force and this increases the risk of you cutting yourself.

Once you've got good knives, treat them with respect. Keep them in a knife block or on a magnetic knife rack not in a cutlery drawer – nothing blunts a knife faster – and don't let anyone else use your knife. Everyone's cutting technique is different and this actually alters the feel of the knife.

Some chefs own dozens of knives, but for most cooks, you only need four.

Cook's/chef's knife [1]

Used properly, a cook's knife becomes like an extension of your arm, and it's the one knife I would be lost without. Its deep, heavy blade is ideally suited to a whole range of chopping tasks, while the curved, rocking profile allows it to chop without ever losing contact with the board, ensuring smooth and rapid cutting. I'd recommend starting with a 20 cm/8 in blade, although those with smaller hands might prefer something a bit shorter, maybe 18 cm/7 in. Quality makes a real difference and you're looking for balance and a comfortable grip. I prefer stainless steel, as carbon steel stains and loses its edge quickly. The blade and handle should be made from a single piece of steel with a riveted or bonded handle. I like the German manufacturer Wusthof for the shape and feel of their blades. I'm not a big fan of Japanese-style knives as I find them bendy and uncomfortable with slippery handles and overly-sharp heels (that's the edge and point of the blade nearest the handle). Though I have to admit, the worst cut I've ever had in the kitchen was from a Japanese knife, so I'm probably biased!

Vegetable/paring knife [2]

Most people automatically use a vegetable knife for preparing food, but it doesn't have the versatility

of a chef's knife. At 10 cm/4 in, it's good for specific jobs like peeling shallots and fine dicing. It's also useful for fiddly jobs with meat and fish, and of course, testing to see if your spuds are cooked!

Boning knife [3]
The beauty of the boning knife is that the long, flexible blade is perfect for following the contour of bones while you're filleting fish or boning a chicken. Normal blade length is 15–20 cm/6–8 in.

Serrated carver [4]
At the school, we're all fans of the Wusthof super slicer, with its super-sharp 25cm/10 in blade. It's perfect for cutting thin slices of smoked salmon or tackling cabbage and loaves of bread. It also excels at carving the Sunday roast.

Steel [5]
If you have a knife, you need a steel. Get into the habit of using it every time you cook – it doesn't sharpen your knife, but will hold back the blunting process. When your knife does eventually lose its edge, it will need to take a trip to the knife grinder or more likely, your friendly neighbour-hood butcher. There are two types of steel on the market: the traditional cylindrical metal steel, and the flat diamond steel. I've long been a supporter of the traditional style, but have recently, and reluctantly, been converted to the silky charms of the diamond steel. Sharpen your own knife as others will do it at a different angle, which blunts the blade (see p62).

Other blades

Vegetable peeler [6]
The key to a good vegetable peeler is a blade constructed from the same steel as your knife. Cheap tin blades tend to rust and go blunt so you end up bruising the veg rather than cutting it. Some people like flip peelers, but for speed and accuracy, I find the traditional fixed blade hard to beat. Good makes are Wusthof and my favourite, Gustav Emil Ern.

Tomato knife [7]
This is a deceptively sharp little critter, so don't be fooled by its innocent looks and diminutive size. Razor sharp serrations allow it to glide through tough tomato skins without squeezing out the juice and it's also good for segmenting citrus fruit. A top value tool when treated with respect, but watch those fingers!

Kitchen scissors [8]
Get a heavy pair so that you can use them to snip through fish fins and fine chicken bones. If they're sharp, they'll be just as effective for more delicate jobs like snipping herbs and chopping bacon. Don't use your kitchen scissors to cut card or paper as they'll go blunt.

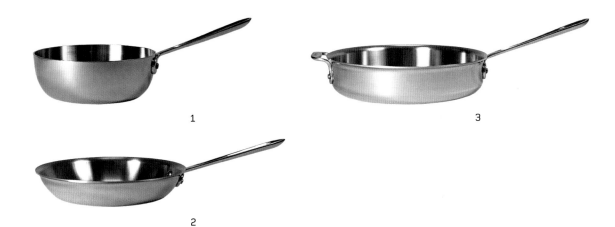

1

2

3

Cookware

Every bit as essential as knives, decent pans not only make your job easier but produce better results. Stainless steel is the best surface to cook on, as it doesn't corrode or scratch easily, but it has bad conductivity so you're best going for something with a bonded steel and alloy construction. The alloy is usually aluminium or copper; great conductors of heat but poor surfaces for cooking on. I'd avoid non-stick, as it doesn't last well and can actually inhibit the process of cooking a good steak (see frying pan, below). Look for pans with close-fitting lids and riveted rather than spot-welded handles. Stainless steel rivets are a must, as aluminium ones corrode sacrificially and become loose. Choose metal handles rather than plastic, so that you can bung the whole pan in the oven. Solid metal handles are best, as they're cleverly constructed to dissipate the heat – used on the stove top, only the first inch or so will get hot. The air in hollow handles tends to conduct the heat right up to your hand, and once scorched, twice shy!

Whether you splash out on a complete new set or opt for one really great pan, the choice of manufacturer is personal. We cook with the US brand, All-Clad at the School, a professional-quality domestic range with a bonded construction of an aluminium core sandwiched between stainless steel. Unlike most pans, the core continues right up to the top of the sides, improving all over conductivity and making it faster for the pan to heat and cool. From their range our favourites are:

Saucier [1]

My pans of choice are the 2qt and 3qt saucier. Similar to a regular saucepan, the secret is the curved edges of the base, which is a far more efficient shape for hot stirring and whisking. You're able to get right into the corners to lift the food up to the surface, and with the silicon spatula (see p52) it's a match made in heaven.

Frying pan [2]

The 25 cm/10 in frying pan is good for steaks, chicken breasts and fish fillets and is the one pan where it really is essential to have stainless steel. Non-stick prevents the food sugars from gathering and becoming sticky, and it's this stickiness that gives steaks etc. that essential, dark, caramelised crust.

Sauté pan [3]

The high sides of the sauté pan make it more flexible than a standard frying pan, ideal for cooking with liquids such as tomato sauce. Great for sautés (of course!), risottos and smaller roasts.

Stockpot [4]

Making large quantities of certain dishes and freezing the excess is a very efficient way to cook, so 6qt is the minimum size of stockpot I'd recommend for stocks and soups. One with a lid is also perfect for bulk-cooking casseroles, which can be started on the hob and finished in the oven.

Other cookware

Wok [5] [6]

An essential for quick-cook Asian stir fries, buy a black iron, round-bottomed variety (for electric and ceramic hobs, you'll have to resort to a flat-bottomed wok, but they don't work quite as well). Season before first use (see glossary). The sloping sides of the wok also make it useful for deep frying (see page 110), and you can even turn it upside down over a hob and use the searing hot curved surface for making naan bread.

Blini pan [7]

A small, black iron 10 cm/4 in frying pan is ideal for making röstis, potato pancakes, fried eggs and erm… blinis.

Griddle pan

A must have if you like chargrilled food. The best are heavy and solid, preferably cast iron. Flimsy ridged pans aren't worth a penny. Invest in a chasseur griddle pan – affordable but long lasting.

Utensils and other equipment

Never go into a kitchen shop without a list. It's like going food shopping when you're hungry; you'll end up with loads of things you don't need. Avoid gadgets that'll just end up at the back of the cupboard along with the foot spa and the popcorn maker. Instead, invest your money in the essential items that will help you to cook better.

Basics

Chopping board

There's been a lot written in recent years condemning wooden chopping boards as harbourers of dangerous and deadly bacteria. But the simple fact is that there's no conclusive evidence to prove that plastic is better than wood, or vice versa. I'd personally use wood, the heavier the better, and bonded end-grain will resist warping. Hard woods like oak or beech are best. It's kinder on the knife, resists tainting and is even vaunted as having anti-bacterial properties. I also keep a red plastic board for raw meat and poultry. I have an aversion to the new wave of glass and ceramic boards which feel weird to chop on and blunt knives. Whatever you choose, scrub by hand after use with an anti-bacterial cleaner, and dry thoroughly at room temperature. My favourite is a great board from Wusthof which has little feet to stop the board skidding around and allows air to circulate underneath. If you can't get one of these, use a non-slip mat under the board. A damp tea towel works too, but can cause the board to warp, as the bottom stays damp while the top remains dry.

Table scraper

A simple device but the single most popular item in our cook shop, this flexible piece of stainless steel is a revelation. Use it to lift chopped onion, garlic, chilli, ginger, herbs etc. and transport them to the pan without dropping little pieces all over the floor. Also great for cleaning chopping boards, barbeques, and even the top of my Aga! It's also useful for lifting and turning delicate pieces of food.

Silicon spatula

Ultra-efficient, and a perfect match for the saucier, the silicon spatula is heatproof to around 300°C/ 570°F, versatile, and has rendered the wooden spoon obsolete in one clean sweep. Shaped to get into all the corners of a pan or dish, it banishes waste, can be used for stirring and lifting and is great for shaping mashed potato portions. It's also perfect for folding, as the sharp edge helps to ensure you don't knock vital air out of your mix. The shape also makes it a great tool for scraping up all those sticky bits in the bottom of the roasting tin when you're deglazing.

Whisk

In the age of food processors and mixers, whisking by hand may seem archaic, but with a 40 cm/16 in balloon whisk and 8 litre/14 pints stainless steel bowl, I can make a better job of whisking egg whites than any machine and get it done in nearly the same time. It's all to do with feel and control (see more on p112). You'll also need a smaller whisk, about 25 cm/10 in, for whisking sauces and smaller quantities. Matfer's a good make as the handles don't fill up with water when washed and the wires don't bend or ping out over time.

Wusthof cranked turner

The best fish slice ever – the flexible blade allows even tightly stuck fillets to be eased out of the pan in one piece. It's also indispensable at BBQs. Just watch the plastic handle: if you leave it in the pan it'll melt and you'll be left with annoying ridges. I also find it's the most nicked piece of chef's kit, so keep your eye on it!

Thermometer

Quick-read digital thermometers, which give a true temperature almost instantly, take the guess work out of how well cooked your food is. Not only essential for timing joints of meat, they're good for steaks, fish, custard, and checking re-heated leftovers so they won't put you in hospital.

Baking sheet

A good quality, heavy-weight baking sheet is less likely to warp under extreme heat. I tend to use aluminium sheets with turned up edges, or flat steel ones. A useful addition is a non-stick silicon mat that fits the baking sheet, such as Silpat or Lift Off.

Bowls

Stainless steel bowls are best for whisking egg whites and cream (see page 112). They also chill more effectively for working with dairy products, and have the added advantage of being durable and stylish. Pyrex bowls are great for general kitchen use, and are actually better for melting chocolate as metal bowls tend to get too hot.

Tongs

Buy with a locking mechanism that stay closed in the drawer. Look for makes with non-stick, silicon tops. They're great for turning meat and fish in the pan.

Ladles

I keep two ladles, the 50 ml/2 fl oz and the 200 ml /7 fl oz. The most versatile is the 50 ml/2 fl oz, which is useful for pressing (chefs call it 'passing') soups and sauces through a sieve or chinois for silky smooth results. It's also the perfect size for making crepes (in a 25 cm/10 in pan), and is great for portion control. The bigger 200 ml /7 fl oz is perfect for serving soups, risottos and stews.

Measuring spoons

While you're learning, you need to stop guessing and get into the measuring habit. Stainless steel spoons mean a long life and get ones that are joined together so you don't lose the ¼ teaspoon.

Apron and oven cloth

Go together like steak and chips. The apron not only keeps you clean, but gives you somewhere to hang your oven cloth. Look for a stylish black Cook School job; proven in the heat of battle!

Bakeware

Start yourself off with a non-stick loose-bottomed tart ring (23 cm/9 in) and a springform cake tin (20 cm/8 in).

Scales

Buy electric, and keep a spare battery. They're a must for accurate measuring.

Grater

I still use a box grater for certain jobs like grating apples, but I've mainly switched to the US-made premium range of hand graters. The two main makes are Cuisipro and Microplane and they come in three sizes: coarse, for shaving shallots, parmesan and garlic, medium for hard cheeses and ginger and fine for zesting. To be truly covered, you need all three, but if you're picking just one, go for the medium.

Clingfilm dispenser

Nothing is more annoying than getting yourself tangled in clingfilm. Benedetti make a great dispenser so you just pull, cut and release. Simple. We use 'full fat' (PVC) clingfilm at the School because it's heatproof. There are non-PVC varieties available if you're worried about plasticisers, though they're not nearly as clingy. You can use the full fat stuff to blind bake (see p88), or a bit of a chef's trick is using it to keep sauces warm: take the sauce off the heat and cover the top of the pan in clingfilm. It hermetically seals the sauce in, stopping steam escaping and keeping it warm. Very clever!

Digital timer

Your senses are best for judging when food is cooked to perfection. But in a frantic household, a digital timer can be an essential for reminding you what's cooking.

Getting a little more serious

Spider draining spoon

An improvement on the old-fashioned slotted spoon, the spider is particularly useful for deep-frying and blanching.

Mousse ring

These are great for creating a professional finish to your dishes. Use them to build towers of crushed potatoes or stacks of smoked salmon and salsa. Great for creating filo baskets and also useful for desserts and little cakes.

Pastry brush

A silicon brush is best as the heat proof 'hairs' don't melt and fall out all over the food. Use for baking and basting, but they're also great for getting sticky BBQ sauces onto ribs and wings.

Mouli

The Mouli is a hand-turned food mill with 3 different sizes of mesh plates. It's great for uber-smooth mash (see page 118) and passing soups when you want to leave a little bit of texture. If you're weaning a baby onto solids, they're pretty much indispensable.

Salad spinner

Necessary for drying washed salad leaves without damage, but also useful for spinach, leeks, cabbage and other leafy veg. I prefer the pull-cord Zyliss model for its speed and durability.

Tea strainer

Use to dust crème brulees with icing sugar before glazing with a blow torch, or for turning desserts into winter wonderlands. But to chefs everywhere, please stop dusting the edges of plates, it's really not clever.

Squeezy sauce bottles

Great for drizzling, just slosh in the sauce and bring out the Jackson Pollock in you! Good for flavoured oils, custard, caramel etc., but give them a quick sniff before using as spicy smells tend to linger. You can use them for reheating sauces in the microwave, but watch out: if it gets too hot, the contents can be jet-propelled out by expanding hot air!

Ice cream scoop

Zyliss produce a good, hefty scoop that makes light work of even the toughest ice cream. Traditional spoons need to be dipped in hot water, but this one's Teflon coated, so the ice cream just won't stick.

Pasta lifter

A slotted spoon with teeth that's perfect for slippery spaghetti, also good for salads. One from Ikea will get the job done perfectly.

Serious chef

Pasta machine
A must if you're making your own pasta, but learn how to make the dough properly (see p266).

Mandoline
There are two main types on the market: stainless steel like the Bron, and plastic like the Japanese Benriner. The plastic ones are brilliant for fine slicing, but I find them unstable and quite dangerous. I much prefer the sturdier and slightly safer stainless steel, but whatever you choose, use a guard and watch those fingers!

Blow torch
For brulee and roasting skins off peppers and tomatoes. Also useful for releasing mousse rings when used to make neat cream desserts.

Chinois
Curdled your custard? Introducing the lump destroyer! A chinois will remove the lumps from most sauces (including white sauce). You can also create incredibly silky smooth results by passing soups and sauces through the ultra-fine metal sieve using a 50ml ladle. Also perfect for purifying stocks.

Electrical equipment

Stick-blender
We use these handy devices all the time on *Ready Steady Cook*. They're good for puréeing, chopping and blending and are great for quick jobs or small quantities. Braun is a good make, and you need one with its own jug. A food processor attachment is also useful.

Food processor
Essential for the serious cook. Magimix is the number one brand. They come with large feeding tubes that can even handle whole potatoes. Slice, dice, process and mix. A truly great labour-saving device.

Blender
High speed blenders do quite a different job than processors. They need some liquid to work and are the only thing that can make proper emulsions, like our speedy hollandaise (see p236). Also a must for smoothies, soups and sauces. Waring are the classic blenders, though Kenwood are also good. Look for a good, solid glass jug.

Mixer
The versatile workhorse in any kitchen, KitchenAid or Kenwood are best.

planning and mise en place

I had a friend who wanted to invite some people round for dinner. He made a few phone calls from work, planned the meal for 8 o'clock, then sat back and relaxed in the convivial glow that comes with planning a gastronomic evening in the company of good friends. Dropping into the supermarket on his way home, he picked up a basket and thought he'd just do that Delia dish with the chicken and pesto he'd seen in a magazine, and maybe that Jamie dessert with the raspberries. He couldn't remember the exact recipes, but they hadn't looked too hard.

An hour later he emerged pushing a massive trolley bulging with top-quality produce, most of which he'd bought 'just in case', and running late because he'd spent all his time looking at Chardonnay.

At home he discovered there wasn't enough space in the fridge for all that food he'd bought and his work surfaces were cluttered with yesterday's dishes. Then the real world paid a visit: the phone rang, someone came to the door collecting for charity, the kids ran in, the dog knocked over the raspberries, and to cap it all off, that chicken recipe he'd been thinking of had long since vanished down the back of the sofa. Things began to go horribly wrong as he guessed the ingredients, turned the oven on too high (he meant to adjust it later), and forgot that he needed toothpicks to hold his pesto-stuffed chicken together. As it cooked, the pesto squirted out all over the elements like toothpaste, catching fire and filling the kitchen with smoke, and my friend, who was now getting hot under the apron, began to wonder why he'd bothered.

It was about this point, so I am told, that the bottle of nice Chardonnay he'd bought began to look very tempting. One glass to steady the nerves led to another as he realised he was out of time, the chicken was burnt and the rasp-berries were on the floor, and it wasn't long before the whole meal and the empty wine bottle were in the bin, and he was on the phone calling for take-out to save the day.

Okay I confess, this story is entirely apocryphal! But the point is that people come away from an experience like this thinking: that was a disaster, you know what? I can't cook! But all that's really happened is they've tried to do too much in too short a space of time without enough planning.

If this all strikes a cord with you then you might be interested to know how big restaurants manage to get out so many meals to so many people on a nightly basis, and without all this panic. There's no big secret, it's just pre-preparation, what chefs call mise en place. Literally translated as 'set in place', to a chef it means having everything ready before you start cooking, and this includes preparing as much as you can in advance. You can't pull a great meal out of the ether, and if you try, chances are you'll end up like my friend: hot, bothered and buying a take away. So we're going to give you a hand. In each of our recipes, we'll tell you what can be made up in advance and to what stage, so that when you take on a big meal, you'll be as stress-free as possible.

Structuring your cooking time like this is not about trying to be perfect, it's about making things easier on yourself. How many times have you tried to do a big dinner party and been stuck in the kitchen with your hair plastered across your face, pink cheeks, everything reeking of frying and listening to the distant sound of tinkling glasses and laughter? You just end up feeling like a kitchen slave.

I look at a dinner party as a re-heat job. I'd also never plan to cook three complicated courses all at once, but rather top and tail the meal with say, a simple soup or cold dish like some Cook School smoked salmon and dressed leaves and then a dessert like a panna cotta that can be made in advance and whipped out the fridge at the last minute. It's helpful to actually sit down and plan your menu out like this, and a lot of it can come from the produce-based theory we've spoken about already. You should also try to dovetail your dishes together so that they work as a whole rather than just as individual courses.

Most of us have quite narrow culinary horizons and a repertoire limited to 5 or 6 dishes. But If you want to progress as a cook, you will eventually have to move out of this comfort zone and cook new things. But my last words of advice would be not to do this wholesale. Don't cook a whole new menu for a dinner party. Stick to a couple of dishes you're comfortable with, and plan to change one at a time to improve your repertoire and increase your skills. Allow yourself to be challenged, and you'll be amazed by the results.

reading a recipe
and critical points

The process of cooking a dish starts when you read the recipe. But what should you be looking for? At the school, we often find that people are so eager to get into the kitchen and start cooking that they pick up recipes and skim them at high speed. They focus in on key ingredients and don't take in all the elements that would help their dish to come together. What's the rush?

Try instead to pick up a recipe and read it through once just to get a sense of what the dish is about. Then read it properly. Start to think all the stages through in your head and imagine yourself actually cooking it. That way you should be able to pre-empt any problems. If it's roast lamb, I'll think, do I have a roasting tin big enough, will it fit in the oven, do I have fresh rosemary in the garden? Then I'll think about the timing: if it's going to take two hours to cook, I'll leave three as it takes time for the oven to come to the right temperature and half an hour for the meat to rest after it comes out.

This sort of virtual cooking is an extremely useful skill to have, particularly if you're going to start thinking outside the box and ultimately create your own dishes. None of our recipes is set in stone, and you should definitely feel free to introduce a degree of variation to suit what's seasonally available, or even your own personal preferences. If you've got a seasonal vegetable stew with courgette, and you don't like courgette, take it out. Hey, if you're the one

that's going to eat it; why not make it the way you like it?

Thinking outside the box also helps to counter all those variations that tend to pop up in the kitchen. It's extremely difficult for you at home to recreate the exact conditions under which our dishes were created. Your oven will be different, your pans may be a completely different shape and size. But these issues are simple to overcome if you can learn to think outside the box. Follow a recipe slavishly, and you may find your food undercooked or slightly singed around the edges. Get to know your oven and you'll know when to add on an extra 5 minutes here, or turn the temperature down a couple of notches there. Use your senses to help you judge things accurately, and your common sense to pick up on the odd error that may have slipped in: hmm, should I really be putting a tablespoon of salt in here, well the recipe says so… If you can pick up on things like this, and start to realise when things don't feel quite right, it means you're becoming an intuitive cook, and this is a hugely positive step in your culinary evolution.

Once you've got this process in your head, you can start to identify the pivotal moments or 'critical points' in the recipe. These are the points where everything can either come together or it can all start to go horribly wrong! If you're making a soufflé, the critical points will be whisking the eggs and folding the mixture in to ensure you retain maximum air. When caramelising a steak, the critical points are getting the pan to the correct temperature, and not moving the meat. These points can be tricky to pick up on if you're not used to looking for them, but hopefully we've given you enough information throughout this book to help you spot them in each of our recipes.

In fact all the information you'll require to prepare the following recipes should be located somewhere in this book: whether it's a piece of culinary terminology we've explained in the glossary, or a description of a cranked turner in the equipment list. So if you find something you don't understand, take a quick trip to the index. Cooking does become easier with experience but what we're offering you here is information and knowledge from our vast pool of culinary experience that will hopefully point you in the right direction, and inspire you to become a better cook.

For me, cooking is like a big jigsaw: every time you cook you learn something new, another piece of the picture slots into place. John, Alan and I still haven't completed our jigsaws. We're still learning, and in fact, you never stop learning.

There will always be something new to pick up in the kitchen, and the only way to become a better cook is to practice.

Speaking of which, it's about time we stopped talking theory and let you put some of it into practice! Our recipes have been divided into vegetables, meat, fish and desserts and we've put in many more basics that can be used and adapted to help you create everything from super suppers to posh dinner parties. Sadly, we don't have a John or Alan clone to send home with everyone, and if you want your own personal Sam or Andy to show you how to pin bone a sea bass, or a Bob, Kevin or Ronnie to help you clear up, then you'll have to come and visit us and take one of our hugely enjoyable classes! But hopefully in this book, we've passed on enough of our combined knowledge to get you started on the road to success.

It's now down to you. So pick a recipe, get your mise en place ready, and happy cooking!

techniques

knives and knifework

Everyone is always impressed when they watch a chef chopping ingredients. The secret is a proper grip, a sharp knife, a basic technique and then practice, practice, practice! If you really want to speed up your technique, buy a big bag of onions and carrots, a supply of elastoplast and get chopping. Using a steel is something you should get into the habit of doing every time you use your knife, as it helps to maintain the edge. Experience will teach you how to feel and hear the correct technique. These instructions are written for right handers.

Using a steel

1

2

1 Hold the steel firmly in your left hand and the knife in your right. Cross them together at the base at a 45° angle (think St Andrew's rather than St George's cross). The blade of the knife near the heel should be gently resting against the edge of the steel at an angle of about 30°.

2 Slide the blade lightly up the steel while simultaneously pulling the steel down the blade. You'll end up with the top of the knife blade at the top of the steel, still at a 30° angle. Move the knife to the other side of the steel and repeat. Repeat this whole action several times.

Holding your knife

1

2

3

1 This is the grip to use for the majority of chopping tasks. Pick up your knife and hold it with a relaxed grip.

2 Place your thumb to the side of the handle, not on top, and grip the handle loosely between your thumb and index finger. Rest your other three fingers underneath the handle.

3 This grip is wrong, you can see the thumb is resting on the top of the handle instead of at the side as it should be.

Basic chopping motion

1

2

3

1 We call the chopping motion 'rock and drop'. Start by resting the end of the blade (but not the tip) on the chopping board.

2 Use your arm to slide the knife forward without breaking contact with the board, and use your wrist to simultaneously bring the knife down so that the heel of the blade makes contact with the board with a 'thunk'. Then, without losing contact with the board, slide and rock the knife back up to its original position, and repeat. You should find that your arm is moving rather like a piston in a steam engine, driving the knife. But it should always be a smooth cutting motion.

3 Practising the rock and drop will result in you chopping faster, so it's important to keep your fingers out of the way using a claw hand grip. Hold your ingredients with the tips of your fingers with finger nails well out of the way. The flat line of your fingers below the knuckle should act as a guide for the knife.

chopping skills

Once you've mastered the rock and drop, chopping and dicing becomes relatively simple. Vegetables can be cut into a variety of shapes for cooking depending on what you're making. Small dice cook quickly and are best for soups and sauces, larger dice are better for casseroles and stews. Batons and Julienne-cut vegetables are good for stir fries or vegetable accompaniments. We've used carrots here, but the basic method is the same for most veg, with a few exceptions, such as onions.

techniques

Chopping vegetables

1   2   3   4

1 Start by peeling, if required. Always peel carefully towards yourself, as when you peel away you tend to apply more pressure on the peeler and take off thick wedges rather than thin, even pieces of peel.

2 Square the vegetable by taking a slice off the side. Rest the top of the blade, but not the tip, on the board and chop down using the forward piston motion. It's important to let the knife do the work, there should be no need to press heavily. Roll the carrot onto this flat side and it should remain stable while you chop it.

3 Chop the carrot in half lengthways. Tip the halves onto their sides and chop lengthways into batons, trying to keep them all the same size to ensure even cooking. Again, use the whole length of the blade for this and remember to rest the top of the blade on the board to give you leverage.

4 Pile the carrot batons together and chop them into dice using the rock and drop method. Notice the claw-hand grip on the carrots. For smaller dice, cut the batons in half again and dice finely.

Chopping herbs

1

2

3

1 To chop herbs like flat-leafed parsley, pick off a few leaves, scrunch them up into a wad and hold them against the blade of the knife. Chop into strips using the rock and drop method, making sure to keep your finger tips curled under.

2 Change your grip so that your thumb is resting on top of the blade, and press the palm of your left hand down on the other end of the blade. Chop by lifting the heel of the knife and bringing the blade down repeatedly on the strips, keeping the point on the board and using it to pivot.

3 Here we have chopped our herbs finely. Use fewer repetitions for roughly-chopped herbs.

slicing and dicing onions

If we were to do a survey of the most common 'lightbulb' moment at the school, chopping an onion would be top of the poll. It's amazing how a simple technique can transform the simplest of tasks. This method stops the onion falling apart while chopping and results in pieces all of the same size. One of the questions we get asked a lot is 'how do I stop onions from making me cry?' The answer is there is no definitive way, although we recommend getting it over with as quickly as possible, good ventilation and possibly sticking your tongue out!

1

2

3

1 Start by chopping the onion in half from root to stem. Cut off the stem end, leaving the root end intact. Remove the skin and first layer of the onion. This underskin is usually a little tough, making it difficult to cut through and to chew!

2 The process calls for a slightly different knife grip. Hold the knife as shown with your thumb resting on top of the blade, and your fingers underneath the handle.

3 Start at one side and place your knife so that the blade is sitting over the onion with the point level with the root. Carefully slice down towards yourself. You should find that, because of the curve of the blade, you don't cut right through the root. Use the natural lines on the onion as a guide as to where to slice.

4   5   6

4 When you're finished, the onion should look like this. Notice that even though it's cut through, the onion is still holding together at the root.

5 Position the onion so that the root is pointing to the left, and carefully chop through the slices horizontally. Do not cut right through, but make sure you leave the root intact. If the onion is very large, make two evenly-spaced horizontal cuts.

6 Change your grip back to normal (with your thumb at the side) and dice the onions using the rock and drop method. All the pieces should come out roughly the same size. You won't be able to chop right to the end, so just discard the root.

slicing and dicing garlic

Garlic can provide a massive oomph of flavour to any dish, but different methods of preparation can result in subtlely different results. The strong pungent flavour of garlic comes from the juice that's stored inside each clove, and the more juice you release the more garlic flavour will infuse your final dish. Crushing a clove breaks down more cells inside it than finely chopping the clove with a sharp knife so the crushed clove will give a stronger taste. Just chopping the garlic gives you a more subtle flavour.

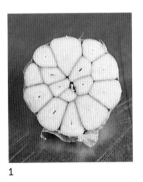

1
2
3
4

1 For stocks, sauces and soups that you strain before serving, chop the entire garlic bulb in half. This will infuse a subtle, sweet garlic flavour.

2 Separate out the individual cloves and peel. For a light garlic flavour, say in a light pasta sauce, simply chop. For a stronger presence, crush the cloves before chopping by placing the flat side of the knife over the top and bang down with the heel of your hand to crush. Chop finely.

3 For garlic paste, sprinkle crushed and finely chopped garlic with a little salt. The salt will help to break the garlic down into a paste, and will also draw out moisture to make the paste creamier.

4 Turn your knife onto its side and press on the flat side using the palm of your left hand. Crush the garlic and salt firmly under the narrower end of the knife using small circular movements. You'll get a fine paste that can be added to anything garlicky – garlic butter, Dauphiniose potatoes etc.

tomato concassé

Skinned, deseeded and neatly diced tomatoes that have had all their acidic juices removed can be used for all sorts of salads and sauces without upsetting the balance of flavour. The success of these depends on the quality of the plum tomatoes.

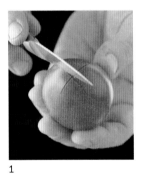

1

2

3

4

1 Remove the skins from the tomatoes. Spear the tomatoes onto a fork or skewer, place them near a naked flame – a gas burner or blow torch – and turn them until the skins start to blacken and blister. Alternatively, cut a little shallow cross in the top of each tomato, place them in a bowl and cover with boiling water. Leave for about 30 seconds, drain and cover with cold water.

2 The skin should then peel off easily.

3 Cut the peeled tomatoes into quarters, and scoop out the seeds.

4 Cut the flesh into very neat 5-mm/¼-in dice. They are best used immediately but will keep refrigerated for 24 hours.

jointing a chicken

It helps to know which end is which and to know the difference between the legs and wings. The legs are the thicker limbs and are made up of the thigh and drumstick and the smaller limbs are the wings. At the leg end you'll find the 'parson's nose', a charming name for the bottom. If you are looking to put any flavourings into a whole bird's cavity, this is the end to do it! One last comment – at no point do you have to cut through bone whilst jointing.

Classic jointing

1

2

1 Start by removing any string or elastic trussing the bird and if the legs are tucked inside, remove them and open the legs out to the side. Cut through the skin between the leg and body on both sides. Bend each leg away from the body until you hear the bone pop out of its socket.

2 The legs will now sit flat at each side of the bird. Use a sharp knife to cut between the thigh and carcass to release the leg. Remove the wings using the same technique: cut skin, dislocate and slice through.

Removing boneless breasts

3

4

3 Using your fingers feel the backbone of the chicken. Starting at the parson's nose end cut down one side of the backbone, using it as a guide, to start removing the breast. The knife will stop when it meets the wishbone. Change the angle of the knife and continue to cut, this time using the wishbone as a guide until you reach the carcass.

4 Gently run your knife along the joint between the breast and carcass, repeating until the breast comes away. Remove the other breast using the same technique.

Drumsticks, thighs and wings

5

6

5 Place the leg on its side with the drumstick pointing up at you. Push the drumstick back until the joint pops out and cut through to separate the drumstick and the thigh.

6 Using a sharp knife cut off the tips of the wings and keep for stock.

Removing the breasts with bone

For grilling, BBQ or certain casserole dishes

Proceed with steps one and two to remove the legs. Then remove the wings. Take a pair of kitchen scissors and with the bird still on its side cut along the side of the bird from parson's nose to neck. This will separate the breast section of the bird from the backbone and parson's nose.

filleting flat fish

Buying whole fish and filleting them yourself is the best way to ensure quality and freshness, so don't be afraid to give it a go. Practice your technique a few times before filleting any carefully sourced fish for an important dinner party! We've used a halibut fish here, but the technique is the same for turbot and sole etc.

techniques

1

2

3

1 Start by making a cut around the head of the fish and continue cutting in a semi-circle. Using your fingers, locate the backbone of the fish and slide your knife gently down one side of it, without cutting through the bones below. Make a cut from head to tail.

2 To remove the fillet, use your filleting knife to get underneath the flesh right down to the bone Using long smooth strokes run the knife along the fish pressing lightly against the bone. The flexible blade should prove invaluable here as it should ride over the bones and get underneath the fillet. Repeat until you've worked the knife right through the fish, and the fillet comes away.

3 Remove the second fillet in the same way as the first, running the knife down the opposite side of the backbone without leaving any of the flesh behind. Sometimes you'll find a little bit of roe in the fish as you're filleting it, just take it out.

4

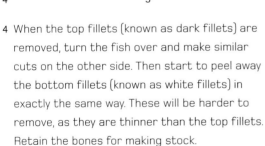

5

6

4 When the top fillets (known as dark fillets) are removed, turn the fish over and make similar cuts on the other side. Then start to peel away the bottom fillets (known as white fillets) in exactly the same way. These will be harder to remove, as they are thinner than the top fillets. Retain the bones for making stock.

5 To skin the fillets, turn them so that the narrow pointed end is towards you, flesh side up. Sprinkle the end with a little salt. This will act as traction to make sure you get a good grip.

6 Carefully make a cut between the flesh and the skin peeling enough back so you can get a good grip. Hold the skin taught and then use the filleting knife to peel away the flesh. Gently wiggle both the skin and the knife and keep the knife flat and lightly pressed against the board or work surface.

filleting round fish

Flat fish and round fish have different anatomies, so the technique for filleting them is a bit different. This method is the one we teach at the school and suited to home cooks. Your fishmonger may use a slightly different technique. We've done this with a wild sea bass, but at home you may be handling a smaller sea bass, salmon or mackerel.

1

2

3

2 Most fish will be sold gutted and scaled. But it's worth running the back of your knife gently from tail to head to pick up any spare scales that the fishmonger has missed.

3 Chop off the head, making your incision just above the gills. Keep the head for making fish stock or soup.

1 Start by snipping off all the fins with a pair of kitchen scissors. With some fish, such as sea bass, you need to watch the spines in the top fin, as they're extremely sharp and cause nasty nicks.

4

5

6

4 Look at the fish side on, you will see the backbone at the top of the body. Insert the knife just above this and start cutting the flesh away from the skeleton right along the body of the fish. Lift the belly of the fish in order to cut through the rib bones tight against the backbone. Adjust your grip as you work along to keep the fillet taut.

5 Repeat on the other side. To remove the rib bones, take one of the fillets and place skin-side down with the head end towards you. Slide your knife under the rib bones, freeing them up and away from the flesh with a slicing movement. Cut them away and trim off any fatty portions of the flesh.

6 Remove the ribs from the second fillet and trim. Then take a pair of tweezers or pliers and remove the pin bones. These are located at the head-end of the fish, towards the centre of the flesh. You should be able to feel them by running your finger along the surface of the fillet from head to tail.

To skin, use the same technique as for flat fish.

preparing lobster

There are various ways of dealing with a lobster, but this is the technique to use for our lobster crumble (see page 191) or thermidor. Take the live lobster (making sure that there are rubber bands around the claws) and stick it in the freezer for about 15 minutes to put it to sleep. Whether this is kinder to the lobster than just killing it outright is difficult to say, but it does make them easier to handle.

techniques

1

2

3

4

1 Sit the lobster on a chopping board. You should see a little cross in the lobster's head. Place the point of your knife here and press the knife point down in the direction of the chopping board. When the point hits the board, bring the knife handle down to the board in an arc, cutting through the lobsters head.

2 Take the bands off the claws and place the lobster immediately in a pan of boiling salted water. Leave to simmer for 4 minutes. Turn off the heat and leave the pan with the lid on for about 15 minutes to cook the lobster gently. Take the lobster out and allow to cool. It will have turned pinkish red.

3 Pull off the claws by twisting them against the movement of the joint. Pull off the legs and retain.

4 Insert your knife into the hole in the head, and cut down towards the tail. The shell will be hard, so use a good chef's knife and a bit of force. Turn the lobster round and slice through the head to separate the two halves. Locate and remove the stomach sack, which is in the head just behind the eyes on both halves.

5   6   7   8

5 Remove the tail meat. You should see a red membrane on the outside of the meat. Peel this back slightly at the top curve of the tail then look for and remove the gut, which will be either a clear or black tube. The greenish paste in the cavity is the tomalley, which provides the liver function of the lobster. This is really tasty, so for lobster crumble, thermidor or other dishes served in the shell, leave it in.

6 Take the claws and dislocate the smaller part of the claw, by pushing it forward, then back and then pulling it down to the side. If you're lucky, the hard cartilage inside the claw will come away with the shell.

7 Place the large part of the claw on your chopping board, holding it up slightly, and using the back of your cook's knife like a hammer, lightly crack the shell several times. You should then be able to pull out the claw meat whole.

8 Tap the other parts of the claw to loosen the meat before picking out the morsels. Try to get as much meat as possible out of the shell. You can use the end of a teaspoon, a pair of pliers or a lobster pick to help you.

When you're finished, you'll end up with the tail and claw meat, and a big pile of the shells and legs. Don't throw these away, but use to make fantastic stock (see page 230).

preparing and cooking mussels

To make sure your mussels are good and fresh, they must be alive when you cook them. Any fishy pong means they're past their best. Discard those with broken shells, and give any open ones a quick tap on the counter or with the back of a knife; they should slowly begin to close up. The first four steps here illustrate the essential process of cleaning the mussels while the final steps show a classic method of cooking.

1

2

1 Mussels have a fibrous 'sea anchor' (called a beard) to keep themselves attached to whatever they're growing from. The beard should be pretty obvious hanging from between the shells, just give it a good tug to remove it. With the back of your chef's knife, knock off any barnacles or debris adhering to the shells.

2 Place the de-bearded mussels into a bowl and fill with cold water. Scrub the mussels well between your hands to remove remaining debris. Drain the water out, re-fill the bowl, scrub and repeat until no more debris comes off. When the water runs clear, drain the mussels into a colander and use straight away.

3

3 Select a big pan with a lid. The mussels should fill it no more than half way. Heat the pan on your hottest ring until roasting. Have your wine or cooking liquid standing by. Lift the mussels into the pan with your hands, don't tip them in or you may pour debris in as well.

4

5   6

4 Pour in any wine that the recipe calls for and put the lid on. Give the pan a couple of good shakes to make sure the mussels cook evenly. They'll release a liquid into the sauce as they open, and this will come quickly to the boil in the hot pan. You'll soon start to see little puffs of steam escaping from under the lid.

5 When the lid starts jumping with the steam (3–4 minutes), the mussels should be ready. Strain through a colander set over a bowl to catch the juice, and discard any mussels that haven't opened during cooking.

6 Strain the juice through a fine sieve lined with muslin to remove any grit. The mussels and stock are now ready for use.

preparing scallops

Like all shellfish, scallops are at their best when fresh, fresh, fresh! The only way to ensure this is to buy them in their shells and shuck them at home. They must be alive when you cook them, so give them a tap to make sure they'll start to close up, and stick your nose in for a good sniff, discarding any with a suspiciously fishy pong. This is the technique for shucking king scallops, not queen scallops which are much smaller.

techniques

1

2

3

4

1 Grip the shell, holding the hinged end at the join of your thumb and forefinger. It may help to balance the shell edge on your work surface, or on a tea towel, but it's not essential.

2 Insert the knife into the side of the shell, close to the flat hinge where there is a natural gap. Now pressing the knife against the inside of the flat shell, sweep the blade across from top to the bottom and you will feel yourself cutting through the muscle that holds the shell in place.

3 When this is done open the flat shell back and twist it off.

4 Hold the shell flat in the palm of your hand, with the flat hinge edge parallel to your thumb. To the top you will see where the muscle (white meat) connects to the shell, and the pink/white roe surrounded by an outer frill with little 'eyes'. Use a spoon to loosen the contents from the shell.

5

6

7

5 Lift the contents, holding the part that was previously connecting the scallop to the shell in your left hand and use your thumb to run back and forth to break the connection with the white muscle.

6 When loosened, you will then be able to push the white meat up, which will simultaneously pop the meat out from its skirt. Pull away the skirt and the rest of the debris leaving the white meat in your hand.

7 Place the scallop meat in a bowl whilst you shuck the others. Wash the meat and roe for no more than 30 seconds and store them on absorbent cloth or paper. The frills can be discarded or well washed under running water to remove the slime, then frozen for use in stocks.

stock

Making your own stocks will change the way you cook forever. It sounds like an extravagant statement, but using homemade stock will have a dramatic impact on the taste and flavour of your dishes. Once made, stocks freeze extremely well, making them every bit as convenient as a cube. Many sauces will require you to reduce stock to intensify the flavour (with a stock cube based sauce this will only intensify the salt levels and little else). Here is one of the most common and versatile stocks, chicken (see page 228 for recipe).

1

2

3

1 Break your carcasses up into pieces and trim off any fat. Place in a roasting tin and roast in the oven until golden brown. Take care not to burn, as this will give your stock a bitter taste.

2 Place the roasted bones in a pot large enough for the bones to take up half its depth. Add vegetables to the roasting tin and roast until caramelised, or cook on the stove top in the tin. Tip the veggies in with the bones and deglaze the pan with 1 litre/1¾ pints of water. Add the water to the pan and top up with enough water to leave 5 cm/2 in of bones/vegetables showing above the water. Bring to the boil. Adjust the heat to a simmer and skim off any fat that has risen to the surface. The simmering stock will now rise and fall through the vegetables, which act as a filter, absorbing all of the gunk from the liquid and leaving it crystal clear. Leave it to simmer like this for 2½ to 3 hours, tasting regularly. You should eventually notice the point at which the flavour stops improving.

3 Strain the stock through a sieve into a large bowl or pan.

white sauce

White sauce is a flour-thickened sauce made with milk that can be used as is, or as a base with other flavourings added, such as in a cheese sauce. This technique can be used for other flour-thickened sauces, such as a velouté (using stock in place of milk) or a more advanced brown sauce, where the roux is taken to a dark brown colour and a base for sauces such as Madeira. White sauce uses 2 parts fat to 1 part flour (see page 240 for recipe), which is a slightly wetter mix than is classic. Making the roux is easier with these proportions and perfect for adding to a souffle mix.

1

1 Melt the butter until just foaming. Add the flour and use a whisk to mix well and remove any lumps. Cook the flour and butter mix until it becomes sandy in texture and colour, which is known as a roux.

2   3

2 The key to the next step is to either have a hot roux and cold milk, or vice versa. If both are warm, lumps are guaranteed! Add a little of the milk to the pan and whisk well. The most common error is to add the milk too quickly. Bring to a simmer before adding the next batch of milk.

3 Add another splash of milk and repeat step 2. Continue this process until all the milk is added. Cook over a medium heat, stirring continuously until boiling. Cook for a couple more minutes until the sauce thickens and shines.

risotto

Put simply, you get out of a risotto what you put into it – that is a little time and patience. You can skive and put in 80% of the effort or even opt to prepare the first stage in advance, but for perfection – meaning creamy sauce combined with just cooked rice – a little elbow grease and cooking from start to finish are essential.
A heatproof spatula comes into its own here, especially twinned with an All-Clad saucier. See page 128 for ingredients.

1

2

3

4

1 Heat the saucier to a medium heat. Add the oil and allow to heat through before adding the onion. Sweat the onion over a medium heat until it has become translucent – this should take about 5-8 minutes – add the garlic and sweat for a further 3-4 minutes. The onion must be properly cooked before adding the rice.

2 Add the rice and stir it around for a couple of minutes until well-coated with the oil and the outside of each grain is translucent. You will hear the rice beginning to 'ping' as it heats and toasts. Don't let it colour at this stage – you are just slightly toasting it until you release the aroma.

3 The 'ping' sound is an important sign – the rice is screaming for more liquid. Add any wine called for in your recipe and use your heatproof spatula to stir the rice and evenly distribute the liquid. Continue to stir until all the wine is absorbed and the rice is screaming for more liquid. Add a ladleful of stock and repeat.

4 When stirring, make sure you get right into the corners to ensure the rice doesn't stick. Continue this process, adding the stock one ladle at a time. The creaminess of your risotto comes from the starch in the rice emulsifying with the stock – the more it is stirred the better the emulsification and the more starch is released so keep stirring!

5

6

7

5 Continue until the risotto is creamy but the grains still firm and on no account chalky or hard in the centre. From the time you start to add the stock, the risotto should cook in about 15-20 minutes, depending on the type of rice used.

6 When the grains are still firm but no longer chalky, remove from the heat, put on a lid and rest for 1 minute. You may have to add another ladleful of stock after this stage as the risotto will have thickened on standing – you're looking for a texture that is soft and yielding, not stiff or dry.

7 Return the pan to the heat and add in butter, Parmesan, an optional squeeze of lemon and seasoning. Beat for a minute or so until really creamy, then remove the pan from the heat. Cover the pan with a lid and leave to stand for a minute to let the risotto relax before serving.

homemade pasta

Homemade pasta is much more delicate than its shop-bought counterpart. It's doesn't have to be homemade everytime – robust sauces are better served with dried pasta. But for more delicate pasta dishes it's really worth that little bit of effort involved in making your own. It's worth remembering that a dish like ravioli would never be made to order in a restaurant, so keep life simple and prepare it in advance. See page 266 for ingredients.

techniques

1

2

3

4

1 Place the flour in a food processor and start giving it a whiz round. Add half of the eggs and keep whizzing until the mixture resembles fine breadcrumbs (it shouldn't be dusty, nor should it be a big, gooey ball). Add the remaining of the eggs and whiz until the mix resembles couscous. This takes 2–3 minutes, but if it doesn't look right you can regulate the texture by adding more flour or egg until it's spot on.

2 Tip out the dough and form into a ball shape. Knead briskly for 1 minute or until smooth and not grainy. Wrap in clingfilm and rest for 1 hour before using.

3 Now cut the dough into 2 pieces. For each piece, flatten with a rolling pin to 5 mm/¼ in thickness.

4 With the pasta machine at its widest setting, pass the dough through the rollers.

5

6

7

8

5 Repeat this process, folding over the dough
after each pass until the pasta is silky smooth
and shiny.

6 Change to the next setting up and pass through
the pasta again, this time without folding.
Change the setting again and pass through
twice without folding and continue working
through the settings until the desired thickness
is achieved.

7 At this stage you can use cutters to make the
pasta shape you are looking for.

8 Or keep it whole as a base for making ravioli
(see page 130).

blind baking

Most tart or flan recipes call for the tart to be blind baked to ensure the pastry is fully cooked.

1

2

3

4

1 Make your pastry and allow it to rest in the fridge (see page 267). Once ready begin to roll out on a lightly floured work surface. Dust your rolling pin with a little flour too, as this will help to stop the pastry from sticking. Rotate and turn the pastry frequently while rolling to ensure the pastry is round and even in thickness. The thickness of a beer mat is ideal.

2 Use your rolling pin to pick up the pastry and manoeuvre it over the flan tray. Working away from you, carefully unroll the pastry over the top of the tin. Placed on evenly, it should overlap on all sides.

3 Gently lift an edge of the pastry to allow you to push the pastry down into the corners without tearing. An easy way to press the pastry into the corners is to use a ball of waste dough, dipped in flour. Don't bother chopping off the spare bits of pastry around the edge. These will be easier to remove once the tart case is cooked.

4 Prick the pastry with a fork, to prevent it rising, then place in the fridge to rest for at least 20 minutes. Line the pastry with clingfilm (not the low cling variety) and fill with dried pulses. Fold in the edges of the film. Place on a baking sheet and bake at 180°C for 10-12 minutes.

5

6

5 Remove from the oven and lift out the clingfilm
  containing the beans or pulses.

6 If your recipe calls for the tart to be brushed
  with egg yolk, this is the time to do it. Return to
  the oven for 4-5 minutes until crisp and golden.
  Leave to cool, then trim off the excess pastry
  from the outside.

7

7 To remove the tart, place the tin on an upturned
  bowl and gently push the ring downwards and
  off the pastry. It should fall away leaving the
  pastry intact and resting on the base. Gently
  slide the case off the base. When completely
  cool, it's ready to be used.

batter

A batter is a mix of flour, eggs, milk or water and, on occasion, sugar and fat. The secret to a good batter comes down to consistency. This technique remains the same whether you are making crêpes, pancakes, batter or Yorkshire puddings.

1

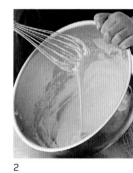

2

1 Sift the flour into a bowl and make a well. Pour the beaten eggs and sugar, if using, into the well and whisk.
2 When the mix has formed a light elastic consistency, add the milk.

3

3 Whisk in the milk or water until the batter has the consistency of single cream. If adding any fat (melted butter or oil) add and whisk until glossy and shiny. Set aside and leave to rest for an hour. If the batter has thickened after resting, thin using a little milk.

frying eggs

We'd be pretty stuffed without eggs in the kitchen. Used whole, or separated into the whites and yolk they're a vital ingredient in hundreds of dishes, from soufflés to ice cream, biscuits to pasta. If you're worried about salmonella, or you are cooking for vulnerable individuals, then forget runny yolks, and cook your eggs right through.

Freshness

1

2

1 Eggs have a permeable shell so with time, more air enters the shell and begins to break down the egg. With a fresh egg, the yolk will stand proud on top of jelly-like albumen. It holds together well, making it perfect for frying and poaching.

2 With time, the albumen becomes thinner and the yolk, more delicate. Note how it spreads over the pan. Though not good for frying or poaching, the white will be perfect for meringues and soufflés (see page 207).

Frying

1

2

1 The chefs all have their own preferences for a fried egg. We're opting for Nick's crispy based egg here. Heat the pan to hot and add a little oil. Crack the egg into the pan, it should start to cook and bubble straight away. Do not touch the egg at all until the white is partially set.

2 Try to apply an even heat to the egg by basting with hot oil. When the white is set, the edges crispy and the yolk still wobbly, use a cranked turner (see page 52) to remove the egg. Drain off any excess oil on kitchen towel and serve immediately.

poaching eggs

Properly cooked, a poached egg is simply one of life's finest pleasures: a firm white ball that cuts open to reveal a thick runny yolk. We are showing Alan's method for poaching eggs, which is foolproof, but gives a whole extra espresso cup to wash up! Nick breaks his egg straight into the pan, holding the shell over the pan using the thin strand of albumen connecting the egg and the shell to hold the egg in place until it sets. It's these little differences that make life a little more interesting!

1

2

1 Crack your egg into a small cup. For the perfect poached egg, the cooking water must not contain salt, but should have a generous splash of vinegar (clear not malt) to help set the albumen. Bring the pan to the boil and using a perforated spoon or a whisk, stir the water to create a whirlpool in the middle.

2 This will take the water off the boil. Immediately lower the cup into the water, holding the bottom of the cup in the water for 20 seconds. Lower the cup completely into the water and empty the egg into the water.

3

3 Poaching water should have no bubbles, but will have steam rising from the surface. For a runny yolk and set white cook for about 5-6 minutes, use a slotted spoon to remove the egg, drain on some kitchen roll and serve.

4

5

4 If cooking in advance, remove the eggs from the pan when slightly under-done (after 3 minutes). Place in a bowl of cold water to stop the cooking process. Drain the eggs off on to kitchen paper and place on a dry cloth on top of a tray and store in the fridge for up to 24 hours.

5 To serve, place in a pan of slightly salted poaching water for roughly 2-3 minutes. Remove with a slotted spoon and drain on kitchen paper. There you have it: the perfect poached egg.

custard

Custard is a milk or cream based sauce, thickened with egg yolks. We're sure you'll agree it's damn fine as it is, but it can also be made with more cream to make crème brûlée or to form the base for creamy ice creams. Heat is the critical factor here: under-cook and the custard could make you ill, if however, the milk becomes too hot then the egg will curdle and you'll be looking at sweet scrambled eggs!

1

2

1 Place the milk, cream and vanilla pod and seeds into a thick-bottomed pan and place on a high heat until boiling. Meanwhile add the sugar to the yolks and beat well. A common mistake is to pour the sugar over the eggs and leave them unmixed while the pan is warming. This will start to cure the yolks and lumps may form.

2 Beat the eggs yolks until they are thickened and pale. This pale egg mix is frequently used in recipes, so it's worth taking a look here to see what you should be looking for.

3

3 Slowly pour half the hot mix onto the bowl of mixed eggs, whisking continually.

4

5

6

7

4 Take the pan off the heat. Use a heat-proof spatula to scrape the egg and milk mix from the bowl back into the pan. Place back on a medium heat and stir with a spatula. Stir in a figure of eight to prevent hot spots forming.

5 The mixture should begin to thicken within about 2 minutes. The perfect temperature is 82°C/180°F, and a thermo probe will prove invaluable here. If you don't have a probe, watch for little puffs of steam escaping from the side of the pan. These are a warning sign that the custard is getting too hot; take the pan off the heat and continue stirring.

6 You're aiming to have a mix that has thickened enough to coat the back of the spatula.

7 When it's the right consistency, take the custard off the heat and strain immediately through a fine sieve to remove any small lumps which may have formed. Serve immediately, or pour into a clean bowl, cover with clingfilm and chill quickly in an ice bath.

caramel

Making a caramel is an excellent basic skill to master. The secret is not to over-stir the sugar as it melts as this will cause clumps to form. One word of caution: please wear gloves whilst making caramel as sugar can give a nasty burn and is almost impossible to remove if it drips onto the skin.

techniques

1

2

1 Heat a medium (10 in/25 cm) heavy-based frying pan. Sift the caster sugar into the centre of the pan to make a pyramid half the diameter of the pan. The heat will slowly start to melt the sugar.

2 The melting sugar will make the pyramid start to collapse. When this happens, give the pan a shoogle (that's a shake to those of you unfamiliar with Scottish vernacular!) and allow the sugar to continue to melt.

3

3 When there is more liquid than dry sugar, use a heatproof spatula to work in the rest of the sugar, breaking down any lumps. Watch out for hot spots – gently push the sugar around with the spatula to incorporate cool sugar into areas that are overheating. Do not over-stir as this can cause it to clump and appear crystalised.

4

5

4 You are looking for a golden caramel colour (the colour of sesame oil is a good guide) and take care not to let it get too dark, as it will make the caramel taste burnt and far too bitter. If you do see it darkening too quickly, simply take the pan off the heat and continue to stir. When you have the right colour, dip the base of the pan in a bowl of cold water for 5 seconds to stop the caramel cooking any further. Many recipes, such as caramelised fruits, will require caramel that is made up to this stage.

5 To make a caramel sauce, once your caramel is golden (as at the start of step 4) remove from the heat and add a little cream and stir through. Be careful as a particularly hot steam will come off. Put the pan back on the heat and stir through the remaining cream and stir until fully incorporated.

chargrilling

Chargrilling is a great way of cooking veggies, fish, shellfish, meat and poultry as it gives them all a wonderful characteristic flavour and appearance. The important factors are making sure the grill is at a high heat, basting the food with oil or marinade and keeping the food still as it chars to give pronounced charred markings. We're using a chargrill here, but the same principles will also apply on a barbecue.

techniques

1

2

1 Begin by brushing the ingredients with oil. Lean meats such as chicken benefit from being marinated to help prevent the meat drying out.

2 If you are dealing with small pieces of meat or veg that will be fiddly to turn, use a skewer or cocktail stick to create a raft or kebab, which will make turning and even cooking easier. Wooden skewers or sticks should be soaked for 30 minutes to prevent them from burning.

3

3 Preheat the griddle until hot. Place your fillets, kebabs or rafts into the griddle pan. Food cooking for a short time only will benefit from a press down using the back of a ladle to ensure good contact with the ridges.

4

5

4 If you would like to give your meat a criss-cross effect, turn your ingredients 90° (without turning them over). Turn over using tongs. Here we have given asparagus chargilled stripes.

5 Repeat the procedure on the other side, turning 90°C/190°F if you want the crisscross lines. If your ingredients look as if they are drying out, baste them with a little oil.

If cooking poultry, check the meat is completely cooked before serving. Thicker cuts can be finished in the oven if more cooking is required.

frying in a 'happy pan'

I feel getting your pan to the right temperature is so important that it warrants a section of its own. When frying, it's important to have a good heat in the pan to allow your food to caramelise, but not so hot that your food burns.

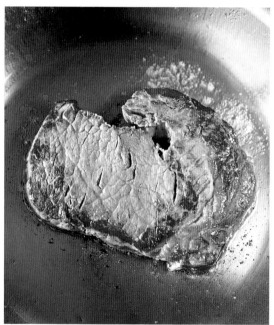

1

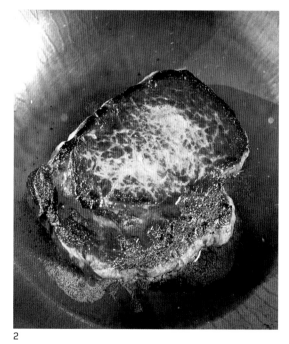

2

1 If your pan isn't hot enough and you add in a lovely piece of fillet, it will heat slowly and eventually stew in its own juices. This will result in a grey piece of meat, lacking the tasty characteristics that caramelisation achieves.

2 If your pan is too hot the oil will spit when adding ingredients. It's likely that your piece of produce will burn before it has had a chance to cook properly, resulting in a bitter burnt crust and undercooked meat in the middle.

3 How can you tell the temperature? Hold your hand over the heated pan. If it's too hot to hold your hand over, take off the heat for a while. If it just feels warm, crank the heat up a little.

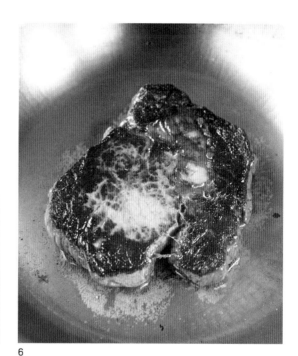

4

5

6

4 Add the oil. If the oil stays in the middle of the pan, it's likely the pan isn't hot enough. If the oil quickly spreads and thins, even starting to discolour or give off a haze, the pan is too hot. At a good temperature it will start to spread: swirl it to coat the base of the pan evenly.

5 Need one more piece of reassurance? Rather than slapping your steak in only to a fierce splatter or to hear nothing at all, touch a corner into the pan – it should make a satisfying sizzle. This is the sign of a good pan temperature.

6 It's also worth considering how big your pan is and how much you are cooking and then using the best burner on your hob. Don't use a big 30-cm/12-in frying pan to cook a single scallop on your 5KW burner as you're unlikely to have great control over the temperature. Conversely if you are cooking 4 steaks, don't try to cook them all in a medium pan on the lowest power burner. The steaks will reduce the temperature of the pan causing them to stew. Either use a bigger pan or cook in 2 batches. With a happy pan, perfect steaks will be on the menu.

frying and caramelisation

We've used a fillet steak to illustrate frying, but the method applies to anything fried from steak to scallops. Don't use a non-stick frying pan as this will curtail the development of the crust.

techniques

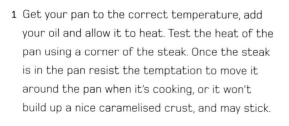

1

2

1 Get your pan to the correct temperature, add your oil and allow it to heat. Test the heat of the pan using a corner of the steak. Once the steak is in the pan resist the temptation to move it around the pan when it's cooking, or it won't build up a nice caramelised crust, and may stick.

2 After a few minutes, you will see a caramelised crust starting to form around the edges. When the crust has developed, turn over your steak. You should find that a nice crust has built up on the bottom. Again, don't play with the steak once it's turned.

3

4

5

3 All meat, fish and shellfish contracts on contact with a hot pan, often meaning that the centre of the meat is off the pan completely. Once the meat has been caramelised on both sides, turn it over and give a quick cook on the first side once more. At this stage you can add butter to the pan for extra colour and flavour. Butter cannot withstand long periods over high heats, so use oil for temperature at the start and add butter towards the end of cooking. Use the melted butter to baste the steaks.

4 Judging how long the steak should cook is difficult. Every steak will be different and chefs do this by feel, but it's easier with a digital thermometer. Immediately upon removing the meat from the pan the temperature should be: rare 40°C/100°F; medium-rare 52°C/125°F, medium 63°C/145°F; well-done will be 74°C/165°F.

5 As important as cooking the steak, is resting it properly. During cooking, the fibres in the meat shrink and the steak tenses up, forcing all the juices to the centre. Resting the meat in a warm place allows the fibres to relax and the juices to re-distribute throughout the meat. A perfect steak should have a good caramelised crust, cooked to your preference in the centre and when cut open, no juices will run out.

roasting

Roasting refers to cooking food in dry heat, i.e. in the oven. This method can be used to slow cook large cuts of meat or smaller fillets, but there are a few key pointers to bear in mind depending on the cut you are using. The big challenge with lamb and beef joints is getting them cooked to succulent perfection, my ideal hovering somewhere between rare and medium-rare. Regardless of what you are roasting it is important to let all fish and meat rest before carving or serving.

1

2

3

1 When slow roasting a leg of lamb or beef joint make sure you have a roasting tin or pan big enough for your chosen cut, and keep the skin and fat on and bone in to retain maximum flavour. Score the fat in a criss cross pattern and season well with salt and pepper.

2 Heat a frying pan or roasting tin to a medium heat but don't add any oil. Stick the joint into the pan fat-side down and leave it alone. The fat should start to melt and sizzle. After about 10 minutes, the fat should be starting to smoke. Carefully turn the meat over and place the whole pan in the oven for 45 minutes to an hour.

3 With a big joint, it's hard to judge how well it's done by oven temperature and cooking time; so insert a meat thermometer into the thickest part of the joint. For rare, it should be 45°C/110°F, for medium-rare, 50°C/120°F, for medium, 55°C /130°F, well-done, 65°C/150°F. If you don't have a thermometer, insert a skewer into the meat and hold for 10 seconds. Take out and place on the underside of your lower lip. If it is cold, the joint is too rare and needs longer to cook; if hot, it's done.

4

5

4 It's essential to rest a roasting joint after cooking to allow the fibres to relax and the juices to re-distribute throughout the meat. A 4-lb/1.8-kg chicken or leg of lamb will need about 20 minutes to rest after cooking, a denser sirloin about 30–40 minutes. Remove from the roasting tin and place on a warm plate then loosely cover with tin foil (don't tuck in the edges or you'll keep the heat in). The joint will stay warm at room temperature, and will be perfectly succulent when you come to serve. Remember to use any juices in a gravy or just pour over the meat.

5 To make a good base for a gravy, deglaze the pan or roasting tin with a glass of red wine, scraping off any crusty bits off the base using a heatproof spatula. Add in any juices from the rested joint. Add these into your gravy recipe (see page 233).

sautéeing

When you sauté, you brown smaller pieces of meat before creating a sauce in the same pan. The ultimate, speedy one-pan meal with less washing up! A sauté pan is always best, but a high-sided non-stick frying pan will do just as well.

techniques

1

2

3

2 Remove the meat from the pan and place on a pre-heated baking tray to keep warm.

3 If your recipe calls for veggies, reduce the heat of the pan a little, add them to the pan and brown all over. You can add some butter for colour and flavour at this stage.

1 Heat your frying pan to medium hot and add sunflower oil. Place your meat in the pan but don't move it around, which will allow a caramelised crust to form. When browned, turn using a cranked turner. Brown on the other side.

4

5

4 Add some wine to the pan. Stir around in the pan with a heatproof spatula to pick up all the caramelised pieces (packed with flavour) from the bottom of the pan. The alcohol will boil off quickly, leaving a nice winey residue. This is called deglazing the pan.

5 Add the stock to the pan and leave the liquid to reduce by about half, return the meat to the pan and add in any herbs (the example here is tarragon chicken) stirring occasionally to prevent the meat and vegetables from sticking to the bottom of the pan.

6

6 Add cream if the recipe calls for it, stirring to combine with the other ingredients. Reduce the sauce by one-quarter and serve.

stir-frying

The important thing with stir-fries is getting the ingredients cut into small, evenly-sized pieces so that they all cook at the same time. Cutting pieces into thin batons increases the surface area, helping things to cook faster. It's also very important to have all your ingredients prepared before you start cooking. At the school we prefer to cook any meat separately from the veggies, as meat can often leak out water, causing the stir-fry to steam instead of fry.

1   2   3   4

1 Heat the wok until it's very hot and add the oil, sloshing it around a little to coat the pan. Make sure you use an oil with a high smokepoint, such as vegetable oil. Olive oil isn't suitable as it will start to smoke before your wok is hot enough for stir-frying.

2 Add the vegetables to the pan. Keep the veggies moving at all times, either by carefully tossing the wok, or by using a heatproof spatula. This ensure that the veggies are evenly cooked.

3 Add your liquid to the pan, such as soy sauce, rice wine, or sherry. Continue to stir.

4 Add any seasoning, fresh spices or herbs and if you were having meat, add this back into the wok. Continue to stir until the vegetables are lightly cooked and softened but not mushy.

stews and casseroles

The secret to a good casserole is the browning and caramelisation of the meat and veg, which will add flavour to the finished dish. Casserole refers to the type of pot it is cooked in, generally a large oven-proof large pot with a well-fitting lid. Slow cooking like this is ideal for slightly tougher cuts of meat, which will tenderise and break down in the cooking process.

1

2

3

4

1 Start by browning off the ingredients in the pan. Start with the meat, removing with a slotted spoon.

2 Next brown the veggies, again removing with a slotted spoon.

3 Add a splash of wine to the pan and use a spatula to scrape up any caramelised remnants of meat or vegetables. Allow the alcohol in the wine to burn off and the liquid to reduce down. This process picks up all the flavours left in the pan from the browning process.

4 Tip the rest of the ingredients back into the pan with the stock and bring to the boil. Reduce to a simmer with the lid on, until cooked through. Remove the lid for the last half hour of cooking to reduce down the sauce and to intensify the flavour.

deep-frying

If you deep-fry regularly, consider an electric deep-fat fryer. Never use an open chip pan, instead use a wok, which is safer because the sloping sides allow the hot oil to bubble up without bubbling over. Unless making crisps or chips, food will have to be coated with batter or crumbs to protect it from the heat. Chips are an exception in technique, as they have to be cooked twice (see page 258).

1

2

1 Prepare your food for deep-frying, whether chopping or covering with batter. If frying food with a high water content e.g. potatoes, it's a good idea to roll them up in a clean tea towel to remove excess water. If coating in batter, dust the food with flour to help it stick and deep fry immediately for best results.

2 Only fill a wok to one-third of its capacity and a fryer to half full. Hot oil is dangerous. Using the correct oil is essential too – a vegetable oil is best as they can withstand heat in excess of 200°C/390°F on average. Remember never to move a fryer or wok with hot oil, wait for it to cool first. Never let oil heat above 190°C/370°F. If it does, turn off the heat source immediately.

3

3 Use a cube of bread to check the oil temperature. On a low heat (or 160°C/320°F) a cube will take 60 seconds to brown, 40 seconds on a medium heat (180°C/360°F) or 20 seconds on a very high heat (190°C/370°F). For vegetable crisps or chips do a test piece, if it starts to cook immediately but not furiously the oil is at temperature.

4

5

6

4 It is very important to deep-fry food in small batches. If the fryer or basket is too full, the temperature of the oil will drop too much and result in soggy, pale food.

5 If using a wok to deep fry, a spider is an essential tool as it will allow you to manoeuvre larger amounts of food at a time and also move food around in the pan so that it doesn't stick together.

6 Always drain food off on kitchen paper. If keeping fried food warm, do not cover it or it will become soggy. Instead, spread it in a single layer on a baking sheet and keep in a warm oven with the door open to allow air to circulate.

whisking

Whisking egg whites basically traps air within the mix, which will add lightness to soufflés, cakes, mousses and many more dishes. The egg white, or albumen is a protein stretched by whisking, this stretched protein holds pockets of air that expand on cooking creating light mixtures.

Egg whites

1   2   3   4

1 Begin by separating your eggs. Break the egg carefully in two and pass the yolk gently between the two parts of shell. Be careful not to damage the yolk, as even a little yolk in the white will prevent it from whisking up correctly.

2 Add a little lemon juice or cream of tartar to the whites. This will help to stretch the whites and make it easier to tease out the long strands without them snapping. This is essential for fluffy whites. Older egg whites will increase in volume much quicker than fresher eggs. The foam is a little less stable than fresh whites, but ideal for meringues.

3 We prefer to use a stainless steel bowl to whisk eggs, but a glass or ceramic bowl will do. Avoid plastic bowls as they can often hold a residue of grease, which will prevent the eggs whisking properly. Tilt the bowl up at an angle and begin to whisk.

4 Lift the egg whites high to allow as much air as possible into the mix.

5

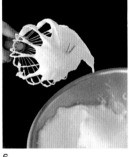

6

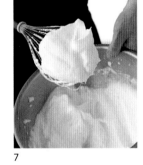

7

6 If you continue to whisk for longer, the mix will start to stiffen a little. A medium peak is just a little firmer that a soft peak, but should still wobble when the whisk is shaken.

7 Meringues require egg whites to be whisked to a stiff peak. Even the strongest arms would give up on this task, so it's best to use a hand mixer, or even better a table top mixer. Stiff peaks appear shiny and moist and when ready will remain in a bowl held upside down.

5 Continue whisking until the egg white stands up in soft peaks. With a soft peak the peaks will curl over rather than stand up stiffly. Eggs reach the soft peak stage relatively quickly, so whisking by hand will allow for the best control. Soft peak mixes are often used to lighten mixtures, for example our moist chocolate cake (page 204).

whisking 'to the ribbon'

You may see reference in a recipe to whisk egg yolks and sugar 'to the ribbon'. This is often called for in baking, where egg yolks are whisked until frothy and pale in colour.

Egg yolk and sugar

1

2

1 This can be done by hand, but is a little quicker and you'll get the same results from using a hand mixer. Place the eggs and sugar into a bowl and mix.

2 As more air is incorporated into the mix, the yellow colour of the yolks will start to become paler until almost white and foamy. The mixture is ready when it can leave a trail on the surface when drizzled from the beater or whisk.

whipping cream

Like with egg whites, you may see the term whip to a soft peak when using cream. Unless otherwise stated, most recipes will look for a soft peak, which we've illustrated before. For cream fillings or toppings, a thicker cream will be needed. You should know when it's at a spreadable consistency, but take care not to over-whip, as shown.

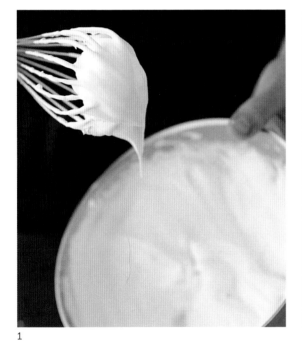

1

2

1 When whipping cream, as soon as the mix starts to thicken keep an eye on it. Most recipes will be looking for whipped cream to be taken to a soft peak stage.

2 If you overwhip cream, as shown here, you can add a little milk to take it back a stage. If it has been whipped to the point of being grainy it is quite difficult to rescue.

folding

If you have to add whisked eggs into a heavier mixture, care has to be taken to avoid knocking the air out, especially after all your hard work. The key is to lighten the heavier mix with a spoonful of whites before using a folding technique to incorporate the rest of the mix.

1

2

3

4

1 First fold a tablespoon of the whisked egg whites and stir it into the heavier mix, this is called 'loosening' the mix.

2 Gently fold the loosened mix into the egg whites using a spatula. Very gently lift egg whites from the bottom of bowl at the side and lift them over into the centre at the top, repeat on the other side, following a figure of eight.

3 The mix shouldn't be fully incorporated and is ready when a marbling of whites is still visible. It is very important not to overwork the mix.

4 Take care when moving the mix into its baking tin, trying at all times not to knock any air out of the mix.

emulsification

Emulsification occurs when you mix fat such as melted butter, or oil with liquid such as water, vinegar, stock or lemon juice. Some emulsified mixes are temporary and will revert back to their separated state after a while. A good example of this is vinaigrette. Egg yolks have an emulsifying quality and are used to create more permanent mixes and help liquids that wouldn't normally combine to do so.

Butter sauce

1   2   3   4

1 Butter sauce contains hard fat (butter) so is more difficult to emulsify successfully than a mix using oil. First add the shallots, white wine and vinegar into a small heavy based pan. Reduce down by three-quarters.

2 It is important that the butter is diced and chilled. If the sauce overheats it will split. Add the butter, keeping the pan on the heat and whisk furiously.

3 Temperature is critical here. If you see any signs of the sauce getting too hot (bubbling at the sides or steam escaping) take the pan off the heat immediately. Try to maintain a temperature around 50°C/120°F (still comfortable to stick your finger in).

4 The sauce is ready when it's smooth, shiny and there is no hint of oiliness on the surface.

mechanical aids: blending and puréeing

The blades on a blender are designed to purée or liquidise, not chop like a food processor. In general, using a blender is as simple as putting in the ingredients, affixing the lid and off you go. If you are dealing with hot liquids, we have a few pointers to save you some scalding. Another indispensable item for smooth foods is a Mouli grater. See also food processor.

Blending hot foods

1 To blend hot liquids, place all the ingredients in the jug and place the lid on. Take out the central cup from the lid to allow steam to escape. If you leave it in the lid is sealed which can cause a dangerous build up of steam.

2 Use a tea towel to completely cover the hole. This will prevent splattering and will allow some of the steam to escape whilst processing. Start to process the soup.

Using a Mouli

1   2

1 Another way to create purées with texture is to use a Mouli. Here we're using a Mouli to create uber-smooth mashed potatoes. It can also be used for any kind of puréed veg and for making really smooth soups.

2 Turn the handle to force the soft potato through the plate. It should start to come out in long threads. This method is far superior to using a potato masher, as it doesn't compress the potatoes and keeps the mix light.

mechanical aids: chopping and slicing

Food processors are great labour-saving devices that can be used to slice, dice, grate, mix and, of course, process. They don't do the same job as a blender, however, so don't use for soups or smoothies. You will see processors being used in many of the recipes here, many for straightforward processing, as in pasta or pastry, but here are a few pointers to bear in mind when using one.

Food processor

2

1 A food processor is handy for chunky sauces where you want to bruise and chop the ingredients while retaining some of the texture. When making pastes and sauces, it's important to scrape down the inside of the jug several times whilst processing.

2 Don't just put the attachments in a drawer and forget about them. We love the versatility of the Magimix 5200 model – should a mandoline seem like an indulgence, the 5200 will slice veg thinly in addition to hundreds of other tasks.

Using a mandoline

1

1 A favourite of chefs everywhere is the mandoline. Nothing slices vegetables as thinly and evenly as this, and in particular it is indispensable for dauphinoise potatoes. Always remember to keep your finger tips raised well away from the blade or use a guard.

harmony

the meaning of harmony

Harmony is something that happens when you combine together fantastic, well-prepared produce, to make something that's greater than the sum of its parts. Put simply, it's about everything on your plate working together and serving a purpose.

Some ingredients will have natural harmony. For example, consider the following:

Tomato and basil

Lime and coriander

Garlic and mushrooms

Vanilla and cream

Lamb and rosemary

Steak and chips

Bacon and eggs

Conversely, there are some combinations you should always stay clear of:

Chocolate and red wine

Fish and mint

Beef and white chocolate

Milk and lemon juice

Anchovies and ice cream (unless you're pregnant!)

There are those who might recommend experimenting and finding new combinations. But I say leave the molecular gastronomy to the handful of superchefs who really understand how it works. Us mere mortals need to stick with the tried and tested. After all, the more elements you try to include in one dish, the harder it will be for your palate to decipher what's going on in your mouth.

Dishes with harmony will offer a perfect, sensuous experience, with a special and often allusive combination of taste, flavour, texture, smell and appearance. But to understand how all these things come together, we need to look more closely at how our senses are affected by the food we eat.

Food and your senses

When you're set to be creative in the kitchen, one of the best things you can do to better your skills is learn how to make use all of your senses. When I'm cooking, I become totally absorbed in the process. I engage fully with whatever I'm making and use all my senses to take in the maximum amount of information possible. I'll listen to the pans, and taste the ingredients, I'll smell and watch things cook, and touch the food to gauge when it's done. It's such an involved process for me that I shut out everything else. In fact, it was a bit of a revelation to my wife that I could actually cook and talk at the same time, though admittedly, I only seem able to do it when I'm in front of an audience or a TV camera!

A lot of people rely solely on their sense of taste while they're cooking. Obviously taste is incredibly important to a chef but if you can learn how to use all of your senses, it will raise the bar on everything you produce. You'll start to judge how well a piece of beef is cooking simply by listening to the sizzle in the pan and watching for subtle changes in colour; you'll be able to smell when that loaf of bread has browned and baked to perfection in the oven; and you'll learn how to feel the tension in a piece of monkfish as it roasts, and use your fingers, not just your watch, to judge when it's perfectly succulent.

Let's start by looking at the key sense of taste, but in particular I want to highlight the difference between taste and flavour. Taste is simply what your tongue tells you about the food you're eating. It's a very powerful sensation but the tongue's ability is limited and can only detect sweet, salty, sour, bitter and umami (a Japanese word, meaning savoury, it is generally accepted as the fifth taste). Now, flavour is something much more subtle and comes not from the tongue, but from your nose.

The best way for you to understand this is to try a simple experiment. Take a piece of fresh herb leaf like coriander, basil or parsley. Hold your nose, place the leaf in your mouth and chew it. Concentrate hard on what you're eating. Taste anything? Then release your nose. Ahh! Spot the difference? That dramatic burst in flavour is all down to your olfactory canal. The herb contains nothing that your tongue could sense as taste, but when you released your nose, air surged up from your oesophagus lifting the molecules from the herb that we recognize as flavour, and these can only be sensed in your olfactory canal, not on the tongue. For me, these subtle nuances are the sexy bit of eating, and the thing that some people don't seem to understand. The inherent character of our food is in its flavour, not its taste, and flavour is all about fragrance. Without it, our eating experience would be lessened, and we'd miss out on the subtleties and complexities of foods like garlic and ginger, herbs and spices.

The problem is that taste is such a strong sense it tends to override all the subtle and sophisticated things your nose is telling you about flavour. Your brain also interprets taste as something positive, and seems hard-wired into thinking that a dish is good to eat if it tastes sweet or salty. This means that manufacturers of food can be a little bit sneaky and rely on pure taste to sell their food, even sometimes making big profits on inferior-quality products by packing them with sugar and salt; good examples being sausages, burgers, processed cheese and sweet fizzy drinks.

However, salt is the real thing to watch out for with processed foods. It's cheap and manufacturers add it to almost everything from baked beans to ice cream. But because it's so prevalent in our basics like bread and cereals, most of us are eating more than the current recommended intake of 6 g/$^1/_8$ oz of salt a day, and often without realising it. Salt does have its uses as a preservative and also holds water in

suspension in products like processed meat. But it also contains sodium, which can cause high blood pressure, so it's always a good idea to check out the salt content of any product you're eating. Complicated labels can make this a challenge, and you'll often see salt listed as sodium (which needs to be multiplied by 2.5 to get the salt level) or as a proportion of the whole packet rather than just what you're eating.

If you want to try cutting down on salt, a great way to do it is to try re-training your taste buds to appreciate all the nuances of flavour. If you can avoid highly-seasoned foods for only three weeks, you should start to notice a real difference in your palate. You'll crave better quality, fresher produce and really notice all the wonderful things your nose is telling you about what you're eating. It'll also help you to become a better cook, as it takes real skill to add flavour to a dish, while anyone can reach for the salt pot or the sugar bowl.

Once you're tuned in to taste and flavour, another sense to start thinking about in the kitchen is touch, which is important for two reasons. First of all, touch can help you to judge when your food is ready. Take a steak for example; as it cooks, the tension across the meat changes and gets tighter, and by feeling the steak with your fingertips while it cooks, you'll be able to sense this. If you want to gauge the level of doneness, tap lightly from the outside and when it feels the same tension all the way across, the steak is ready. Simple! You can use the same technique for fillets of chicken or fish, but also for cakes, flans and tarts.

Touch is also important because of mouth-feel. Your tongue not only senses taste, but also the texture of what you're eating. And why is texture so important? Well, just think of something like sago pudding: to my palate, it has no texture at all but just slides over the tongue like slimy frogspawn. On the other hand, think of something like puff pastry with its intermingled crunchy and chewy layers, or compare the experience of munching through a fabulous crunchy salad as opposed to eating something limp and soggy. Even soup can be lifted by the addition of a few croutons or a slice of crusty bread. I love to tantalize the whole of my mouth with the feel of food, and I find that again, it really does heighten the experience of what you're eating.

Sight is another sense that's often forgotten about by cooks, and again, it's vital for two reasons. Firstly, it's useful while you're actually in the process of bringing all your ingredients together. Put simply, when something you're cooking looks right, it probably is right. That chocolate sauce, for example, looks just right when it's uniformly thick and glossy with an even, luscious colour. Conversely, there's something very wrong with that custard with the ominous lumps floating around on the surface! Trust your eyes and get the chocolate sauce out of the pan and onto a plate (incidentally, a sieve is the best tool for rescuing your lumpy custard).

But sight is also important for when you come to serve. A lot of the pleasure in food actually happens before you start eating. It's in the anticipation. Food should make you hungry, and the best dishes are the

ones you enjoy from the moment you catch sight of them. So never just slop food onto a plate, a bit of accuracy can make a big difference to what you're serving. It's not about being poncy and making little neat towers of things either (though sometimes it can be fun to create something spectacular! See Alan's Apple Sorbet page 217). Think rather of presenting the food to its best advantage. Properly cooked fresh fish will look fantastic on the plate and doesn't need any messing about. When you've got great natural ingredients let them shine. A bit of careful presentation can give a big boost to your eating pleasure.

So now you're thinking about taste and flavour, you're thinking about touch and texture and you are thinking about the visual appeal of your food, considering all these things will go some way towards helping you to create fabulous meals. But to me, flavour is god in the kitchen, and if you can learn to appreciate flavour, then you're on your way to creating truly great food.

recipes

risotto
with peas, mint and crispy bacon

ingredients

about 1.5 litres/2¾ pints
  chicken or vegetable stock
2 tablespoons olive oil
130 g/4½ fl oz cubed
  pancetta (cubetti di
  pancetta or lardons in
  supermarkets)

1 medium onion, peeled and
  finely chopped
1 garlic clove, peeled and
  finely chopped
400 g/14 oz Italian risotto rice
150 ml/5 fl oz dry white wine
200 g/7 oz fresh or frozen
  peas

50 g/1¾ oz unsalted butter
freshly grated Parmesan
  cheese, plus extra to serve
  (optional)
50 g/1¾ oz chopped fresh
  mint, plus extra to serve
  (optional)

crispy bacon/pancetta, to
  garnish
Maldon salt and freshly
  ground black pepper

serves **4**

technique
risotto page 84

mise en place
• If time is pressing cook the
  risotto base up until the
  wine is absorbed, remove
  from the heat and hold
  until ready. Make sure the
  stock is hot if you do so.

Alan says: Use the right pan
for the job, not too deep and
not too shallow – a saucier
is best. Use with a flexible
spatula (see page 52) – this
makes for even stirring.
Timing is crucial – do not
overcook or you will have
rice porridge. The rice should
be 'screaming out' for each
ladleful of stock, so make
sure the previous ladleful
has been well absorbed by
the rice.

method

1 Have the stock at a constant, very gentle simmer in a pan beside your
   risotto pan and have a ladle to hand.
2 Follow the technique for making risotto on page 84.
3 After 12–15 minutes stir in the peas. Check the texture of the rice. When
   firm, but not chalky, take the pan off the heat and allow to rest for a minute.
4 Beat in the butter, Parmesan, seasoning and mint. Beat for a minute or so
   until really creamy, then remove the pan from the heat. Cover the pan with a
   lid and leave to stand for a minute to let the risotto relax. You may have to
   add another ladleful of stock at this stage as the risotto will have thickened
   on standing – you're looking for a texture that is soft and yielding, not stiff
   or dry. Uncover, stir again, then serve immediately, sprinkled with a little
   more Parmesan and chopped mint if you like. Divide between four serving
   bowls and top with some crispy pancetta slices.

butternut squash ravioli
with sage butter

ingredients

1 x recipe pasta dough
(see p266)
1 medium butternut squash
1 whole red chilli, halved and
deseeded
3 whole garlic cloves, skin on
3 tablespoons extra virgin
olive oil

1 teaspoon chopped fresh
thyme
25 g/1 oz freshly grated
Parmesan cheese, plus
extra to serve
semolina flour, for dusting

for the sage butter:
150 g/5½ oz unsalted butter
about 20 fresh sage leaves
freshly squeezed juice of ½
a lemon
Maldon salt and freshly
ground black pepper

serves **4**

vegetable recipes

techniques
homemade pasta page 86

mise en place
• Make the ravioli in advance,
cook, refresh in cold water,
dry and lay out on a clean
tea towel. Cover with oiled
clingfilm and keep in the
fridge for up to 6 hours.
Reheat in boiling water for
2 minutes.
or
• Make the ravioli and
freeze uncooked. Allow
5-7 minutes cooking time
after defrosting.

John says: Instead of
cutting discs, you can keep
the pasta strip whole,
dotting spoonfuls of the
filling along the length (well
spaced). Dampen the long
edges and between the
mounds and fold over the
pasta lengthways. Cut into
individual ravioli.

method

1 Preheat the oven to 200°C/400°F/gas mark 6. Using a large cook's knife,
cut the butternut squash in half lengthways. Scoop out and discard the
seeds, then peel the squash and cut the flesh into 2 cm/¾ in dice. Place in
a roasting tin, add the halved chilli and whole garlic cloves, pour over the oil
and season well. Toss to coat, then roast in the oven for about 30 minutes
or until soft and starting to caramelise. Take out of the oven, pop the garlic
cloves out of their skins and mash the whole lot together with a fork or
potato masher. Beat in the thyme and Parmesan and allow to cool.

2 Now unwrap the pasta dough and cut into two pieces. Work with one piece,
rewrapping the other half. Follow the technique for rolling out pasta on
page 86. I use the thinnest setting on the pasta machine, as you are
sandwiching two layers together.

3 Lay the length of pasta on a work surface dusted with semolina. Using a
10 cm/4 in cutter, cut circles along the length of the pasta. Working quickly,
place scant teaspoons of butternut squash filling in the middle of each
round. Dampen the edges with very little water on a pastry brush and fold
over to create a semi-circle, pressing in and around the mound to exclude
air as you do so. Lay in a single layer on a clean dry tea towel until ready to
cook – no longer than 2 hours or they turn soggy. Repeat the whole process
with the second ball of dough.

4 Place a large pan of salted water on to boil ready to cook the pasta. Drop
the ravioli into the boiling water to cook for 2 minutes. Refresh the ravioli in
a pan of cold water, remove using a slotted spoon or 'spider' and lay on a
clean tea towel until required. These can be covered with oiled clingfilm and
kept in the fridge for up to 6 hours .

5 For the sage butter, melt the butter in a small pan and heat gently. Add the
sage, turn up the heat and cook the butter until it turns palest brown and
the sage leaves start to crisp. Do not over-brown or burn the butter or sage.
Remove from the heat, cool and season with lemon juice, salt and pepper.

6 Cook the pasta for 2 minutes in boiling water, lift out with a slotted spoon
onto a warmed plate. Pour over the sage butter, toss and serve immediately
with plenty of Parmesan.

seasonal vegetable stew

ingredients

230 ml/8 fl oz marinated vegetable stock (see p230)
40 g/1½ oz butter
50 g/1¾ oz baby carrots, peeled and thinly sliced, diagonally
½ garlic clove, peeled and very finely chopped

3 baby leeks, very finely sliced
8 thin asparagus spears, trimmed and sliced into 5 cm/2 in lengths
50 g/1¾ oz baby courgettes, diced
30 g/1 oz mange tout, sliced

2 tablespoons fresh or frozen peas
1 tablespoon chopped fresh flat-leaf parsley
30 g/1 oz spring onions, sliced diagonally
8 cherry tomatoes, halved
finely grated zest of ½ lemon

serves 2

mise en place

• Prepare all the vegetables: nothing more otherwise it will lose its delicate flavour.

Nick says: Add some sliced monkfish or scallops to the stew and cook until opaque for a fresh, delicious starter.

method

1 Place a large pan over a medium heat. Add the butter and vegetable stock, whisking until the butter is fully incorporated. Add the sliced carrots and garlic and cook for 1½ minutes.

2 Next add the baby leeks, asparagus and the courgettes – you may need to add a little water here if the sauce has reduced too much. Give this a further 1½ minutes to cook.

3 Now add the mange tout and peas and cook for about 20 seconds. Add the parsley, spring onions, tomatoes and lemon zest. Stir well, bring to the boil and serve immediately.

potato and watercress soup

ingredients

30 g/1 oz unsalted butter
1 medium onion, peeled and
finely diced
2 garlic cloves, peeled and
finely chopped
2 medium floury potatoes
(about 200 g/7 oz), peeled
and cut into 5 cm/2 in dice

1 litre/1¾ pints chicken
stock (a stock cube will do)
275 g/10 oz watercress
Maldon salt and freshly
ground black pepper
crème fraîche and chopped
fresh chives, to serve

serves **4**

techniques
using a blender p118

mise en place
• Make the potato and stock
base and freeze, or cool
and store in the fridge for
up to 3 days. Reheat to
boiling and add the fresh
watercress.

John says: Add some raw
spinach before liquidising
for a really intense colour.

method

1 Heat a medium saucepan over a medium heat and add the butter. When melted and foaming, add the onion and sweat for 4–5 minutes over a low heat so that it cooks but doesn't colour. Add the garlic and sweat for a further 2–3 minutes. Add the diced potatoes and chicken stock and bring to the boil. Reduce the heat to a simmer and cook for 10–15 minutes. Season with a little salt and pepper. The soup can be prepared to this stage, cooled and stored in the fridge for up to 3 days, or frozen if more convenient.

2 Wash the watercress really well in cold water and pick over to remove any discoloured leaves. Stalks are fine, but do remove any extra-thick ones.

3 Add all the watercress in one go and boil for 2 minutes: this will set the colour and bring out the fresh, zingy flavour. Pour the soup into a blender and liquidize until smooth (see page 118), passing it through a sieve for a smooth texture or through a chinois for a super-silky texture.

4 Serve immediately with a dollop of crème fraîche, chopped chives and extra freshly ground black pepper.

vegetable recipes

french onion soup

ingredients

75 g/2³⁄₄ oz unsalted butter
500 g/1 lb 2 oz medium white
  onions, peeled and sliced
  (not Spanish onions: these
  are too sweet)
1 teaspoon caster sugar
1 garlic clove, peeled and
  crushed in a little salt

1 tablespoon flour
900 ml/1½ pints hot brown
  chicken stock (see p228)
1 bouquet garni of bay leaves,
  thyme and parsley stalks
½ teaspoon light soy sauce
1½ teaspoons Cabernet
  Sauvignon vinegar

Maldon salt and freshly
  ground black pepper
4 slices of baguette,
  1 cm/½ in thick
1 whole garlic clove, peeled
  and lightly crushed
150 g/5½ oz Gruyère cheese,
  coarsely grated

vegetable recipes

serves 4

techniques
slicing p66

mise en place
• Make the whole thing
ahead of time and reheat
with bread and cheese.

Nick says: I like to use cider
in this recipe, instead of
the vinegar. I add it after
softening the onions, allowing
it to reduce down and add a
strong base flavour to the
soup. You are looking for an
even caramelisation of the
onions – you don't want
white onions stewing in a
pool of liquid, and conversely
no burnt edges.

method

1 Set a pan on a medium heat and add the butter. When the butter is melted
and foaming but on no account browning, add the onions. Cover and cook
for 5 minutes, stirring only occasionally to stop them sticking, and allow
them to cook evenly. Cooking with the lid on traps the steam inside the pan
and helps extract the juices and vegetable sugars from the onions. When
you remove the lid, the onions should look quite moist and translucent, but
not coloured.

2 Increase the heat slightly, remove the lid and stir in the sugar. The moisture
in the pan will now evaporate and the onions will start to caramelise. Cook
and stir steadily for another 20–30 minutes until the base of the pan is
covered in a rich, nut-brown caramelised film and the onions are golden
brown. Keep a close eye to make sure they don't burn.

3 Now add the crushed garlic and the flour. Mix well and cook for a couple
of minutes. Next add the stock slowly, mixing well. Once all the stock is in,
bring the soup to a simmer and add the bouquet garni and soy sauce.

4 Simmer for 15 minutes before adding the vinegar. Simmer for a further
5 minutes, taste and season with salt and pepper. Keep warm.

5 While the soup is bubbling away, toast the baguette slices under a
pre-heated grill until crisp and brown. Then rub the surfaces of the
toast with the bruised garlic clove.

6 Ladle the soup into four heatproof bowls and float a piece of toast on
top of each one. Sprinkle the cheese liberally over the top and set the
bowls on an oven tray. Place under a preheated grill until the cheese is
starting to brown and bubble, but don't allow it to burn.

7 Carefully remove the bowls from under the grill and serve immediately
whilst the soup is piping hot – watch out for burning-hot onion strands!

twice-baked goat's cheese soufflés

ingredients

60 g/2¼ oz unsalted butter, plus extra for greasing
4 tablespoons fresh white breadcrumbs
2 small sprigs of fresh thyme, leaves finely chopped
260 ml/9 fl oz full fat milk

40 g/1½ oz plain flour
50 g/1¾ oz freshly grated Parmesan cheese, plus extra to serve
225 g/8 oz ripe goat's cheese log (such as Sainte Maure), crumbled

3 medium egg yolks
5 medium egg whites
pinch of cream of tartar
Maldon salt and freshly ground black pepper
200 ml/7 fl oz double cream

serves **6**

techniques

making a roux p83

mise en place

• Can be made up to the end of stage 6 in advance.

Nick says: Ring the changes by swapping half of the breadcrumbs for some chopped hazelnuts.

method

1 Heavily butter six deep 7.5 cm/3 in soufflé ramekins, taking care to cover the rim (if your soufflé is going to catch anywhere, it's here). Use the breadcrumbs to coat the inside of each ramekin – the breadcrumbs will stick to the soufflé mix and the melted butter will prevent them sticking to the side of the ramekin. Set them on a tray in the fridge for a maximum of 1 hour.

2 Add the thyme to the milk and warm through for a few minutes. Remove the thyme stalks and use the infused milk and the butter and flour to make a roux (see page 83). At the final stage add the Parmesan and goat's cheese, then season and mix through. Remove the sauce from the heat and pour into a large bowl. Preheat the oven to 220°C/425°F/gas mark 7.

3 When the base has cooled for 5 minutes, but is not cold, beat in the egg yolks. The base (chef's term: panade) for the soufflés is now finished. If you're not baking them immediately, dot the top with butter to prevent a skin forming or cover with clingfilm directly on to the surface.

4 Next whisk the egg whites and cream of tartar to soft peaks (see technique page 112). Loosen the soufflé base with the whites and fold in the remainder (see page 116).

5 Remove the ramekins from the fridge and arrange them on a baking tray, leaving enough space between each one for the heat to distribute evenly as they cook. Fill the ramekins to the top with the mix.

6 Slide the tray into the oven and bake the soufflés for 9–10 minutes until puffy and well-risen, but still a little wobbly. A 'standard' soufflé would be served now, but we are opting for the twice-baked method, so leave them to cool for about 10 minutes.

7 Turn out (top side down) on to individual shallow ovenproof dishes and pour a small amount of double cream around the soufflés. Sprinkle a tablespoon of fresh Parmesan over each and bake again at 220°C/425°F/gas mark 7 for approximately 5–6 minutes and serve immediately.

vegetable recipes

filo flan
with courgette and tomato

ingredients

4 large sheets of filo pastry
  (Greek-style is the best)
about 100 ml/3½ fl oz
  melted butter or olive oil
6 plum tomatoes
170 g/6 oz feta cheese, cubed
4 tablespoons homemade
  pesto (see p241)

3 tablespoons olive oil,
  for sautéing
1 garlic clove, peeled
4 medium courgettes,
  very thinly sliced
2 tablespoons pine nuts
2 tablespoons finely
  shredded fresh basil

Maldon salt and freshly
  ground black pepper

vegetable recipes

serves 4

techniques
making a roux p83

mise en place
• Construct the tarts in
  entirety in advance. Make
  up to stage 6, simply
  finishing off in the oven.

John says: For larger
numbers it may be more
economical to layer full filo
sheets one on top of the
other, brushing with butter
in between each and cutting
4 disks from the layered
sheets.

method

1 Carefully unwrap the filo pastry and lay it on a flat surface, covering it with a cloth or clingfilm to avoid it drying out and crumbling. Take a sheet of filo and using a pastry brush, brush lightly but evenly with butter or olive oil. Carefully fold the filo in half to form a rectangle. Again brush half of the rectangle and fold over to form a square. Repeat for each filo sheet.

2 Using a saucer or small plate (about 10–14 cm/4–5½ in diameter) as a guide, cut each layered pastry square into a circle, using the point of a sharp knife. Arrange the discs on a baking sheet and set aside.

3 Blanch, peel and deseed the tomatoes (see page 69). Cut the flesh into small dice and add to the cubed feta. Lightly mix in half of the pesto and season with salt and pepper. Set aside.

4 Add the 3 tablespoons of olive oil, or melted butter to a 'happy' (see page 100) large shallow pan and add the garlic clove. Cook for 5 minutes to flavour the oil, then remove the garlic and discard. Add the courgettes and sauté for about 1–2 minutes until barely half-cooked as they still have further cooking to do in the oven. Spread out the courgettes on a tray to cool completely.

5 Preheat the oven to 200°C/400°F/gas mark 6.

6 When the courgettes have cooled, arrange them in concentric circles on top of the filo discs, starting 5 mm/¼ in from the edge and overlapping each slice slightly, until each disc is covered.

7 Spoon the tomato and feta mix into the centre of each tart and sprinkle with pine nuts.

8 Bake for approximately 8 minutes or until the pastry is golden and crisp. Serve scattered with shredded basil and drizzled with the remaining pesto.

nick's macaroni cheese

ingredients

2 x recipe basic white sauce
  the thick version (see p240)
1 teaspoon Dijon mustard
225 g/8 oz strong Isle of
  Mull Cheddar cheese,
  grated
225 g/8 oz dried macaroni or
  similar pasta shape

1 x recipe quick tomato
  sauce (see p233)
butter, for greasing
Maldon salt and freshly
  ground black pepper

serves 4

mise en place
• Make the dish in advance
  and reheat.

Nick says: I've always used
Marshall's macaroni for this
(as did my Mum!); fancy pasta
shapes just don't feel right
here.

method

1 Preheat the oven to 200°C/400°F/gas mark 6.
2 If you've made the sauces in advance, reheat the white sauce. Beat in the
  Dijon mustard and three quarters of the cheese, season to taste with salt
  and pepper and keep warm.
3 Bring a large pan of water to a fast rolling boil and add a teaspoon of salt.
  Pour in the pasta and give it a good stir so that it doesn't stick together.
  Bring back to the boil as quickly as possible and keep at a rolling boil for
  8–12 minutes depending on the type of pasta (check on the packet), stirring
  half-way through cooking. Fish out a piece and taste it – it should be very
  'al dente' – have a distinct bite to it. You are looking for slightly undercooked
  pasta here, as it will finish cooking and absorb the cheese sauce when it's
  finished off in the oven.
4 When the pasta is almost cooked, drain it well and stir in the tomato sauce
  (this needn't be hot: the heat of the pasta will bring it up to temperature).
5 Butter an ovenproof dish and tip the tomato macaroni into it. Pour over
  the cheese sauce and give the dish a good shoogle ('shake' if your Scottish
  vernacular isn't up to scratch) to get the sauce down into the macaroni.
  Scatter the remaining cheese on top. Bake for 20 minutes until golden
  brown and bubbling. Serve with a big bowl of crunchy salad.

john's perfect gnocchi

ingredients

400 g/14 oz floury potatoes, to give 300 g/10 oz after baking and peeling
1 medium egg
1 egg yolk
25 g/1 oz unsalted butter, melted
100 g/3½ oz plain flour

to serve (method 1):
at least 100 g/3½ oz clarified butter (see p246)
freshly grated Parmesan cheese

to serve (method 2):
2 tablespoons olive oil
200 g/7 oz baby leaf spinach, washed
freshly grated nutmeg
1 small goat's cheese log with rind, ends trimmed, cut into 4 slices

150 ml/5 fl oz double cream
Maldon salt and freshly ground black pepper

serves **4**
as a starter

techniques
using a Mouli p118

mise en place
• Make and cook the gnocchi, toss in oil and keep in the fridge for 2 days.

John says: Lightly fried gnocchi can make a perfect potato garnish for fish dishes.

method

1 Bake the potatoes in their jackets in the oven at 200°C/400°F/gas mark 6 for about 1 hour, or the microwave for about 10 minutes. Allow to cool for 5–10 minutes. Halve the potatoes and scoop out the flesh, removing any green or spotted bits, then pass through a potato ricer, Mouli or medium-to-coarse sieve into a large bowl. Do not mash it as this compacts the potato make the gnocchi heavy. You will need 300 g/10 oz of the hot potato for the gnocchi.

2 Add the egg, egg yolk, butter, flour and seasoning while the potato is still hot and beat lightly, bringing the ingredients together until smooth and even-textured. Let the mixture cool slightly and roll into long sausages about 1.5–2 cm/⅝–¾ in thick. Place them on a lightly floured work surface then, using a sharp knife, cut into 1.5–2 cm/⅝–¾ in pieces (the action of cutting them will make them look like pillows; give them a gentle squeeze in the centre to make them into little fat bow ties). Lay them on a tray covered with a clean tea towel as you make them. Now they are ready to cook. If you like, lightly roll them over the back an upturned fork to give them a ridged effect to help a sauce cling to them – this takes practice!

3 Bring a large pan of salted water to the boil, lift up the gnocchi in the tea towel and drop them into the pan. Bring back to the boil and they are cooked as soon as they float to the surface. Scoop them out with a slotted spoon or spider, and drain well on another clean tea towel. Toss in a little oil and keep in the fridge or even freeze until you are ready to serve them.

Serving method 1: Heat a frying pan and add at least 100 g/3½ oz clarified butter. When nutty, add the cooked gnocchi and toss in the butter over a steady heat for about 5–6 minutes or until they are golden brown on the outside. Tip out on to warmed serving dishes with any remaining butter and serve with masses of freshly grated Parmesan cheese.

Serving Method 2: Heat a saucepan with a dash of olive oil and sauté the spinach until just wilted, then season with salt pepper and freshly grated nutmeg. Arrange the spinach on the base of four gratin dishes and divide the cooked gnocchi on top. Slice the goat's cheese and sit a slice of cheese on top of the gnocchi. Spoon over the cream, season and shove under a blazing hot grill for 2-3 minutes or until browned and bubbling. Eat straight away with a crunchy bitter salad and some freshly grated Parmesan.

chargrilled asparagus
with a fried egg

ingredients

450 g/1 lb medium asparagus
2 tablespoons extra virgin
  olive oil, plus extra for
  drizzling
4 organic eggs
50 g/1¾ oz Parmesan
  cheese, freshly shaved

Maldon salt and freshly
  ground black pepper

serves **4**

techniques
chargrilling p98;
poaching and frying eggs
p91-92

mise en place
• Shave the Parmesan.
  Chargrill the asparagus in
  advance and reheat in a
  warm oven for 4 minutes.
• Fried eggs should be
  cooked to order, but you
  could opt for poached
  eggs and hold in cold water
  to reheat later.

Nick says: I always fry my
eggs until a really good crispy
crust appears – the added
contrast in texture is
perfect here.

method

1 Preheat a ridged griddle pan until very hot/smoking.
2 To prepare the asparagus, snap the woody ends off the spears and, using a
  potato peeler, shave the ends (if hard and woody) to a point. Brush the
  spears lightly with olive oil. Lay three spears together side by side so that
  all the tips are pointing the same way. Take a wooden cocktail stick and push
  it through all three spears, starting near the base, until they hold together.
  Repeat further up with another cocktail stick (you may need to use three
  cocktail sticks if your spears are particularly long).
3 Griddle for about 3 minutes on each side, turning only once – don't keep
  moving them! Use the cocktail sticks to help you turn the 'rafts' over. Leave
  the asparagus on the griddle for long enough to brand with griddle marks.
  The asparagus should be tender and lightly charred. Keep them warm while
  you cook the eggs.
4 Fry the eggs.
5 To serve, remove the cocktail sticks from the asparagus and divide the
  asparagus between four warmed plates. Top with a fried egg, drizzle with
  olive oil, season with salt and pepper and finish off with a scattering of
  shaved Parmesan.

vegetable recipes

slow-baked leg of lamb

ingredients

2-3 large sprigs of rosemary
4 large garlic cloves
  (or more if you like garlic!),
  cut in half lengthways
1.8 kg/4 lb leg of lamb
8 good-quality anchovy
  fillets, halved

100 ml/3½ fl oz olive oil
250 ml/9 fl oz dry red wine
Maldon salt and freshly
  ground black pepper

serves **6**

meat recipes

techniques
roasting p104

mise en place
• A real winner for cooking
  ahead as no real critical
  timing issues here. Ideally
  kick-start the recipe
  6 hours before your
  guests arrive!

Nick says: This cooking
method is more akin to
braising, as the meat cooks
slowly in its own juices over a
long period in a low oven,
cooking down like confit
until it's super-moist and
practically falling apart.

method

1 Preheat the oven to 220°C/425°F/gas mark 7.

2 Pull the small sprigs off the rosemary branches and set aside with the garlic. Using the tip of a paring knife, make up to 20 well-spaced cuts into the flesh of the lamb, about 2.5 cm/1 in deep. Divide the rosemary sprigs, garlic and anchovies and push down into the cuts. Place the leg in a large roasting tin and pour over the oil, massaging it all over the joint. Season well with salt and pepper and pour the wine and 250 ml/9 fl oz water into the tin.

3 Put into the oven and sear for 15 minutes, then turn the temperature right down to 130°C/270°F/gas mark ½ and roast for 4–5 hours, basting every 30 minutes or so. Basting frequently helps to keep the meat moist and encourages the build-up of a good glaze on the outside. Add more liquid (wine or water) if the tin looks dry – there should always be liquid in the tin throughout this cooking process.

4 The meat is ready when it is starting to fall off the bone, at which point it should have a core temperature of 90°C/190°F. Remove from the oven, transfer to a warmed carving dish, cover loosely with foil and leave to rest in a warm for 30–45 minutes before carving.

5 Pour the juices from the tin into a tall hi-ball glass and allow to settle. Spoon the fat from the top of the glass. There should be enough sticky, reduced juices for an intense gravy hit – if not, pour the juices you have back into the roasting tin and put it over the heat, pour in a splash of water or wine and deglaze the tin scraping up all the sticky bits from the base. Boil fast until syrupy, taste and correct the seasoning.

6 To serve, I like to cut the lamb into big chunks. I do this by cutting along the length of the joint, following the bone, and then across into big 4 cm/1½ in chunks.

roast sirloin of beef

ingredients

1.5 kg/3 lb 5oz boned sirloin,
  not rolled
Yorkshire puddings
  (see p267)
red wine gravy, to serve
  (see p233)

serves **6–8**

techniques
roasting p104

mise en place
• Make the red wine gravy
  the day before and re-
  heat. Make and rest the
  Yorkshire pudding batter
  up to 6 hours in advance.
  1.5 kg/ 3lb 5oz roast needs
  at least 30 minutes to
  relax after cooking,
  leaving time to cook the
  Yorkshires and heat
  the gravy.

Nick says: You'll want to
know the best cut for this.
I like rib eye, which is taken
from the thick end of
the strip loin, and has a
great marbling of fat for
succulence and flavour. If
you prefer leaner meat, go
for the thin end of the strip
loin. Delicious served with
horseradish sauce!

method

1 Start by making the Yorkshire pudding batter and allow to rest whilst you
   prepare and cook the beef.
2 Preheat the oven to 200°C/400°F/gas mark 6.
3 You'll need an ovenproof frying pan or heavy roasting tin that's big enough
   to take the joint. I keep a 30 cm/12 in frying pan specifically for roasting – it
   fits perfectly in the oven. Trim the meat, leaving a decent layer of fat (about
   3 or 4 mm/⅛ in at least) on the outside. Using a sharp knife, score the fat in
   a criss-cross pattern and season well with salt and pepper, rubbing the
   seasoning into the scored fat.
4 Heat the frying pan to a medium heat but don't add any oil. Stick the joint
   into the pan fat-side down and leave it alone. The fat should start to melt
   and sizzle in the pan. After about 10 minutes, the fat should be starting to
   smoke. Carefully turn the beef over and place the whole pan in the oven for
   about 45 minutes to an hour.
5 Use a digital thermometer with a probe or an oven thermometer to
   measure the core temperature of the meat. For rare, the temperature
   should be 45°C/110°F, for medium rare, 50°C/120°F, for medium, 55°C/130°F
   and for well done, 65°C/150°F. If you don't have a temperature probe, stick
   in a metal skewer and keep it there for at least 10 seconds. Pull out the
   skewer and place it on your bottom lip – for medium rare it should feel
   warm. If it's hot, I'd say it's overcooked; if it's cold cook a little longer. When
   the meat is at the correct temperature for your taste, remove it from the
   oven and transfer to a warmed dish, loosely cover with foil and allow to rest
   for 30–45 minutes.
6 Pour any juices from the pan into a tall glass. Deglaze the pan with a glass
   of red wine, scraping any crusty bits off the base using a spatula. Add this
   to the glass, allow to settle and spoon off any fat. The contents of the glass
   can be added to your red wine gravy.
7 Meanwhile, make the Yorkshire puddings (see page 267) and the red wine
   gravy (see page 233).
8 Finally carve the beef into thick slices, adding any juices into the red wine
   gravy. Serve with the Yorkshire puddings and red wine gravy.

chicken in red wine casserole

ingredients

2-3 tablespoons olive oil
1 medium chicken (approx
    1.5 kg/3lb 5 oz), jointed
seasoned flour, for dusting
120 g/4 oz lardons of dry-
    cured pancetta (cubetti
    di pancetta)

200 g/7 oz small whole
    shallots or button onions,
    peeled
150 g/4 oz button
    mushrooms, quartered
250 ml/9 fl oz good quality
    dry red wine

4 garlic cloves, peeled and
    sliced
3 sprigs of fresh thyme
500 ml/18 fl oz brown
    chicken stock (see p228)
2 fresh bay leaves

Maldon salt and freshly
    ground black pepper
chopped fresh parsley,
    to garnish

serves **4**

techniques
jointing a chicken p70

mise en place
• Like any casserole, this
  benefits from being made
  in advance.

John says: If the sauce
doesn't want to thicken, add
2 teaspoons of arrowroot
and stir through.

method

1 Heat a large, heavy-based casserole on the hob until medium hot, then add
  the olive oil and heat. Dust the chicken in the seasoned flour. Cooking in
  batches, place the chicken pieces skin side down into the hot oil and gently
  fry until really golden – do not be tempted to move them. When they are
  nice and golden brown, turn the pieces over and brown on the other side.
  Once the chicken is really well coloured, remove from the pan. Repeat until
  all of the chicken is browned.

2 In the same pan, fry the pancetta gently until starting to colour. Add the
  shallots or onions and fry until they start to colour. Then add the
  mushrooms and fry for 2–3 minutes.

3 Preheat the oven to 180°C/350°F/gas mark 4.

4 Deglaze the casserole with the red wine, then add the garlic and thyme and
  boil to reduce by one third. Add the stock and bay leaves and season well
  with salt and pepper. Bring to a gentle simmer and add the chicken pieces.
  Cover with a tight-fitting lid and cook in the oven for 30 minutes.

5 Remove the lid and cook for a further 20 minutes to help reduce and
  thicken the sauce. Make sure the chicken is cooked through by piercing one
  of the thighs with a skewer and pressing down on the flesh using the back
  of a fork: the juices should run clear.

6 Remove the casserole from the oven and check the consistency of the
  sauce. It should be thick; if it's a little on the thin side, lift out all the chicken
  and vegetables using a slotted spoon and keep warm in a covered bowl.
  Place the casserole over a high heat on the hob and bring back to the boil,
  skimming off any unwanted fat. Reduce slowly to make the sauce richer and
  more intense in flavour. When it has reduced, return the chicken and
  vegetables to the casserole and reheat before serving, garnished with the
  chopped parsley.

7 This is perfect with creamy mash (see page 255) and some green veg.

braised pork belly

ingredients

1.5 kg/3lb 5oz pork belly,
  skin removed

for the brine mix:

1.4 litres/2½ pints water
1 onion, peeled and sliced
200 g/7 oz salt
175 g/6 oz golden caster
  sugar

6 juniper berries
1 bay leaf
1 teaspoon black peppercorns
4 whole cloves
3 sprigs of fresh thyme
1 small piece of nutmeg
1 red chilli

for braising:

1 onion, peeled and chopped
4 celery sticks, chopped
2 carrots, chopped
2.5 litres/4½ pints chicken
  stock
5 tablespoons soft brown
  sugar
1 tablespoon soy sauce

1 teaspoon lemon juice
⅛ teaspoon ground cloves
1 teaspoon chopped fresh thyme

for the sauce:

100 ml/3½ fl oz dry cider
100 ml/3½ fl oz beef or chicken
  stock
Maldon sea salt and freshly
  ground black pepper

serves **6–8**

meat recipes

mise en place

- The pork can be prepared up to the end of stage 6 and heated through and glazed at the last minute. The sauce and mash can be made in advance and heated through in saucepans.

John says: This recipe may seem lengthy, but many of the stages are prepared in advance. The depth of flavours are well worth the effort. Try serving this with perfect mash (page 255) and cabbage and carrots (page 261).

Nick says: To serve, place a mound of mashed potato on each of four plates. Add a pile of cabbage and place the pork on top. Serve with the sauce drizzled around the outside of the plate. We've also served ours with a piece of pork crackling.

method

1 Take a pan that's large enough to hold the pork, and add the water, onion, salt and sugar. Bring to the boil and stir until the salt and sugar have dissolved. Take off the heat, add the remaining brine mix ingredients (except the pork) and allow to cool.

2 When the brine mix is completely cold, add the pork. Cover and leave in the fridge for 10 hours or overnight. Remove the pork, pat dry with kitchen paper, and discard the liquid.

3 Preheat the oven to 160°C/325°F/gas mark 3. Take a clean, ovenproof pot and add the chopped onions, celery, carrots and chicken stock and pork. Bring to the boil over a medium heat. Cover and transfer to the oven. Leave to braise for 1½–2 hours. The pork is ready when soft to the touch.

4 Remove from the liquid and place in a cold roasting tin or other container to cool. Strain the juices through a chinois or tea strainer and reserve 100 ml/3½ fl oz to make the sauce. The rest can be frozen. When the pork is cold, cover with clingfilm and rest a heavy chopping board on top. Place weights on top of the board and leave in the fridge overnight.

5 When almost ready to serve, remove the pressed pork from the fridge and cut into 5 x 10 cm/2 x 4 in rectangles, scoring a criss cross pattern on the fatty top using a sharp knife.

6 Preheat the oven to 200°C/400°F/gas mark 6. Heat an ovenproof frying pan to a medium heat. Place the pork pieces skin side down until the fat starts to melt out of them, this should take about 2 minutes. Repeat on the remaining five edges of the pieces until the majority of the fat has been released, which should take approximately 12 minutes.

7 Add the glaze ingredients to the pan and as they melt paint the glaze on to the pork using a heatproof pastry brush. The glaze will be thin at first but will thicken; continue to baste the pork until the glaze has the consistency of sticky ribs and is sticking to the pork. Transfer the pan to the oven and roast for 20 minutes, continuing to baste frequently.

8 To make the sauce, take a clean pan and place it on a high heat. Add the cider and boil. When it has reduced by half, add the stock and reserved braising liquid and reduce by half once more. Season with salt and pepper.

sautéed tarragon chicken
with mushrooms

ingredients

2 free-range chicken breasts
2 tablespoons olive oil
20 g/³⁄₄ oz unsalted butter
80 g/3 oz button/chestnut
mushrooms, quartered
100 ml/3½ fl oz dry white
wine

100 ml/3½ fl oz Nick's roast
chicken stock (see p228)
100 ml/3½ fl oz double
cream
1½ teaspoons chopped fresh
tarragon

lemon juice, to taste
Maldon salt and freshly
ground black pepper

serves 2

techniques
sautéeing p106

mise en place
• No major advance prep
here: just have all the
ingredients ready before
you start.

Nick says: If cooking for a
dinner party, keep the chicken
breasts whole, with skin on
and cook these in a separate
pan from the sauce.

method

1 Skin the chicken breasts and slice across the grain of the meat (vertically)
into thin escalopes to give roughly six pieces per breast. Season with salt
and pepper.

2 Heat a frying pan to medium and add the oil. Add the chicken pieces one at
a time, ensuring they are not on top of each other. Leave them alone in the
pan and don't move them around too much. This will allow them to form a
crust. Turn the chicken pieces over and cook for another 2–3 minutes.
Remove them from the pan and place on a warmed plate.

3 Add the butter and mushrooms to the pan, moving them around to ensure
they take on a nice colour. Pour in the wine and deglaze using a heatproof
spatula to scrape all the flavour off the bottom of the pan. Reduce the
liquid by half, then add the stock and reduce by half again.

4 Add the cream, tarragon and a squeeze of lemon juice and bring to a
simmer. Add the chicken to finish cooking, and further reduce the sauce by
a quarter or until the sauce has a good consistency and coats the chicken.
Check the seasoning and serve on two warmed plates with boiled new
potatoes and buttered green beans.

cook school steak
with cabernet sauvignon vinegar and rocket

ingredients

2 x 225g/8 oz rib-eye steaks
2 tablespoons sunflower oil
20g/¾ oz butter
2 garlic cloves, peeled and
  crushed
1 teaspoon chopped fresh
  thyme

4 tablespoons good quality
  Cabernet Sauvignon
  vinegar
2 tablespoons beef stock
2 tablespoons olive oil
2 handfuls of rocket

Parmesan cheese, freshly
  shaved
Maldon salt and freshly
  ground black pepper

serves 2

techniques
frying p102

mise en place
• Bring the meat to room
temperature before guests
arrive. For dinner parties,
cook the steaks while
preparing the starter. Set
aside the frying pan and
rest the steaks whilst you
eat the starter. Reheat
the pan and deglaze it
prior to serving.

Alan says: A good vinegar is
essential for a recipe as
simple as this. When we cook
this on a class our Forum
Cabernet Sauvignon vinegar
jumps off the shop shelves.

method

1 Place a large, heavy frying pan on a high heat. Season the steaks well with
  salt and freshly ground black pepper. Add the sunflower oil to the hot pan.
  When it starts to smoke, lay the steaks in the pan and don't move them.
  It's important to leave the steaks to create a good-coloured crust on the
  outside, so resist the temptation to move them around.

2 After 2–3 minutes little spots of blood will start to appear on the top of
  the steaks; they're now ready to turn. Turn and cook again for another
  2–3 minutes.

3 Turn the heat down, add the butter, crushed garlic and thyme and baste
  the steaks. If your steaks have a particularly fatty edge, hold each steak
  on its side with kitchen tongs, press the fatty edge into the pan and allow
  to colour. Remove the steaks from the pan and place on a warm metal tray
  in a warm place to rest for at least 5 minutes.

4 Take the pan off the heat and allow to cool slightly. Add the vinegar and
  place the pan over a medium heat, deglaze the pan and reduce the vinegar
  by half. Add the stock (water or chicken stock will work just as well here)
  and again, reduce by half. Add the olive oil, give a stir and remove from the
  heat. The vinaigrette will separate, but that's fine.

5 Meanwhile place the rocket into a bowl and toss with some of the warm
  vinaigrette. Place each steak on a warmed plate, pour the rest of the
  vinaigrette over them and top with the salad and some freshly shaved
  Parmesan. Serve with creamy Dauphinoise potatoes or chips. Pour a glass
  of gutsy, fruity red wine and enjoy!

meat recipes

asian stir-fried duck

ingredients

2 female Gressingham duck
  breasts
1 garlic clove, peeled and
  finely sliced
3 red chillies, finely shredded
20 g/¾ oz finely shredded
  fresh ginger

12 shitake mushrooms, finely
  shredded
120 g/4 oz carrots, finely
  shredded
100 g/3½ oz fresh bean
  sprouts

4 shredded spring onions,
  cut into long strips
2 tablespoon fresh lime juice
2 tablespoons chopped
  fresh coriander
1 packet medium egg
  noodles, to serve

for the chilli sesame dressing:
4 teaspoons sesame oil
4 teaspoons Linghams sweet
  chilli sauce
4 teaspoons soy sauce
4 teaspoons rice wine
  vinegar

serves **4**

techniques
stir-frying p108;
slicing vegetables p64

mise en place
• Be prepared. Chop and
  shred everything, ready
  for stir-frying.

John says: If the sauce
doesn't want to thicken, add
2 teaspoons of arrowroot,
and stir through.

method

1 Trim the duck breasts, removing excess fat and sinew, then score through
   the fat diagonally, making sure you don't cut into the breast meat. Place
   skin side down into a warm frying pan and cook slowly for 5 minutes,
   checking that the skin is crisping and browning but not burning.

2 At this stage the pan will be full of rendered duck fat and the skin golden
   and crisp. Pour out some of the fat and reserve, leaving a small amount
   behind. Turn the breasts over and cook for about 5 more minutes, turning
   as required; they should be cooked medium. Remove from the pan and allow
   to rest for 5 minutes.

3 To make the dressing, mix all the ingredients together in a bowl.

4 Heat a wok until smoking and add a splash of the reserved duck fat.
   Add the garlic, chillies, ginger and shitake mushrooms and quickly stir-fry
   for 30 seconds. Add a good splash of water. Then add the carrot strips
   and bean sprouts and stir-fry once more for 1 minute, but no longer or
   the vegetables will start to go soggy.

5 Finally add the spring onions and the dressing. Remove from the heat and
   add the lime juice and chopped coriander. Slice the duck breast thinly
   across the grain, add to the stir-fry and toss well. Serve with the egg
   noodles in a deep bowl.

chang mai curry

ingredients

500 g/1lb 2 oz blade steak
cut into 1 cm/½ in slices
500 ml/18 fl oz coconut milk
1 x recipe perfect basmati
rice (see p254)
lime wedges, to serve

for the aromatic paste:
2 shallots, peeled and finely
chopped
4 stalks of lemongrass, finely
chopped
6 garlic cloves, peeled and
chopped

1 tablespoon chopped fresh
ginger
⅓ teaspoon dried piri piri
chillies
1 green bird's eye chilli, or
more if you want it hotter!
2 tablespoons curry powder

2 tablespoons yellow bean
sauce (optional)
1 tablespoon grated palm
sugar
1 tablespoon shrimp paste
1 teaspoon tamarind paste
60 ml/2 fl oz water

serves **2–3**

meat recipes

techniques
processing p119

mise en place
• Make the whole thing in
advance and warm through.

Alan says: I sometimes add
some freshly squeezed lime
juice, chopped coriander
and extra chilli. Add these
to taste.

method

1 Heat a frying pan with a lid to a medium heat. Place the slices of beef in
the pan, then pour on the coconut milk and cover. Simmer for 45 minutes.

2 While the beef simmers, make the paste. In a blender, process the shallots,
lemongrass, garlic, ginger, piri piri chillies, green bird's eye chilli, curry powder,
yellow bean sauce, grated palm sugar, shrimp paste, tamarind paste and
water to make a paste.

3 After the beef has simmered for 45 minutes, add the paste and stir
in until completely incorporated. Simmer with the lid on for a further
30 minutes to cook out the flavours.

4 Remove the curry from the heat and allow to rest for 10–15 minutes.
Meanwhile prepare the rice. Warm the curry through again and serve
with the rice and lime wedges.

chicken liver pâté

ingredients

225 g/8 oz chicken livers,
  fresh or frozen
220 g/7¾ oz unsalted butter
3 tablespoons port
4 teaspoons brandy
4 teaspoons brown chicken
  stock (see p228)

3 small or 2 large egg yolks
125 ml/4 fl oz double cream
1 garlic clove, peeled and
  crushed
1 sprig of fresh thyme, finely
  chopped

½ teaspoon Maldon salt and
  freshly ground black
  pepper
clarified butter, to serve
  (optional)

serves **6**

techniques
blending p118

mise en place
• The whole thing can be
  made in advance and
  chilled until serving.

method

1 Preheat the oven to 180°C/350°C/gas mark 4. Lightly butter six medium ramekins, place in a deep roasting tin and set aside. Check over the livers, making sure they are free of any fat, sinew and green-looking gall bladders, and place in a blender.

2 Melt the butter slowly in a small pan – do not allow it to become too hot. Remove from the heat to cool a little.

3 Pour the port, brandy and chicken stock into another pan and reduce over a medium-high heat until thick and glaze-like. Using a heatproof spatula, scrape this out of the pan and into the blender with all the remaining ingredients, except the melted butter.

4 Blend for 2–3 minutes to a very smooth paste. Running the blender on its slowest setting, slowly pour in the cooled melted butter: it should be warm, not hot, or the livers will cook.

5 Strain the mix through a sieve and pour carefully into the ramekins, leaving a 5 mm/¼ in gap at the top. Fill the tin with hot water to come just over half-way up the ramekins. Cook in the oven for 20–30 minutes and then check – the centre of the mix should be slightly risen and wobbly with the edges set. If the edges are not fully set, return the tin to the oven for another 5–10 minutes.

6 When the pâtés are cooked, remove the ramekins from the tin and let them cool. When they are cold, pour over a little clarified butter if you wish and chill in the fridge overnight. These will keep for 2–3 days in the fridge.

meat recipes

john's spanish chicken

ingredients

1 chicken (about 1.5 kg/3 lb 5 oz), jointed

for the marinade:

80 ml/2½ fl oz red wine vinegar

3 garlic cloves, peeled and crushed

24 pitted green olives

4 tablespoons salted capers, rinsed

12 prunes, diced

1 teaspoon dried oregano

Maldon sea salt and freshly ground black pepper

80 ml/2½ fl oz olive oil

sunflower oil, for frying

2 tablespoons light brown sugar

150 ml/5 fl oz dry white wine

1 fresh bay leaf

3 tablespoons chopped fresh flat-leaf parsley

Pilaf rice, to serve

serves **4**

techniques

jointing a chicken p70

mise en place

· Make the whole thing in advance and heat through.

method

1 Make two or three slashes through the skin of each chicken piece, cutting a little way into the flesh. Mix the vinegar, garlic, olives, capers, prunes, oregano, salt, pepper and olive oil together. Lay the chicken in a shallow glass or stainless steel dish and spoon over the marinade, rubbing it into the cuts. Cover with clingfilm and chill overnight.

2 Preheat the oven to 200°C/400°F/gas mark 6.

3 Lift the chicken from the marinade and drain well, reserving the marinade.

4 Heat a frying pan to the 'happy pan' state (see page 100) and add a small amount of sunflower oil to the pan. When the oil is hot, fry the chicken pieces in the pan, skin side down, until the skin is a light golden brown. Be careful here as the chicken is likely to spit when the marinade hits the hot oil. Turn over the chicken, remove the pan from the heat and allow to cool a little. Pour the marinade over the chicken then sprinkle on the brown sugar.

5 Pour the wine around the chicken in the pan and tuck in the bay leaf, cover with a lid and cook in the oven for about 25 minutes, basting two or three times.

6 To test if the chicken is cooked, prick its thickest part with a skewer and check that the juices run clear with no trace of blood. Lift the chicken on to a warm serving dish and return the pan to the heat. Bring the juices to the boil and add the parsley. Reduce until thick, but don't allow to go syrupy. Mix well and check the seasoning, then pour the pan juices over the chicken. Serve immediately with Pilaf rice.

confit duck legs
with wilted greens and puy lentils

ingredients
8 Barbary duck legs

for the 'pickle':
2 tablespoons Maldon salt
1 tablespoon whole white
 peppercorns, crushed
4 sprigs of fresh thyme
2 teaspoons juniper berries,
 chopped

2 garlic cloves, peeled and
 crushed

for the cooking fat:
750 ml/1¼ pints duck or
 goose fat, melted and
 cooled, to cover (or
 however much you can
 get topped up with oil)

½ garlic bulb, sliced across
 the equator
2 sprigs of fresh thyme
1 fresh bay leaf

1 x recipe red wine gravy
 (see p233)
2 x recipe wilted greens
 (see p260)
200 g/7 oz cooked puy lentils

serves **8**

mise en place
• Prepare to the end of
 stage 4 in advance.

Alan says: Give the dish an
Asian flavour by basting
the duck breasts in a
combination of soy sauce and
honey and serve with stir-
fried soy greens.

method

1 The day before serving, make the pickle by mixing the salt, peppercorns, leaves from the thyme sprigs, juniper berries and crushed garlic together. Season the prepared duck legs liberally with this mixture, rubbing it into the flesh. Place flesh side uppermost in a shallow dish, cover and refrigerate for 4 hours.

2 Wash the excess salt and spices off the legs, then pat with kitchen paper to remove any traces of moisture (a watery brine will have developed around the duck).

3 Preheat the oven to 150°C/300°F/gas mark 2. Place the duck legs in a heavy, ovenproof casserole with a tight-fitting lid. Pour over enough melted fat (or oil and fat) to cover and add the garlic, thyme and bay leaf. Bring the mixture up to barely simmering point. Cover with the lid and cook in the oven for 2–3 hours. It is very difficult to give an exact cooking time as the thickness of the legs and heat of the oven will vary. However, the legs should be tender and succulent and the meat just starting to fall off the bone.

4 Lift the legs out of the fat and place in a wire rack, allowing the excess fat to drip off. Transfer to a plate and cover. This will keep in the fridge for up to 3 days.

5 Preheat the oven to 220°C/425°F/gas mark 7.

6 When you are ready to serve the duck, transfer it to a roasting tray and set it in a hot oven for 10–12 minutes to brown and crisp, draining off any fat that appears after 6 minutes or so. The legs should now be heated through and the skin beginning to crisp.

7 To serve, heat through the red wine gravy and stir through the puy lentils. Just before serving, crisp up the duck skin further, under a spanking hot grill and serve with the lentil gravy and some wilted greens.

scallops
with crispy pancetta and lemon butter sauce

ingredients

12 slices of thin-cut
  pancetta
100 ml/3½ fl oz beurre
  blanc/ butter sauce (see
  p236)
finely grated zest of ½ lemon
2 tablespoon sunflower oil

12 hand-caught scallops,
  white meat only
4 handfuls of mixed organic
  salad leaves
2 tablespoons good-quality
  olive oil
1 teaspoon lemon juice

Maldon salt and freshly
  ground black pepper

serves **4** as a starter

techniques
frying p100

mise en place
• Make the lemon butter
sauce in advance and keep
in a pre-warmed, small
vacuum flask for up to
8 hours. Cook the bacon
in advance, simply serving
at room temperature. For
very large numbers keep
the scallops whole and
sear them quickly on both
sides, leaving them very
underdone. Chill, then bring
back to room temperature
before finishing in a hot
oven for 4 minutes.

John says: This is one
of our modern classic
combinations of flavours
and textures – the sweet
scallops contrasting with
the salty, crispy bacon; the
clean salad with the richness
of the lemon butter sauce.

method

1 Preheat the oven to 200°C/400°F/gas mark 6. Lay the slices of pancetta on
to baking parchment and bake until crisp and golden, about 4–5 minutes.
Drain off the fat, gently scrunch up the slices and keep just warm. Have
the butter sauce ready and stir in the lemon zest.

2 Heat a heavy-duty frying pan. Add the sunflower oil. Slice the scallops
across the equator and place into the pan, cut side down. This is the side
that has never been in direct contact with water and it will caramelise
perfectly. Do not put too many scallops in the pan at one time, but cook
them in two batches (or more if cooking for a larger number). Sear the
scallops for 60 seconds, turn over and sear for 45 seconds. Turn once more
and give them a final 60 seconds, then remove on to a clean tray and keep
warm. The reason for this three-step process is that scallops shrink
on contact with a hot pan, and the centre of the scallops arch up, losing
contact with the pan. Flipping the scallop over will reverse this, meaning
that the full surface of the scallop will be caramelising in the final second,
as opposed to the edges only.

3 In a large bowl, toss the salad leaves in the olive oil and lemon juice
and season.

4 Set a mound of salad in the centre of each of four warmed plates. Arrange
the scallops around the salad, three to a plate, and pour a thin stream of
sauce around the scallops. Top the salad with three slices of the crispy
pancetta and serve.

crab tart

ingredients

1 x recipe shortcrust pastry
  (see p267)
2 eggs
2 egg yolks
150 ml/5 fl oz double cream
2 tablespoons olive oil
2 leeks, finely shredded
4 spring onions, sliced

½ teaspoon cayenne pepper
300 g/10½ oz crabmeat
60 g/2¼ oz freshly grated
  Parmesan
Maldon salt and freshly
  ground black pepper

serves **6**

techniques
pastry making p88;
blind baking p88

mise en place
• Perfect for entertaining.
  Make the whole thing in
  advance.

Nick says: Pasteurised or
frozen white crabmeat
makes an extremely worthy
tart, but if you want to
create the ultimate eating
experience opt to cook a
live crab and pick your own
meat. If good fresh crab
meat isn't available, you can
substitute undyed smoked
haddock that's been
poached in milk and flaked.

method

1 First make the pastry shell.
2 Preheat the oven to 180°C/350°F/gas mark 4.
3 Whisk the eggs, egg yolks and cream together.
4 Heat the olive oil in a pan and sweat the leeks and spring onions until softened, but not coloured. Season with salt, pepper and cayenne. Allow to cool slightly and fold into the egg mix.
5 Add the crab and Parmesan, mix well and turn into the cooled tart case. Set the tart on a baking sheet and bake for approximately 45 minutes or until the filling is just firm. Serve with dressed leaves and a tomato salsa.

shrimp fritters
with romesco sauce

ingredients

3 tablespoons self-raising
  flour
¼ teaspoon paprika
125 g/4½ oz small shrimps
  or prawns
1 tablespoon chopped
  shallots

1 tablespoon chopped fresh
  flat-leaf parsley
6 tablespoons sparkling
  water or soda water
2 tablespoons olive oil
vegetable oil, for frying
Maldon salt

lemon wedges, to serve
1 x recipe Romesco sauce,
  to serve (see p254)

serves **4**
as a starter or canapé

techniques
deep frying p110

mise en place
• Parcook the fritters and
  drain. When ready to serve,
  plunge them into hot oil
  and fry until crisp and
  golden. Make the Romesco
  sauce and spoon into a jar;
  covered with a layer of oil,
  it will keep for a week.

Nick says: These are brilliant
made using Morecambe Bay
brown shrimps, however if
you can't get your hands on
the little brown morsels,
North Atlantic pink prawns
make a good second best.

method

1 Sift the flour, paprika and a pinch of salt into a bowl. Roughly chop the
   shrimps or prawns and stir into the mix with the shallots and parsley. Make
   a well in the centre and pour in the oil and ⅔ of the water. Mix or whisk the
   flour slowly into the liquid to form a smooth batter, adding more water if
   required. Set aside.

2 Heat a deep-fat fryer to 180°C/350°F (or use a wok, see p108). When the oil
   is hot enough, carefully drop walnut-sized blobs of batter from a spoon into
   it. Try to get the spoon quite close to the hot oil, or it will splatter. After
   about a minute, take the fritters out of the basket and press them lightly,
   either with a big wad of kitchen paper or the back of a spoon. This flattens
   them and helps them to cook through.

3 Return the fritters to the oil for another 2 minutes, then lift and drain on
   kitchen paper. Season with salt and serve immediately with the Romesco
   sauce for dipping and lemon wedges to squeeze over them.

fish recipes

mousseline of scallop and sole

ingredients

250 g/9 oz very fresh boned and skinned sole fillets, chilled

250 g/9 oz fresh hand-caught scallops, white meat only (see p26), chilled

2 egg whites, chilled

400 ml/14 fl oz double cream, chilled

Maldon sea salt

pinch of cayenne pepper

1 tablespoon lemon juice

melted butter, for greasing

150 ml/5 fl oz fish cream, to serve (see p237)

3 tablespoons chopped fresh chives, plus extra to serve

3 tablespoons Avruga caviar

serves 8

techniques

filleting flat fish p72

mise en place

• Make the mousselines up to step 3, cover with clingfilm and refrigerate; they'll hold this way for 8 hours. Or, cooked, the mousselines will hold for 30 minutes if kept warm – the best way to do this is to remove the water bath from the oven and leave to sit at room temperature.

John says: Heat is the enemy of the mousseline, so keeping everything cool is most important. This means putting food processor bowls and blades in the freezer beforehand, having a bowl of ice on standby and giving the fish and the cream 15–30 minutes in the freezer before starting.

method

1 Remove any sinew from the fish, and check for bones. Cut the sole and scallops into chunks and place into a chilled food processor. Blitz for one to two minutes until smooth and thick, stopping to scrape down the sides a couple of times. Add the egg whites. Process the mixture for another 1–2 minutes until really fine and thick. Lift off the bowl and chill in the fridge for 30 minutes.

2 Take out of the fridge and place back on the food processor. Run the mixer and gradually begin to add the cream, until the mix is as soft as possible, but still holding its shape. Take care not to overwork the mix or it will split. Once the cream is incorporated, season with salt, cayenne and lemon juice to taste. The salt and lemon juice will help thicken the mix.

3 Preheat the oven to 170°C/325°F/gas mark 3. Lightly grease eight 100 ml/3½ fl oz dariole moulds or ramekins, and fill with the mousseline mix to within 5 mm/¼ in of the tops. Give each a firm tap on the worktop to release any trapped air.

4 Arrange the moulds in a roasting tin and pour in enough boiling water to come halfway up the sides of the moulds. Then cover the whole thing in buttered kitchen foil. Bake for 10–12 minutes or until very slightly raised on top. They should feel springy, but if they still feel a little soft in the centre, pop them back in the oven for a couple of minutes. Springy doesn't mean rubbery, which equates to overcooked mousselines.

5 If serving straight away, heat the fish cream gently in a saucepan and add the chives and Avruga. Turn out the mousselines into the centre of four warmed plates. Spoon some of the warm sauce on top and finish with a sprinkling of chives.

mackerel kebabs
with crunchy spiced potatoes

ingredients
2 medium fresh mackerel

for the marinade:
2 tablespoons curry paste
finely grated zest and juice
  of 1 lemon
1 tablespoon chopped fresh
  coriander
2-3 tablespoons olive oil

**for the crunchy spiced
potatoes:**
450 g/1 lb floury potatoes
  (King Edward, Desirée)
2-3 tablespoons sunflower oil
½ teaspoon cumin seeds
½ green chilli, deseeded and
  very finely chopped

½ teaspoon ground cumin
¼ teaspoon cayenne pepper
¼ teaspoon ground turmeric
1 teaspoon garam masala
Maldon salt and freshly
  ground black pepper

serves 4
as a starter

techniques
chargrilling p98;
filleting round fish p74

mise en place
• The potatoes can be
  pre-cooked, cooled and
  reheated in a warm oven.
  Marinate the fish. Soak the
  wooden skewers in water
  to prevent them from
  burning. Thread the fish on
  to the skewers and cook at
  the very last minute.

Alan says: If using a
barbecue, get it going before
you start the recipe. This
way the coals will have time
to become red/grey embers
that will give just the right
heat for searing.

method

1 First fillet your spanking fresh mackerel fillets then slice into 2 cm/¾ in strips.

2 Blend all the marinade ingredients together in a large mixing bowl and season well. Toss in the fish and gently turn to coat in the marinade. Cover and allow to stand in a cool place for about an hour to allow the fish to absorb maximum flavour.

3 Peel the potatoes and cut into large cubes. Place in a pan of boiling salted water and boil for about 5–6 minutes until almost cooked but still a bit firm in the middle. Drain well and leave to cool.

4 Heat the sunflower oil in a large frying pan. Add the potatoes and fry over a medium heat for about 5 minutes, turning from time to time until a light golden brown. Sprinkle over the cumin seeds and the chopped green chilli and continue to cook for 3–4 minutes. Now add the ground cumin, cayenne and turmeric and cook for another 5 minutes, tossing and turning the potatoes until they build up a nice spicy crust. Sprinkle over the garam masala and season with salt and pepper. Keep warm.

5 Preheat your griddle pan.

6 Thread the pieces of fish tightly on to wooden skewers. (This will help to prevent the fish from cooking too quickly.) Lightly brush the mackerel with a little olive oil and place them on to the griddle pan for about 3 minutes on the first side. Baste with a little of the marinade while they are cooking, then turn them and cook for another couple of minutes, but take care not to overcook or they'll fall apart.

7 Serve the mackerel kebabs with the hot potatoes, some dressed salad leaves, warm naan breads (cook for 30 seconds on both sides on the griddle or barbecue) and loads of lemon wedges to squeeze over the fish.

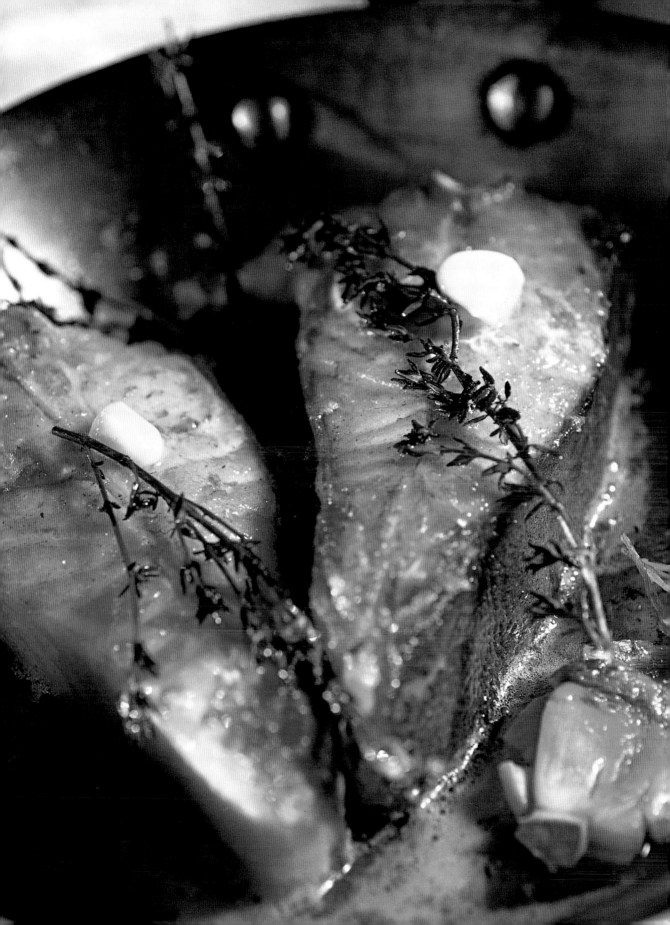

roast turbot
with shrimp cream

ingredients

4 turbot steaks, bone in
50 g/1¾ oz unsalted butter
freshly squeezed juice of 1
  lemon
1 teaspoon finely chopped
  fresh thyme
1 garlic clove, peeled,
  crushed and finely chopped

Maldon salt and freshly
  ground black pepper
for the shrimp cream:
300 ml/10 fl oz double cream
100 g/3½ oz peeled brown
  shrimps
1 tablespoon of lemon juice
½ teaspoon Dijon mustard

2 tablespoons chopped
  fresh chives

serves **4**
as a starter or canapé

techniques
roasting p104

Nick says: Brown shrimps
are a must for this recipe
as the shrimp cream relies
on their full flavour. Roasting
the turbot on the bone
keeps the fish moist as well
as intensifying the flavour,
however if the steaks are
being elusive, farmed fillets
would make a good second
choice. If you find a really
fresh small turbot, you can
roast it whole. Cut off the
head and fins with kitchen
scissors, then place in a
well-buttered roasting tin
with the lemon juice, thyme
and garlic. Dot the top of
the fish with butter and
roast for 20 minutes. Allow
to rest before carefully
lifting the fillets off the
bone to serve.

method

1 Preheat the oven to 180°C/350°F/gas mark 4.
2 Heat two ovenproof frying pans until hot, then add a little olive oil. Fry the
   turbot steaks two to each pan until lightly coloured, turning once. Add half
   the butter, lemon juice, thyme and garlic to each pan and season lightly.
   When the butter has melted, baste the fish with the juices. Place the pans
   into the oven and cook for about 4 minutes, depending on the thickness of
   the steaks. Remove the turbot from the oven, cover and leave to rest for
   4–5 minutes. This allows the juices to re-distribute back into the flesh.
3 Meanwhile, make the shrimp cream. Bring the cream to the boil in a medium
   pan and stir in any collected pan juices from the turbot. Boil briskly for
   2 minutes.
4 Now stir in the peeled shrimps, lemon juice, mustard and chives.
   Warm through, but be careful not to boil. Check the seasoning, though it
   shouldn't need any.
5 Serve the steaks (with or without the bone: entirely up to you) with boiled
   new potatoes, steamed broccoli florets and the shrimp cream spooned
   over the top.

steamed mussels
with white wine and cream

ingredients

2 kg/4lb 8 oz fresh mussels
25 g/1 oz unsalted butter
2 shallots or 1 small onion, peeled and finely diced
2 garlic cloves, peeled and finely chopped

150 ml/5 fl oz dry white wine
1 fresh bay leaf
sprig of fresh thyme
75 ml/2½ fl oz double cream
2-3 tablespoons chopped fresh parsley

1 teaspoon lemon juice
Maldon salt and freshly ground black pepper

serves 4

as a main dish or 6–8 as a starter

techniques

preparing mussels p78

mise en place

• Clean the mussels a maximum of 20 minutes ahead. You can make the reduction up to 12 hours ahead, decant, cool and refrigerate. Then simply heat in a large pan until very hot, add the mussels and cook as described.

Nick says: White wine and cream has to be my all time favourite flavour combo for mussels. It just doesn't get any better than this.

method

1 Clean and prepare the mussels (see p78). Choose a very large saucepan with a lid, and place over a moderate heat. Add the butter and, when it has melted, toss in the shallots or the onion and the garlic. Cook uncovered for about 5 minutes until the vegetables are soft and beginning to turn opaque. Pour in the wine, add the bay leaf and thyme and bring to a rolling boil. Reduce to a thick glaze consistency, then add the cream and reduce again until thick.

2 Using a slotted spoon, lift (don't pour) the squeaky-clean mussels into the pan, slam on the lid, turn up the heat and bring to the boil. When the lid starts jumping, give the pan a couple of good shakes to make sure the mussels are cooking evenly. After 4 minutes, take the pan off the heat and lift the lid slightly to see if the mussels have all opened. If not, cook for a few seconds longer, but not more than 5 minutes in total, or you'll end up with overcooked, shrivelled mussels.

3 Take off the lid and stir in the parsley, lemon juice, salt and freshly ground black pepper to taste. Divide the mussels (discarding any that have failed to open) and the sauce between four bowls and serve immediately with piles of crusty bread.

roast monkfish
with pancetta and red wine sauce

ingredients

400 g/14 oz monkfish tail,
   skinned and cut into
   2 fillets
lemon juice, to taste
2 sprigs of fresh thyme
10–12 thin slices of smoked
   pancetta

25 g/1 oz unsalted butter
4 tablespoons white wine or
   water
Maldon salt and freshly
   ground black pepper

for the red wine sauce:
150 ml/ 5 fl oz light red wine
   (I like Beaujolais)
1 teaspoon black treacle or
   dark brown sugar
300 ml/10 fl oz fish stock
   (see p229)
25 g/1 oz chilled butter, diced

2 teaspoons lemon juice
1 x recipe Dauphinoise
   potatoes (see p255)

fish recipes

serves **4**

techniques
roasting p104

mise en place
• Make the sauce and
  reheat when you're ready.
  Wrap the monkfish in the
  pancetta.

John says: For lemon
Dauphinoise, add the zest
of a lemon to the cream
mix before baking.

method

1 First prepare the monkfish. Take the two fillets and pat them dry with kitchen towel to remove excess moisture. Season with pepper and lemon juice. Don't add salt at this stage as it draws out moisture and stops the bacon from sticking to the fish. Strip the leaves off the thyme sprigs and roll the monkfish in the leaves. Set one fillet on top of the other, tapered end on top of fatter end. Wrap the whole thing with overlapping slices of pancetta, making sure the fish is completely covered. Tie up at 2.5 cm/1 in intervals with fine string to make a small gigot or "joint". Cover and refrigerate until needed, remembering to take it out of the fridge 20 minutes before you start cooking to allow it to come to room temperature.

2 Make the red wine sauce. Bring the wine to the boil in a saucepan, add the treacle or sugar and boil until it is reduced by about three quarters to a thick and foamy syrup. Add the stock and boil until reduced to about 150 ml/5 fl oz.

3 Now add the diced butter, a few pieces at a time, swirling the pan as the butter melts. The sauce needs to be dark and glossy, so don't be tempted to whisk in the butter, as this would make it too foamy. Keep swirling the pan until the butter has been incorporated, then season the sauce, cover it with clingfilm and keep it warm. If it begins to look as if it might split, heat it up a bit and give the pan a good swirl until you have a glossy sauce again.

4 Preheat the oven to 230°C/450°F/gas mark 8. The oven needs to be this hot to prevent moisture from leaking out of the monkfish as it cooks. Heavily butter a baking dish and place the tied monkfish roast/gigot in it. Sprinkle with the rest of the lemon juice, dot generously with butter and season. Add the wine or water and bake for 10–12 minutes or until just cooked through. Remove from the oven and leave to rest for 7–8 minutes.

5 Slice the monkfish thickly and arrange on four warmed serving plates. Strain any juices into the sauce and spoon over the fish. Serve with wilted spinach and some lemony gratin Dauphinoise.

pan-fried salmon
with peas, lettuce and pancetta

ingredients

2 tablespoons sunflower oil
4 x 175 g/6 oz salmon fillets,
  cut from the top of the
  fish, not the belly
250 g/9 oz diced pancetta
  (cubetti di pancetta)
2 Cos lettuce hearts, roughly
  shredded

200 ml/7 fl oz chicken or fish
  stock (see p228-229)
225 g/8 oz fresh or frozen
  peas
3 tablespoons chopped
  fresh parsley
25 g/1 oz butter

freshly squeezed lemon juice,
  to taste
Maldon salt and freshly
  ground black pepper

serves 4

techniques
frying p100

mise en place
• None to be done – best
  cooked fresh. Have
  ingredients prepared
  before starting.

Alan says: To save some
time, use two frying pans
and cook the salmon at the
same time as the peas,
lettuce and pancetta.

method

1 Heat a medium frying pan until hot and add the sunflower oil. Add the
  salmon, skin side down, and cook for 2–3 minutes. Turn the salmon over and
  cook for a further 2 minutes. Reduce the heat a little and add the butter,
  swirl it around to melt and use it to baste the salmon for a minute. Using
  a fish slice, transfer the fillets to a warm roasting tray and place into a
  low oven to rest while you make the peas, lettuce and pancetta.

2 Heat the same frying pan until fairly hot and add the pancetta cubes.
  Turn down the heat and cook for 2–3 minutes, stirring around, until the fat
  starts to run and they begin to take on a bit of colour. Throw in the lettuce
  and stir around for a minute to coat with the fat from the pancetta. Pour
  in the stock, season and bring to the boil, then turn down the heat and
  simmer for 3–4 minutes.

3 Add the peas and parsley, give the pan a good shake while it comes to the
  boil and add the butter. Let this melt into the 'stew', taste and add a
  squeeze or two of lemon juice to lift it. Don't allow it to cook too long,
  or the lettuce will become limp and soggy.

4 Serve the vegetables with the salmon in warmed shallow bowls, with new
  potatoes or crusty bread.

fish and chips

ingredients

for the beer batter:
225 g/8 oz self-raising flour
300 ml/10 fl oz chilled lager
    or ice cold sparkling
    mineral water
pinch of Maldon salt
vegetable oil, for deep-frying

for the tartare sauce:
150 ml/5 fl oz mayonnaise
    (see p239)
1 tablespoon chopped
    gherkins
1 tablespoon chopped capers
3 shallots or spring onions,
    finely chopped

1 tablespoon chopped
    flat-leaf parsley, dill or
    chervil
Maldon salt and freshly
    ground black pepper
freshly squeezed lemon
    juice, to taste

1 x recipe chips (see p258)
4 x 175 g/6 oz thick haddock,
    cod or ling fillets, skinned
100 g/3½ oz flour seasoned
    with 1 teaspoon salt and
    20 grinds of pepper
lemon wedges, to serve

serves **4**

techniques
deep frying p110

mise en place
• Prepare the fish. Blanch
the chips ready for
the second frying and
refrigerate until needed.
Make the batter up to an
hour in advance.

John says: For this dish the
fish must be fresh, skinned
and a decent thickness so
that it doesn't overcook.

Nick says: Haddock is my fish
of choice here and I also like
my chips to be dry and fluffy,
so it's Golden Wonder or
Kerr's Pinks. If you prefer a
mushier chip opt for Maris
Piper or similar. The secret
to this is not to overload the
fryer, as this will cool the
down the oil temperature
and result in oily fish and
chips. The average home
fryer is only big enough to
cook one piece of fish at a
time, which makes this a dish
for smaller numbers. I get
round this by having two
fryers at home and cooking
the fish and chips at the
same time.

method

1 To make the beer batter, gradually whisk the flour into the lager or water
   with a good pinch of salt until you have a smooth, thick batter.
2 Heat the oil in an electric deep-fat fryer to 160°C/325°F.
3 Make the tartare sauce by mixing the mayonnaise, gherkins, capers and
   spring onions and herbs together. Season well and add the lemon juice.
4 Prepare the chips and keep them in a warm oven with the door slightly open.
5 Dip the fish in the seasoned flour to coat each piece, shaking off the
   excess. Then dip the fish in the batter, lift and allow any excess to drip off.
   Fry the fish pieces one at a time, for about 5 minutes until golden brown
   and lift out onto the kitchen paper to absorb any excess oil. Keep the
   cooked fish warm while you fry the rest.
6 Get the chips out of the oven as soon as the fish is cooked and serve with
   tartare sauce and lemon wedges.

lobster crumble

ingredients

4 live lobsters, no more than
  600 g/1 lb 5 oz each
4 shallots, finely chopped
2 garlic cloves, finely sliced
200 ml/7 fl oz dry white wine
1 bay leaf

100 ml/3½ fl oz nick's roast
  chicken stock (see p228) or
  fish stock (see p229) or
  vegetable stock (see p230)
260 ml/9 fl oz double cream
4 tablespoons chopped
  fresh flat-leaf parsley
1 teaspoon lemon juice

for the crumble:
2 tablespoons extra virgin
  olive oil
2 tablespoons clarified
  butter (see p246)
100 g/3½ oz stale
  breadcrumbs

60 g/2¼ oz freshly grated
  Parmesan cheese
2 tablespoons chopped
  fresh flat-leaf parsley
Maldon salt and freshly
  ground black pepper

serves 4
as a main dish
or 8 as a starter

techniques
preparing lobster p76

mise en place
• Make the sauce and the
  breadcrumb topping up
  to 24 hours in advance.
  The lobsters can be cooked
  30 minutes before your
  guests arrive, but it's best
  not to refrigerate them.

Nick says: We came up
with this dish whilst
experimenting on my
lobster thermidor for the TV
programme *Great British
Menu*. This is a far simpler
version and lighter too.
All it demands as an
accompaniment is some
crusty bread, salad and a
cool glass of white wine.

method

1 Prepare the lobsters (see p76).

2 To make the sauce, place the shallots, garlic, wine and bay leaf into a pan and simmer until the wine has evaporated by two thirds. Add the stock to the pan and simmer again until the liquid has reduced by half. Add 200 ml/7 fl oz of the cream and return to a simmer for about 5 minutes until thickened. Remove from the heat and stir in the chopped parsley and lemon juice. This sauce base can be made in advance for later use.

3 Make the crumble. Heat a frying pan until hot and add the oil and clarified butter. Throw in the crumbs and toss in the pan until crisp and golden. Remove from the heat, drain through a sieve and dry on kitchen paper. Cool, then mix in the Parmesan and parsley.

4 Preheat the oven to 180°C/350°F/gas mark 4. Remove the sauce from the heat and fold in the lobster meat. Lightly whip the remaining double cream and fold it into the sauce. Place the half shells onto a baking sheet and spoon the mix equally between them, reserving 4 tablespoons. Cover with the crumble mix and pop them into the oven for 4–6 minutes to warm through. The top should be a golden brown colour, finish under a hot grill if a little more colour is needed.

5 Serve one lobster per person, spooning over the reserved sauce and serve with some good granary bread and salad.

arbroath smokie fishcake
with tomato salsa

ingredients

1 x tomato salsa (see p238)

for the fishcakes:

2 x Arbroath smokies (see p23), or enough to give 400 g/14 oz when prepared

200 g/7 oz cooked mashed potato (see page 255), cold but not chilled

4 spring onions, finely chopped

finely grated zest of 1 lemon

4 tablespoons finely chopped fresh flat-leaf parsley

3 tablespoons mayonnaise (see page 239)

100 g/3½ oz plain flour, for coating

4 tablespoons olive oil, plus extra for drizzling

serves **4**

as a main dish or 8 as a starter

techniques

frying p100

mise en place

• Make the fishcakes in advance and chill for up to 3 hours. Make the salsa up to 3–4 hours ahead.

Alan says: These are also great made with smoked haddock or hot smoked salmon.

method

1 Peel the skin from the smokies and flake the flesh with a fork, being careful to locate and remove any bones.

2 Mix the flaked fish into the mash with the spring onions, lemon zest, parsley, mayonnaise and plenty of black pepper.

3 Divide the mixture equally into eight and shape into cricket balls, then, using the palm of your hand, gently flatten them to make cake shapes. Place the cakes on a tray, cover with clingfilm and chill in the fridge for 1–3 hours to firm up.

4 Preheat the oven to 150°C/300°F/gas mark 2. Sift the flour on to a large bowl or on to a plate. Take the fishcakes out of the fridge and roll them in the flour until evenly coated. Lift and pat gently to remove excess flour.

5 Heat a medium frying pan to hot. Add half of the olive oil and heat, swirling it around a little to coat the bottom of the pan. Carefully slide four of the fishcakes into the pan. Turn the heat down to medium and cook for about 5 minutes until a nice brown crust has formed. As always, if you're looking to get a good crust, don't be tempted to fiddle with the cakes. Carefully turn them over and fry for another 5 minutes. Lift out of the pan and drain on kitchen paper, then place on a baking tray and keep warm in the oven with the door slightly ajar (this helps to keep the coating crisp).

6 Turn up the heat in the pan and add the olive oil and the four remaining fishcakes. Turn the heat down to medium and cook and drain as before. Spoon the salsa mix on to individual plates and top with one or two fishcakes, drizzle around a little olive oil and serve.

pan-fried market fish
with lemon butter sauce

ingredients

2 tablespoons light olive oil
4 x 120 g/4 oz fresh thick
   fish fillets (the best
   available on the day)
20 g/¾ oz unsalted butter

Maldon salt and freshly
   ground black pepper
1 x recipe of wilted greens
   (see p260)

for the lemon butter sauce:
1 quantity butter sauce
   (see p236)
zest of 1 lemon
1 tablespoon of lemon juice

serves **2**

fish recipes

techniques
frying p100

mise en place
• Make the sauce up to
  6 hours in advance and
  store in a warmed vacuum
  flask.

Nick says: A simple
combination that just works!

method

1 First make your butter sauce. Stir through the lemon zest and juice and
   keep the sauce warm. (A vacuum flask rinsed out with hot water will provide
   the ideal storage and allow you to make the sauce well beforehand.)

2 Heat a medium frying pan to medium hot. Add the oil and swirl to coat
   the pan. Lightly season the fish and place into the hot pan skin side down
   to crisp the skin. On contact the pan and fish should make a good sizzle
   noise. Leave the fish to cook for approximately 3-4 minutes without fiddling
   with it. Once you see a caramelised brown edge appear, carefully turn over
   the fish.

3 Add the butter to the pan, which will help colour the fish and give a richer
   flavour. Cook for a further 2–3 minutes, depending on the thickness of the
   fish. To test the fish, give it a gentle poke with your finger: it should still be
   a little springy in the middle. Remove the fish on to a warmed plate or
   baking sheet and allow to relax for a couple of minutes.

4 While the fish is relaxing, make the wilted greens.

5 To serve, divide the wilted greens between the serving plates, top with the
   fish and spoon over some lemon butter sauce.

seared smoked salmon

with apple and watercress salad and horseradish cream

ingredients

4 pieces of best-quality
smoked organic salmon,
sliced at an angle to about
5-7 mm/¼ in thickness
1 tablespoon sunflower oil

for the horseradish cream:
40 g/1½ oz freshly grated
horseradish
2 tablespoons mayonnaise
2 tablespoons crème fraîche
a squeeze of lemon juice

**for the apple and
watercress salad:**
125 g/4½ oz white cabbage
2 teaspoons rice wine
vinegar
1 teaspoon caster sugar
2 spring onions, finely sliced
diagonally

½ green eating apple, grated
with the skin on
about 1 teaspoon freshly
squeezed lime juice
80 g/3 oz watercress, thick
stalks removed
pinch of Maldon salt

serves **4**

techniques
chopping p64

mise en place
• Make horseradish cream
up to 3 days ahead.
Marinate the cabbage for
40 minutes. Slice the
salmon.

John says: The salmon for
this recipe should be cut at
an angle, to give good-sized
pieces. Using a serrated knife
(the Wustof Super Slicer is
the best man for the job),
hold the knife at an angle of
45 degrees to the salmon
and slice at that angle. Cut
the slices 5-7 mm/¼ in thick
to give the best contrast in
textures and to prevent the
salmon cooking through. I
also like to cut the brown
fat off.

method

1 Make the horseradish cream by mixing all the ingredients together well.

2 For the salad, shred the white cabbage as finely as possible. Mix the
shredded cabbage with the rice wine vinegar, sugar and a pinch of salt.
Leave to marinate for 40 minutes at room temperature. At the last minute,
add the spring onions, grated apple and lime juice to taste and stir in well
with a fork.

3 Just before serving, heat a frying pan to medium hot. Add the sunflower oil
and flash-fry the smoked salmon for about 30 seconds – but no longer as
we are looking simply to sear one side and not cook the fish through.

4 Mix the watercress into the cabbage salad, then divide the salad into four
portions and arrange on the left-hand side of each of four plates. Place the
salmon next to the salad, with a dollop of horseradish cream alongside.
Serve immediately.

fish recipes

potato and herb pancake
with smoked haddock and a poached egg

ingredients

10 g/¼ oz unsalted butter
olive oil, for frying
4 x 120 g/4 oz undyed
  smoked haddock fillet
  (thick pieces)
a squeeze of lemon juice

for the potato pancake :
300 g/10½ oz mashed
  potatoes, cold but not
  chilled (see p255)
2 free-range eggs
50 g/1¾ oz self-raising flour
2 tablespoons milk
80 ml/3 fl oz double cream

spring onions, green part
  only, finely shredded
2 tablespoons chopped
  fresh herbs, (parsley,
  chervil, basil, chives)
Maldon salt and freshly
  ground black pepper

4 poached eggs
  (see page 92)
1 x recipe hollandaise sauce
  (see p236)

serves **4**

mise en place

• Make the pancakes ahead
of time, wrap in foil and
reheat for 5 minutes in the
oven. Pre-poach the eggs
and hold in cold water –
reheat for 2 minutes in
boiling water. Make the
hollandaise and keep it
warm in a vacuum flask.

Nick says: A classic example
of harmony on a plate, the
pancake, smoked haddock
and soft-poached egg
compliment each other
perfectly. You need really
fresh eggs here, and buy
farm fresh if you can get
them, organic if you can't.
The rich hollandaise sauce
transforms this into a
special occasion dish, but
those counting the calories
may wish to leave it out. Me?
I'd keep it in and schedule a
30 minute walk in later!

method

1 To make the pancakes, place the mashed potatoes in a bowl, beat in the eggs
and fold in the flour. Heat the milk with the cream but do not allow to boil.
Add most of the hot cream and milk to the potatoes and stir. The amount
of milk needed will vary depending on the type of potatoes, size of the eggs
and so on. You're looking for a dropping consistency. Add more milk or cream
if necessary. Fold in the spring onions and chopped herbs, taste and season.
Cover and set aside. This mix will hold for a couple of hours if you are not
cooking immediately.

2 To cook the pancakes, you will require either two blini pans or an ovenproof
20 cm/8 in frying pan. I use blini pans, but if making a single larger pancake,
simply allow an extra 10 minutes in the oven and also flip the pancake over
after 15 minutes to make sure it's cooked through; slice to serve.

3 Preheat the oven to 180°C/350°F/gas mark 4.

4 Heat the pans and add a tablespoon of oil. Ladle some of the mixture into
the pans to produce a cake about 10 cm/4 in across and 5 mm/¼ in thick
(I find a 70 ml/2½ fl oz ladle is the perfect amount). Cook over a moderate
heat for approximately 2 minutes, until bubbles start to appear around the
edges. Place the pan into the oven for about 8–10 minutes to cook through
and colour. Remove from the oven and allow to sit for 1 minute, before
turning out the pancakes on to a baking sheet lined with non-stick baking
parchment. Repeat the process until you have enough pancakes plus a
couple of spares to cover any last-minute disasters!

5 Place an ovenproof frying pan over a medium heat and allow to warm. Add
a splash of oil and the butter. When the fat is foaming, add the haddock and
leave to caramelise on one side for 2–3 minutes, depending on the thickness
of the fish. Turn over and place the pan in the oven for about 2–3 minutes
until just cooked. Take care not to overcook the fish.

6 While the fish is in the oven, put the poached eggs in boiling water for
2 minutes, drain and put to the side. Remove the fish from the oven and
squeeze over some lemon juice. Place a pancake on each of four warmed
plates. Set a smoked haddock on top and a poached egg on top of this.
Coat with the hollandaise sauce and serve immediately.

cherry and almond tart

ingredients

1 x recipe sweet shortcrust
  pastry (see p269)
250 g/9 oz unsalted butter,
  softened
250 g/9 oz caster sugar
25 g/1 oz plain flour
250 g/9 oz ground almonds

4 medium eggs, at room
  temperature
Cook School custard, to
  serve (see p271)
600 g/1 lb 5 oz tin of pitted
  black cherries, drained
3-4 tablespoons apricot jam

serves **8–10**

techniques
blind baking p88

mise en place
• Make the tart up to 2 days
in advance and keep
refrigerated.

Nick says: We've used tinned
cherries here (look out for
amarena), but you can use
raspberries, brambles,
apricots or pears.

method

1 Use the pastry to line a 25 cm/10 in flan ring and bake blind.

2 Reduce the oven temperature to 160°C/325°F/gas mark 3.

3 To make the almond frangipane, cream the butter and sugar together in
a large mixing bowl until very pale and thick. Beat in the flour and a quarter
of the ground almonds until smooth. Then beat in the eggs, one a time, until
each one is absorbed – if you do this gradually (and all the ingredients are
at room temperature) there is less chance of the frangipane splitting
(curdling), which could make the baked sponge heavy and greasy. Carefully
fold in the remaining ground almonds. (You can successfully freeze the
mixture at this stage if you wish.)

4 Spread the almond frangipane mixture in the tart case and smooth the
surface. Dot the cherries over the frangipane mix. There's no need to press
them in as they'll start to sink in as the tart bakes. Put the tart in the oven
and bake for 45 minutes–1 hour or until risen and golden brown all over.
To test if it's ready, gently press the frangipane near the edge – it should
feel springy. Move closer to the centre with each gentle press: if cooked,
the tart will have the same springiness all the way across.

5 Put the apricot jam into a small pan and leave to melt over a low heat.
Add a little water if it is very thick. Push it through a sieve to remove any
lumps and then brush it liberally over the top of the tart to glaze. Serve
the tart warm with cold Cook School custard (see page 271).

dessert recipes

vanilla cream
with seasonal fruits

ingredients
300 ml/10 fl oz milk
1 vanilla pod, split
50 g/1¾ oz caster sugar
3 gelatine leaves
500 ml/18 fl oz double cream

**for the caramelised
seasonal fruits:**
225 g/8 oz caster sugar,
   sifted
450 g/1 lb apples, pears,
   plums, peaches or berries,
   prepared and chopped

1 vanilla pod or 1 cinammon
   stick (optional)

dessert recipes

serves 6

techniques
caramel p96

mise en place
• Make the vanilla cream up
  to 3 days ahead and keep
  in the fridge. Make the
  fruit compote up to 2–3
  hours in advance.

Alan says: This is all about
the contrast of flavour and
texture between the lightly
set cream and the intense
fruitiness of the compote.
We've opted not to play it
safe with too much gelatine,
as this is best wobbly and
barely set.

method

1 To make the vanilla cream, put the milk, split vanilla pod and sugar into a
   saucepan and bring to the boil. Soak the gelatine in cold water for 5
   minutes or until it goes soft, then lift out of the water, let it drain, drop it
   into the hot milk and stir until dissolved.

2 Pour in the double cream, cool, then place in the fridge until it *just* begins
   to thicken. At this stage, stir to distribute the vanilla seeds throughout and
   lift out the vanilla pod.

3 Pour the vanilla cream into six stemmed glasses or individual flexible moulds,
   set on a tray and refrigerate for at least 5 hours or until set.

4 To make the caramelised fruit, pour the sugar into a conical mound on the
   base of a small saucepan and heat over a medium heat. Don't muck about
   and stir the sugar now or you will get lumps – just let it gradually melt down
   and turn to caramel, stirring once. Once the sugar is melted and starts to
   boil, take it to a blond or pale caramel, then whack in the chosen fruit and
   cook for 2–3 minutes (adding a vanilla pod or stick of cinnamon depending
   on the fruit used). Cool, cover and refrigerate until needed.

5 If the cream has been made in moulds, press the top of the vanilla cream
   and gently pull away from the edge of the mould (this breaks the seal) and
   carefully invert on to cold dessert plates. If it still won't budge, dip very
   briefly into warm water and then unmould. Spoon the fruit alongside. These
   are great served with a tuile biscuit on the side (see page 269).

moist chocolate cake

ingredients

200 g/7 oz unsalted butter, plus extra for greasing
200 g/7 oz good-quality plain chocolate (60% cocoa solids)
140 g/5 oz caster sugar

7 eggs, separated (see p112)
sifted icing sugar, for dusting
crème fraîche, to serve
caramel sauce, to serve (see p272)

serves 12

techniques
whisking egg whites p112; folding p116

mise en place
• Make the day before, wrap and refrigerate, then bring back to room temperature before serving.

John says: With something as simple as this, the quality of ingredients is paramount. Use the best butter and eggs you can get your hands on. The chocolate shouldn't be too rich: around the 60% solids is ideal, anything higher will be too bitter. Experiment with brands to find your favourite, we like Green and Blacks for this recipe, or the widely-available Lindt.

method

1 Preheat the oven to 160°C/325°F/gas mark 3.

2 Lightly butter a 25 cm/10 in springform cake tin and line the base with a circle of baking parchment and the edges with a long strip.

3 Break the chocolate into a bowl and add the butter. Sit this over a pan of simmering water, making sure that the bowl does not touch the water. Leave to melt, stirring until it is smooth and glossy. Make sure the chocolate doesn't get too hot or it will 'seize' and thicken. Turn off the heat, leaving the pan in position to keep it warm.

4 Put the sugar and egg yolks into a medium bowl and whisk to the ribbon stage (p114). This should take 4–5 minutes. Gently fold this into the melted chocolate.

5 In a large bowl, whisk the egg whites into soft peaks (p112). Loosen the chocolate mix with some egg white and fold the mix into the remaining whites (p116).

6 Pour into the tin and bake for 45 minutes. It will soufflé up during cooking and just crack when it's ready but then collapse once you bring it out of the oven. Don't worry: this is just the way it should be. Leave to cool in the tin, then carefully remove from the tin by placing the palm of your hand over the cake and inverting it. Peel off the paper, flip the cake back on to a board and dust with a little icing sugar. Cut the cake into wedges and serve with a dollop of crème fraîche and a heavy drizzle of caramel sauce.

banana and lemon soufflés

ingredients

softened butter, for
  greasing the ramekins
sifted icing sugar, for
  dusting
2 ripe bananas
2 tablespoons freshly
  squeezed lemon juice

1 free-range egg yolk
5 free-range egg whites
3 tablespoons caster sugar

serves **6**

techniques
whisking egg whites p112,
folding p116

mise en place
• Butter and dust out the
  ramekins with sugar – that's
  all; these are very easy to
  make.

Alan says: Once you have put
the soufflé mix into the
ramekins, run the handle of a
teaspoon around the edge.
This will help prevent the
soufflé catching as it rises.

method

1 Preheat the oven to 200°C/400°F/gas mark 6. Place a baking sheet in the
  oven to heat.
2 Butter six ramekins and dust out with icing sugar.
3 Peel the bananas and place in a bowl with the lemon juice. Using the back of
  a fork, mash the bananas down to a mushy texture. Add the egg yolk and mix
  with the fork until thoroughly combined.
4 In a large bowl whisk the egg whites until they form soft peaks. Gradually
  add the sugar, whisking until stiff between each addition, and continue
  whisking until the mixture is thick enough to leave a pretty firm ribbon trail
  when the whisk is lifted.
5 Stir a couple of spoonfuls of whisked egg whites into the bananas to loosen
  the mixture, then gently fold in the rest, taking care to keep the volume and
  not to overwork the mixture.
6 Fill the ramekins right to the top with the mixture. Set the ramekins on
  the hot baking sheet and place in the oven. Cook for 10 minutes, until the
  soufflés have risen by about 2.5 cm/1 in. To serve, place each soufflé on
  the centre of a plate and dust with icing sugar.

dessert recipes

alan's tarte tatin

ingredients
150 g/5½ oz caster sugar
30 g/1 oz unsalted butter
4 Granny Smith apples
120 g/4 oz pre-rolled frozen
   puff pastry, defrosted
ice cream, to serve

serves **4**

techniques
caramel p96

mise en place
· Make the caramel in
  advance and keep in the
  fridge. Although best
  cooked immediately, the
  uncooked tarts will keep
  in the fridge for 1-2 days.

John says: Wearing a pair of
latex gloves is a good idea
when making caramel, as hot
sugar can give a very nasty
burn if you're not careful.

method

1 First make the caramel following the technique on page 272. Take care not to let it get too dark, as it will make the caramel taste burnt and far too bitter. If you do see it darkening too quickly, simply take the pan off the heat and continue to stir. When you have the right colour, dip the base of the pan in a bowl of cold water for 5 seconds to stop the caramel cooking any further.

2 Next, fold the butter into the caramel until fully incorporated. Pour the caramel into the base of four blini pans and cool.

3 Preheat the oven to 180°C/350°F/gas mark 4.

4 Peel and core the apples. Cut each apple into three equal segments and place each piece, outer rounded edge down, into a blini pan. Try to leave a space in the centre, as this is where the ice cream will sit. Bake in the oven for about 10–12 minutes, or until the apples soften slightly. Remove from the oven and cool completely. Cover and refrigerate.

5 Roll out the puff pastry to a thickness of 4 mm/¼ in. Using a medium bowl or side plate as a guide, cut four discs out of the pastry, which should each be just a little bigger than a blini pan.

6 Place a pastry circle over each blini pan, gently pressing it down over the apples. Use a spoon handle to tuck the pastry edges into the pan, which will create a nice pastry shell for the filling. Cover and chill until required. Bring to room temperature before baking.

7 To cook, uncover the pans and sit them on a baking sheet. Bake for 10–15 minutes or until the pastry is golden brown. Remove from the oven and allow to cool slightly.

8 The blini pans will be hot, so make sure you use an oven cloth or glove to handle them. Before inverting the tarts onto serving plates, gently tip the pans and drain off and reserve any excess caramel, as this will make the next stage a whole lot safer! Place a serving plate on top of the blini pan and holding the plate with the palm of your hand, quickly invert the plate and pan to leave the blini pan on top.

9 Remove the pan and drizzle with the extra caramel. Serve with a scoop of ice cream sitting in the middle.

crème brulée

ingredients
600 ml/1 pint double cream
1 vanilla pod, split lengthways,
 seeds scooped out and
 reserved
6 medium egg yolks
75 g/2¾ oz caster sugar
sifted icing sugar, to glaze

dessert recipes

serves **6**

techniques
making custard p94

mise en place
• Cook and chill the creams,
 but glaze only at the last
 moment or the caramel
 can dissolve.

Nick says: Make this with
grated milk chocolate stirred
into the hot mix and spoon
some crushed raspberries
into the bottom of the
ramekin before carefully
pouring on the custard.

method
1 Heat the cream, vanilla pod and seeds together in a saucepan to just below
   boiling. Meanwhile place the egg yolks and sugar into a heatproof bowl and
   set this over the pan containing the cream. Whisk the yolks until they
   become really pale, thick and foamy: this should take 4–5 minutes. At the
   last minute, remove the bowl and increase the heat under the cream until
   it starts to boil. Just as it begins to rise up the sides of the pan, pour two
   thirds into the bowl with the egg mix (see page 94).
2 Whisk thoroughly, then pour the remaining mix back into the remaining
   cream in the hot pan.
3 Place the pan back on the heat and stir, from side to side, with a silicone
   spatula for one or two minutes until the mix thickens sufficiently to coat
   the spatula. Once steam starts to appear, the mix is ready to take off the
   heat (if you have a thermoprobe the optimum temperature is 82°C/180°F)
   If the mixture starts to split, immediately pour the whole lot through a fine
   sieve into a cold bowl and that should do the trick. After you have removed
   the mix from the heat, continue stirring for a further couple of minutes.
4 Divide the mix between six 150 ml/5 fl oz (no.1) ramekins, filling them to the
   brim. Cool, then allow the mixture to set in the fridge for at least 6 hours
   or preferably overnight.
5 To serve, dust the surface of the creams evenly with a thin layer of icing
   sugar (a tea strainer is good for this). Then apply the heat of a blow-lamp
   to glaze – not one of those mini ones which take ages. Alternatively, if you
   don't have a blow-lamp, place the brulées under a hot grill, but watch them
   very carefully because they burn very easily. When glazed, they should be a
   nice mahogany-brown colour – and don't be tempted to poke your fingers
   into the top, because not only will the hot sugar burn you but you will also
   ruin your presentation! Place the brulées in the fridge for 5 minutes before
   serving, to allow the caramel to cool.

fresh fruit pavlova

ingredients

100 g/3½ oz egg whites
1 tablespoon cornflour
a squeeze of lemon juice
100 g/3½ oz caster sugar
400 ml/14 fl oz double cream
250 g/9 oz strawberries
100 g/3½ oz raspberries

sifted icing sugar, for dusting
raspberry sauce, to serve
  (see p275)

serves **4**

techniques

whisking egg whites p112

mise en place

• The meringue can be made and stored in a large container with a tight-fitting lid for about 1–2 days. If serving for a dinner party, have the meringue ready, lightly whip the cream and assemble at the last minute.

Nick says: My favourite fruit combination for pavlova is fresh strawberries with raspberry sauce – a real taste of summer! I don't bother piping the meringue – I just spoon it into a mound and make a hollow in the centre. It might take a bit longer to cook this way. You can also make a large rectangular pavlova and cut out portions to serve.

method

1 Preheat the oven to 140°C/275°F/gas mark 1.

2 Place the egg whites in a clean stainless steel bowl. If you have a tabletop mixer, this is the time to get it out as there is a lot of whisking involved here. Set the mixer on a slow setting and beat the whites to the soft-peak stage.

3 Dissolve the cornflour in the lemon juice and add this with half of the sugar. Increase the speed of the mixer and beat for 2 minutes until the mix reaches the medium-peak stage.

4 Finally add the remaining sugar and beat again for 5 minutes until all sugar is incorporated and the meringue is very, very thick and shiny or forms stiff peaks.

5 Mark a 25 cm/10 in circle on a sheet of non-stick baking parchment and place it on a baking sheet. Fill a piping bag, fitted with a plain wide nozzle, with the meringue. Starting in the centre of the circle, pipe the meringue on to the paper, working outwards in a spiral (a bit like a childish snail drawing); continue until the circle is filled with meringue. Next pipe blobs on top of the circle all the way around the edge and make a second circle of blobs inside the first.

6 Bake for 25 minutes, turn off the oven and leave the meringue inside for a further hour, where it will carry on cooking and then cool down very slowly. Remove from the oven when completely cold.

7 To serve, whisk the cream until it reaches the soft-peak stage. Carefully remove the baking parchment from the meringue, set it on a serving plate and spread the cream over the top, swirling it with a palette knife to cover the surface.

8 Slice the strawberries thinly and arrange on top of the cream, leaving the centre free for the raspberries. Pile the raspberries into the centre and dredge the whole thing with icing sugar. Serve with raspberry sauce.

shirley's marmalade pudding and drambuie custard

ingredients

150 g/5½ oz fine brown breadcrumbs

25 g/1 oz self-raising wholemeal flour

120 g/4 oz light brown soft sugar

120 g/4 oz unsalted butter, plus extra for greasing

175 g/6 oz well-flavoured, coarse-cut marmalade

3 large eggs

1 rounded teaspoon bicarbonate of soda

for the Drambuie custard:

1 x recipe custard (see p271)

3 tablespoons Drambuie

serves 6

mise en place

• This is perfect for entertaining as it can be made in advance and given a quick heat through for a couple of minutes in the microwave. The custard can be made earlier and kept warm in a vacuum flask.

John says: For an extra special presentation, melt a little more of the marmalade and drizzle over the pudding before serving.

method

1 Butter a 3 pint/1.7 litres pudding basin really well and choose a saucepan large enough to hold the pudding basin comfortably. We use a heatproof plastic basin with a matching lid: perfect for this recipe.

2 Place the breadcrumbs, flour and sugar in a large mixing bowl. Melt the butter and marmalade together in a saucepan over a gentle heat, but do not boil. Pour the melted ingredients into the dry ingredients and mix together thoroughly.

3 Lightly whisk the eggs until frothy and beat gently into the mixture until well blended. Last of all, dissolve the bicarbonate of soda in 1 tablespoon cold water. Beat this into the pudding mixture, which will increase in volume as it absorbs the bicarbonate of soda. Transfer the mixture to the prepared pudding basin and leave to stand for 5 minutes for the bicarb to work.

4 Cover the basin with a double sheet of buttered foil, making sure there is a pleat in it for expansion, or put the lid on if your basin has one.

5 Place the pudding basin in a saucepan of boiling water. The water should reach half-way up the side of the basin. Simmer the pudding steadily for 2 hours. The water will need topping up throughout the cooking period. Make the custard and stir the Drambuie through.

6 Uncover the pudding and turn it out on to a warmed serving dish. Serve hot with the warm Drambuie custard.

apple sorbet
with praline crisps and cider syrup

ingredients

300 g/10½ oz Granny Smith
  apples, skin on, cored and
  thinly sliced
2 x recipe stock syrup (see
  p271)
freshly squeezed juice of
  1 lime

for the cider syrup:
120 ml/4 fl oz dry cider
120 g/4 oz caster sugar
freshly squeezed juice of
  ½ lemon
½ red apple, skin on, cored
  and very finely diced

for the praline crisps:
200 g/7 oz sugar
60 g/2¼ oz flaked almonds
for the apple crisps
2 Granny Smith apples
400 ml/14 fl oz stock syrup

serves **4**

techniques
stock syrup p271, making
caramel p96

mise en place
• Make the all the elements
  earlier in the day for serving
  at a dinner party and
  assemble at the last minute.

Nick says: This is a genius
and incredibly easy way of
making sorbet and this apple
version is just like biting into
a crisp green apple straight
from an ice cold fridge. Alan
had a bit of fun with the
presentation for this recipe,
but it's just as comfortable
being served up on its own
as a summery end to a meal.
I make this with cloudy apple
juice instead of water for a
stronger apple flavour. For
the kids just spoon the
crushed apple sorbet into
glasses and let them dig in!

method

1 Spread the apple slices on to a tray lined with non-stick baking parchment
   and freeze.
2 Make the apple crisps. Bring the syrup to the simmer and remove from the
   heat. Cut the apples in half across their equator and lay on a chopping board
   cut side down. Using a 35 mm/1¼ in cutter cut a disc of apple from the
   centre of the halves. Slice the cut apple sections on a mandoline and drop
   the slices into the warm syrup. Allow the slices to soak in the syrup for half
   an hour then carefully lift out and shake off excess. Lay the slices onto non-
   stick mats and place into a cool oven (150°C/300°F/gas mark 2) to dry (this
   should take about one hour). Remove from the oven to cool and crisp up.
3 Make the stock syrup at this stage, if you haven't already done so. For the
   cider syrup, pour the cider into a pan and add the sugar and lemon juice.
   Bring to the boil and simmer for 5 minutes. Cool, then add the diced apple.
4 To make the praline crisps, place the sugar into a warm heavy pan and allow
   to colour slowly. When the sugar changes colour, gently stir to distribute
   the cold sugar. Do not over-stir, as the sugar will form into clumps. When
   a good light caramel is achieved, add the almonds and thoroughly mix.
   Then transfer to an oiled metal tray and allow to cool and set hard. Blitz
   in a food processor until it becomes a fine dust.
5 Preheat oven to 200°C/400°C/gas mark 6. To form the crisps sprinkle a thin
   layer of the praline dust onto silicone sheets and bake in the oven for
   2–3 minutes, remove and cut or form shapes before the mixture sets again.
6 To finish the sorbet, place the frozen apples, lime juice and the second
   quantity of basic stock syrup (not the cider syrup!) into a food processor
   and blitz until a smooth iced purée forms. Serve immediately, or keep in the
   freezer for up to 3 months. To serve, scoop the sorbet into neat balls or
   oval quenelles and arrange on individual plates as follows: start with a
   praline crisp, then add a scoop of sorbet, add a crisp; repeat these layers
   twice more and finish with an apple crisp. Spoon the cider syrup around the
   base and serve immediately.

vanilla parfait
with seasonal fruits

ingredients

280 g/10 oz caster sugar
6 egg yolks
2 teapoons vanilla extract
600 ml/1 pint double cream,
  whipped
280 g/10 oz seasonal berries

2 tablespoons caster sugar
a squeeze of lemon juice
6 brandy snap biscuits
  (see p270), cut to size
  of parfait moulds

serves **6**

techniques
folding p116

mise en place
• Make up completely and
freeze for up to 2 weeks.
Add the sugar to the fruits
when serving your starter.

John says: A parfait is
basically an ice cream that
hasn't been churned. There
are 2 ways to present this –
opt for individual moulds or
make a terrine and cut into
slices to serve. You can add
any flavouring in here from
coffee or honey to liqueurs.
Alcohol of any description
will act as an antifreeze,
allowing you to serve straight
from the freezer – Grand
Marnier is my personal
favourite.

method

1 Put the sugar with 2 tablespoons water in a saucepan. Slowly heat until the
   sugar is dissolved, then bring to the boil and boil for 3–4 minutes. At the
   same time, using an electric hand whisk or tabletop mixer, whisk the egg
   yolks at full speed until pale, light and fluffy.

2 Pour the boiling syrup on to the yolks while still whisking them. Take care
   in this operation not to burn your hands with the boiling sugar. Continue
   beating at high speed for 10–12 minutes. The mix should now be thick,
   smooth and pale yellow.

3 Fold the vanilla extract into the egg mixture, then carefully fold in the
   whipped cream. Spoon or pour the mix into a terrine mould or individual
   containers and freeze for several hours or overnight.

4 Put the fruits in a bowl and sprinkle with sugar and lemon juice. Stir and
   leave for 30 minutes for the flavours to merge.

5 To serve, turn out the parfait and slice, using a knife dipped in hot water.
   Place on to chilled plates, with the summer berries arranged on top and
   a brandy snap on the side.

crêpes
with lemon syrup

ingredients

2 medium eggs
25 g/1 oz caster sugar
90 g/3¼ oz plain flour
250 ml/9 fl oz milk

20 g/¾ oz unsalted butter,
  melted, or clarified butter
  (see p246)
1 tablespoon sunflower oil,
  plus extra for greasing

for the lemon syrup:
1 x recipe stock syrup
freshly squeezed juice of
  2-3 large lemons
2 long strips of pared lemon
  zest

serves 4

mise en place

• You could make and freeze
the pancakes, but part of
the joy of pancakes is the
making and serving straight
out of the pan! Make the
batter and chill up to a day
ahead; stir before using.
Make the lemon syrup in
advance.

Nick says: If you make
crêpes regularly, it's worth
keeping a pan specifically for
the task – never wash it in
soapy water; just wipe it
down with kitchen paper.

method

1 Break the eggs into a bowl and whisk in the sugar and all the flour until
the mixture hangs in thick, lump-free, elastic strings from the whisk and
has the consistency of single cream. Now whisk in all the milk and the
melted butter or oil. Set aside and leave to rest for an hour.

2 To make the lemon syrup, bring the stock syrup to the boil and add the
lemon juice and zest, then allow to cool before decanting into a squeezy
bottle. This can be stored in the fridge for up to a week.

3 Heat a 15–18 cm/6–7 in frying pan until it's medium hot (the temperature is
crucial here – too hot and the batter will splutter and go lacy and burn; too
cool and the pancakes will be pale and leathery). Put some sunflower oil onto
a piece of kitchen towel and rub over the pan. Pour in about 2 tablespoons of
the batter (I use a 50 ml/2 fl oz ladle – not quite full – to make the perfect
crêpe) and tilt the pan until the mixture covers the base in a thin, even layer.
Swirl any excess to the edges as this give the crêpe thicker edges (a good
thing!). Cook over a medium-high heat for 30 seconds–2 minutes, depending
on the heat of the pan.

4 Using a palette knife or spatula, lift the edge of the crêpe and hold it between
your thumb and forefinger. Flip over the crêpe, using the palette knife in the
other hand to help. Cook the other side for 30 seconds–1 minute, until it has
lightly browned. Repeat this process until all of the batter is used up.

5 If keeping the crêpes for any length of time, place a square of non-stick
baking parchment between each one to stop them sticking together as
you stack them.

6 Place each crêpe on a serving plate and squeeze over the lemon syrup.
Fold in half and give another squeeze of syrup before folding into quarters
and serving.

poached pear
and crème fraîche mousse

ingredients

1 vanilla pod, split and seeds scraped out
190 g/7 oz crème fraîche
60 g/2¼ oz caster sugar
finely grated zest of 2 lemons
freshly squeezed juice of 1 lemon

1⅙ gelatine leaves, soaked in cold water for 10 minutes
190 g/7 oz double cream
tuiles, to serve (see page 270)

for the caramel poached pears:
500 g/1 lb 2 oz granulated sugar
1 vanilla pod, split and seeds scraped out
6 small Comice or Conference pears

serves 6

techniques
caramel p96

mise en place
• Make the pears a few days in advance: they benefit from sitting in the syrup. Make and set up the mousses and reduce the syrup and chill up to 6 hours in advance.

Alan says: Use the scraped-out vanilla pods as a garnish for desserts. Cut them lengthways into fine strips and arrange on top of your dessert. This dish is only as good as the pear you use. Look out for comice or conference pears that are slightly under-ripe. The pears should be poached to perfection – soft and yielding to the spoon, but still holding their shape. There's just no excuse for a rock-hard pear!

method

1 Put the vanilla seeds, crème fraîche, caster sugar and lemon zest into a bowl and mix thoroughly.
2 Warm the lemon juice with the drained gelatine until dissolved, leave to cool slightly and stir into the crème fraîche mixture.
3 Whip the double cream to the soft-peak stage and fold into the crème fraîche mixture. Spoon or pour the mixture into individual moulds or a terrine, cover and chill for at least 2 hours.
4 To make the poaching syrup, put the granulated sugar in a saucepan and make caramel. When the caramel is a good colour, but not too dark, remove from the heat and quickly pour in 500 ml/18 fl oz water. It will hiss and splutter, so take care. Place over the heat again, add the vanilla seeds and stir until the caramel lumps have dissolved and the vanilla seeds are evenly distributed.
5 Peel the pears, leaving on the stalks. Using a melon baller, scoop out the seeds and pith from the bottom of the pears before placing them into the boiling syrup, stalks upwards. Bring back to the boil. Turn down the heat and simmer for at least 10 minutes (depending on their size and ripeness), then remove from the heat and allow to cool in the syrup. Do this 24 hours in advance for the best results.
6 The next day, lift out the pears and boil down the liquid rapidly until it forms a medium-thick syrup. Cool.
7 To serve, remove the mousse from the tin and cut into wedges. Stand a pear upright next to each mousse and serve with a pool of syrup and a tuile.

dessert recipes

cook school's ultimate bread-and-butter (panettone) pudding

ingredients

100 g/3½ oz unsalted butter, softened
500 g/1 lb 2 oz Italian panettone, cut into 3 cm/1¼ in thick slices
500 ml/18 fl oz full cream milk
500 ml/18 fl oz double cream
1 vanilla pod

finely grated zest of ½ medium orange
4 free-range eggs
4 free-range egg yolks
180 g/6 oz caster sugar
small pinch of salt
icing sugar, for dusting
pouring cream, to serve

serves 6–8

techniques
making custard p94

mise en place
• Assemble the pudding and leave to soak for up to 4 hours. Put in the oven when serving your starter. Although best served just after cooking, the pudding can be cooked in advance, then either warmed through or served at room temperature. If doing this, reduce the cooking time by 5-7 minutes.

Nick says: After Christmas, panettone are at bargain basement prices. The texture and the fruit make this the best bread and butter pudding around. You can make it with just about everything in the bread department – brioche, croissants, fruit loaf, pain au chocolats. If making it with bread – stick to a humble open-textured white bread that has dried out a bit – new soft bread tends to turn to slime when soaked in the custard. I like to scatter extra sultanas or raisins that have been soaked in brandy or rum over the panettone before pouring over the custard.

method

1 Preheat the oven to 160°C/325°F/gas mark 3.
2 Generously butter an ovenproof serving dish about 4–5 cm/1½–2 in depth and a 1.5 litre/2¾ pints in capacity.
3 Lightly butter the slices of panettone and lay them in the serving dish, slightly overlapping, in a single layer. Do not be tempted to add a second layer (a common mistake) as the slices will expand in cooking and too much dough will make the pudding heavy.
4 To start the custard base, put the milk and cream in a saucepan and bring to the boil. Split the vanilla pod in half, scrape out the seeds and add these to the milk pan with the orange zest. Whisk the eggs and egg yolks with the sugar and a small pinch of salt until pale. Pour on the hot milk and cream, mixing well.
5 Strain the cream mix over and around the panettone and let stand for 3–4 hours.
6 Place the dish in a roasting tin and carefully pour in hot water so that it half-fills the tin and comes part way up the outside of the dish. Dust the top of the pudding with icing sugar and bake for about 45 minutes. The exact time will depend upon the type of oven used and the warmth of the custard when the pudding goes into the oven. When cooked, it will have a slight crust on top, but will still be slightly wobbly inside.
7 Remove the pudding from the oven and let stand for 5 minutes before serving.
8 Spoon portions of the pudding on to a warmed plate, dust with a little more icing sugar and serve with pouring cream.

dessert recipes

basic recipes

nick's roast chicken stock

makes **1.25 litres/2¼ pints**

ingredients

1 roast chicken carcass with
  leftover skin, bone and jelly
1 large carrot, quartered
2 celery sticks, halved
  lengthwise
1 onion, skin on, quartered
1 Knorr chicken stock cube

1 bay leaf (optional)
1 sprig of thyme or parsley
  stalks (optional)
6 black peppercorns
  (optional)

method

1 Place the carcass in a pot large enough for the bones to take up half its depth. Just cover them with about 2.25 litres/4 pints of cold water and bring to the boil.
2 Once boiling, skim off the fat and any scum from the surface. Add the rest of the ingredients, all of which should lie on top of the carcass. Adjust the heat to a gentle simmer and skim once more. The simmering stock will now rise and fall through the vegetables, which act as a filter, absorbing all the impurities from the liquid and leaving it clear.
3 Leave to simmer for 2–3 hours, tasting regularly. You should eventually notice a point at which the flavour stops improving. This means it's ready.
4 Remove from the heat and pour the stock into a colander set over a bowl. Now pass the stock through a fine sieve into a tall container or 2.5 litre/4½ pint jug. Cover and cool quickly, placing it in a sink of cold water.
5 When cool, leave in the fridge overnight so that any fat settles and sets on top. When set, lift off the fat and spoon out the jellied stock into tubs. This will keep in the fridge for 4–5 days, or frozen for up to 3 months.

Nick says Save up your roast chicken carcasses for this recipe. Just pop them in a plastic bag and freeze them as you collect them, then you can make a really big pot of stock.

brown chicken stock

makes **1.25 litres/2¼ pints**

ingredients

4 kg/9 lb raw chicken
  carcasses
1 pig's trotter, split
4 carrots, diced
3 onions, diced
3 sticks celery, diced
½ fennel bulb, diced

1 garlic bulb, cut in half
  across the equator

method

1 Trim the chicken carcasses of any excess fat and discard the fat. Place carcasses in a roasting tin and roast in a hot oven until golden brown, but don't allow them to burn or they'll taste bitter.
2 Place the roasted chicken bones and the pig's trotter in a large pot (tall narrow pots work best for stocks).
3 Add all the vegetables, except the garlic, to the roasting tin. Roast in the oven (or place on the hob over a high heat) and brown the vegetables, stirring occasionally until golden and caramelised but on no account burnt. Remove the vegetables and set aside. Deglaze the roasting tin with 1 litre/1¾ pint of water. Mix well, scraping the bottom of the tin with a heat-proof spatula to release all the caramelised debris from the bottom of the tin.
4 Add the browned vegetables to the bones in the pot with the halved garlic bulb and top up with enough water to leave 5 cm/2 in of bones showing above the water level (these will shrink down as the stock cooks) and bring up to a simmer. Cook the stock for 2½ hours, skimming occasionally, then strain through a colander into a clean pot.

John says Stocks are one of the building blocks of modern cookery, so get into the habit of making your own at home.

basic recipes

chicken and beef stock

makes **about 2 litres/3½ pints**

ingredients

3 tablespoons sunflower oil, for browning
400 g/14 oz shin of beef, diced
1 turkey thigh, boned and diced
3 carrots, diced
2 celery sticks, diced

2 onions, peeled and diced
2 tablespoons tomato purée
300 ml/10 fl oz dry red wine
1 quantity brown chicken stock (see p228)
200 g/7 oz tinned plum tomatoes, chopped
a small bunch of fresh thyme

method

1 Heat the oil in a large frying pan or roasting tin and brown the meat and vegetables. You may need to do this in small quantities to make sure it browns and doesn't stew.
2 Stir the tomato purée into the mix and allow to caramelise until it changes from red to brown.
3 Deglaze the pan with the red wine. Meanwhile, bring the brown chicken stock to a simmer in a stock pot.
4 Add the browned meat and vegetables to the pot.
5 Add the tomatoes and thyme and return to a simmer, regularly skimming off any scum that may appear.
6 Cook the stock for a further 2 hours and strain; first through a colander, then through a fine strainer, and cool quickly.
7 Once cool, the stock will solidify into a jelly which can be refrigerated in covered containers for 4–5 days, or frozen for up to 3 months.

basic fish stock

makes **about 1.5 litres/2¾ pints**

ingredients

1 kg/2 lb 4oz fish heads, bones and trimmings
2 tablespoons olive oil
100 g/3½ oz white vegetables, finely chopped (onions, leeks, mushrooms, fennel etc)

100 ml/3½ fl oz dry white wine

method

1 Check that the bones and trimmings contain no gill filaments or eyes, as these will make the stock cloudy. Wash thoroughly and put them into a colander to drain.
2 Put the oil and vegetables into a heavy pan with a lid, and place over a low heat. Stir well then cover and leave to sweat in their own juices for 10 minutes.
3 Uncover, pour in the white wine, turn up the heat and boil for 1 minute. Now add 1.2 litres/2 pints of water and the fish, and bring up almost to the boil, then skim well.
4 Reduce the heat and simmer very gently for 20 minutes.
5 Take off the heat then carefully pour out the stock through a very fine sieve, or preferably double muslin, cover and refrigerate until needed, up to 3 days. It can also be frozen for up to 3 months.
6 For instant stock cubes, strain the stock then reheat the liquid until boiling. Reduce by about half until a strong flavour is achieved, then cool quickly and freeze in ice cube trays. When frozen, pop out and store in zip-lock bags.

basic recipes

shellfish stock

marinated vegetable stock

makes **about 2.5 litres/4½ pints**

makes **about 1.2 litres/2 pints**

ingredients

3 tablespoons olive oil
1 kg/2 lb 4 oz langoustine or
   lobster heads, legs, shells
1 onion, peeled and chopped
1 carrot, peeled and chopped
1 stick of celery, chopped
1 garlic bulb, cut across the
   equator

2 tomatoes, chopped
2 star anise
1 teaspoon fennel seeds
1 teaspoon coriander seeds
1 tablespoon tomato purée
200 ml/7 fl oz dry white wine
2 litres/3½ pints fish,
   chicken or vegetable stock

ingredients

1 medium onion, peeled
4 celery sticks
2 large carrots, peeled
1 small leek
1 fennel bulb
1 small garlic bulb
300 ml/10 fl oz dry white
   wine

zest of 1 orange
10 coriander seeds
2 star anise
10 pink peppercorns
1 sprig each of thyme, chervil,
   chives and tarragon
1 bay leaf

basic recipes

method

1 Heat a large, heavy-based pan over a high heat and add the olive oil. Throw in the lobster/langoustine heads, legs and shells and stir around the pan for 4–5 minutes until they start to caramelise and turn golden brown.

2 Add the chopped vegetables, star anise, fennel seeds, coriander seeds and tomato purée, give it a good stir, turn down the heat slightly and sauté for 5 minutes.

3 Pour in the white wine, bring to the boil and cook for one minute.

4 Pour in the stock, bring to the boil again then reduce the heat and simmer for 40 minutes.

5 Allow to cool without straining. When cold, strain through a fine sieve or double muslin. Discard the debris and chill until ready to use. This will keep for up to 3 days in the fridge or up to 3 months in the freezer.

6 For instant stock cubes, strain the stock then reheat the liquid until boiling. Reduce by about half until a strong flavour is achieved, then cool quickly and freeze in ice cube trays. When frozen, pop out and store in zip-lock bags.

method

1 Wash and trim the vegetables. Cut into even dice about 1 cm/½ in square. Place the vegetables into a heavy-based pan with 1.8 litres/3 pints of water, white wine, orange zest, coriander seeds, star anise and peppercorns.

2 Bring the mixture to the boil skimming carefully, then turn down to very low heat for about 8–10 minutes to allow slow infusion of the vegetables.

3 Add the herbs to the stock and simmer for another 4 minutes.

4 Remove from the heat, cool and allow the vegetable and stock mixture to infuse in the pan in the fridge for 48 hours to allow the flavours to combine. Once marinated, it can be used immediately, refrigerated (unstrained) or frozen (strained).

5 To use, strain the stock through a fine sieve lightly pressing the vegetables and herbs to extract maximum flavour. The liquid may now be used for vegetable cooking, fish poaching or as the basis of light sauces and soups.

Nick says Make big batches of this useful stock when you can. It freezes well for up to three months.
John says Leaving the vegetables to marinate for a couple of days and then straining off the stock gives a wonderful rich, sweet flavour that works well with most fish dishes.
Alan says This stock can be sweet, so add lemon juice for balance.

quick tomato sauce

makes **400 ml/14 fl oz**

ingredients
6 tablespoons olive oil
2 x 400g/14 oz tins Italian
  plum tomatoes, chopped
  (see p40)

method
1 Take a heavy-based saucepan and place on a
  medium heat. Add the olive oil, then the chopped
  tomatoes.
2 Bring to the boil then turn down and leave to
  simmer for around 20 minutes until reduced
  by half, and the sauce is thick and a coating
  consistency. Stir from time to time to ensure
  the sauce doesn't catch and burn.
3 Serve immediately, or cool quickly and keep in
  the fridge for up to 1 week. Alternatively, freeze
  using the ice cube tray method (see p43), and
  keep for up to 3 months. For a more robust
  sauce, sweat off some chopped garlic and onions
  in the pan before adding the tomatoes. Fresh
  basil and a splash of good quality balsamic
  vinegar will enliven the sauce still further.

Nick says This is a versatile sauce in my kitchen, from pizza
toppings to pasta sauces. I always have some in the freezer.

red wine gravy

makes **440 ml/16 fl oz**

ingredients
300 g/10½ oz beef bones
1 tablespoon sunflower oil
200 g/7 oz beef trimmings
2 whole shallots, skin on,
  chopped
1 sprig thyme
1 bay leaf

5 black peppercorns, lightly
  crushed
300 ml/10 fl oz dry red wine
400 ml/14 fl oz chicken and
  beef stock (see p229)

method
1 Preheat the oven to 180°C/350°F/gas mark 4
  and place the bones in a roasting tin.
2 When the oven is hot, whack in the bones and
  cook until browned, but don't allow them to burn.
3 Meanwhile, heat a large frying pan over a high
  heat. Add the sunflower oil and then the meat
  trimmings and fry until browned.
4 Add the shallots, thyme, bay leaf and crushed
  peppercorns and cook on a medium heat until
  nicely coloured.
5 Pour in the wine and deglaze the pan, scraping
  the bottom of the pan with a heatproof spatula
  to pick up all the caramelised pieces, before
  reducing it until all the liquid has gone.
6 Add the bones and the stock and gently simmer
  for approximately 40–50 minutes, skimming
  constantly. For maximum colour, simmer slowly
  without allowing the liquid to boil.
7 Pass everything through a fine sieve and allow
  the gravy to stand until the fat floats to the
  surface. Skim off the fat and reheat the gravy
  to serve. Or, make a day in advance, cool quickly
  and leave to stand overnight in the fridge to
  make it easier to lift off the fat.
8 If cooled quickly, the gravy can be kept in the
  fridge for 4 to 5 days, or in the freezer for up
  to 3 months.

Nick says Reduce the gravy until the final flavour is perfect.
If a little thin, the gravy can be thickened with arrowroot.

tomato water

basic recipes

makes **about 300 ml/10 fl oz**

ingredients

1 tablespoon white wine
  vinegar
1 tablespoon caster sugar
360 ml/12 fl oz water
20 really ripe plum tomatoes
¼ teaspoon Maldon salt
½ teaspoon Tabasco sauce
1 teaspoon Worcestershire
  sauce
15 fresh basil leaves

method

1 Put the vinegar and sugar into a small saucepan, mix well then place over a medium heat and simmer for 3 minutes until syrupy. Remove from the heat and stir in the water. Set aside.

2 Quarter the tomatoes reserving any juice, and mix the tomatoes and their juices with the syrup and all the remaining ingredients. Line a colander or large sieve with a sterilised double thickness of muslin, and set over a bowl.

3 Pour the tomato mix into a liquidiser and blend the mixture in batches. Pour each batch into the colander or sieve and leave the water to drain through into the bowl (or use a jelly bag hung over a bowl and allow the mixture to drain overnight). Whichever method you use, make sure it will fit into the fridge!

4 The tomato water can be used as a basis for a tomato consommé or as a component of fish and white meat sauces. It will freeze well for up to 3 months, or will keep in the fridge for 4 or 5 days.

Nick says This freezes well, use the ice cube tray method (see p43).

sauce vierge

serves **4**

ingredients

150 ml/5 fl oz extra virgin
  olive oil
½ teaspoon coriander seeds
1-2 small shallots, peeled and
  finely sliced into rings
1 garlic clove, peeled and
  finely sliced
2 really ripe tomatoes, peeled,
  deseeded and cut into
  1 cm/½ in dice (see p69)
freshly squeezed lemon juice
2 tablespoons chopped
  fresh herbs, such as basil,
  flat leaf parsley, tarragon
  etc

method

1 Mix together the olive oil, coriander seeds, shallots and garlic in a pan and set over a gentle heat. When barely simmering, remove from the heat and allow to infuse for 3 hours.

2 To serve, add the tomatoes, lemon juice to taste, and herbs. Heat through and serve immediately.

Nick says For maximum flavour, chose the best olive oil you can afford. I sometimes use cherry tomatoes when good tomatoes are hard to find. Quarter, peel and deseed them.
John says This is a good sauce to serve with oily fish.
Alan says I like this with char-grilled chicken.

the cook school definitive butter sauce

makes **350 ml/12 fl oz**

ingredients
30 g/1 oz very finely chopped shallots
30 ml/1 fl oz white wine vinegar
45 ml/2 fl oz dry white wine
30 ml/1 fl oz water
15 ml/½ fl oz double cream

120 g/4 oz unsalted butter, cubed and chilled
freshly squeezed lemon juice
Maldon salt and freshly ground black pepper
cayenne pepper

method
1 Place the shallots, vinegar, white wine and water in a small heavy-based saucepan and reduce over a medium heat until just over a quarter remains. Add the cream and boil for one minute.
2 The classic way to prepare this dish is to take the pan off the heat and add the butter piece by piece. But our method is to keep it on the heat, dump in all the chilled, diced butter at once and whisk for all you're worth. This will work, but the temperature is critical: if you see any sign of the sauce boiling at the edges (conspicuous puffs of steam are a sure indication that the mix is too hot) then remove it from the heat, but keep whisking. The target temperature for the mix is 50°C/120°F. If the temperature becomes too high, the sauce will boil and split, too low and the butterfat will start to set and also split. The sauce should be smooth and shiny but with no sign of an oily film on the surface; this would mean that the butter has not been successfully emulsified into the sauce.
3 Season to taste with lemon juice, salt and pepper and cayenne and keep warm ready for use. A preheated vacuum flask will provide the ideal storage and allow you to make the sauce up to 1 hour in advance.

Nick says Purists may want to sieve out the shallots before the third stage, but I leave 'em in.
John says The butter must be very cold, preferably directly from the fridge, and cut into small pieces, otherwise the butter may melt too quickly and the sauce may separate.

speedy hollandaise sauce

makes **400 ml/14 fl oz**

ingredients
3 egg yolks
3 tablespoons boiling water
325 g/11½ oz clarified butter (see p246)
15 ml/½ fl oz white wine vinegar
pinch of cayenne pepper

freshly squeezed lemon juice
Maldon salt and freshly ground black pepper

method
1 Warm the jug of the blender by filling it with boiling water and allowing it to stand for 1 minute. Tip the water out and place the jug on the base of the machine.
2 Add the egg yolks and the boiling water to the jug. Cover with the lid minus the central stopper. Cover the open hole with a tea towel to stop the sauce splashing and whiz for about 30 seconds until the yolks start to go fluffy.
3 Heat the clarified butter in a small saucepan. When it is really hot – almost boiling – and with the blender still running, pour the hot butter through the hole in a steady, continuous stream. The hot butter will start to cook and thicken the egg yolks.
4 Keep the blender running and add the vinegar and season well with salt, pepper, cayenne and lemon juice, to taste. When ready, serve immediately. Note that the eggs in this sauce will only be partially cooked (see page 36).

nick's quick cream sauce

makes **200 ml/7 fl oz**

ingredients
150-200 ml/5-7 fl oz double
  cream
1 teaspoon Dijon mustard
a squeeze of fresh lemon
  juice
Maldon salt and freshly
  ground black pepper

method

1 Nick 'borrowed' this recipe from his mate and
   Cook School guest chef Paul Rankin. It was such
   a simple recipe we couldn't resist adding it in.
   Put the cream, mustard and lemon juice
   together in a small saucepan and place over a
   low–medium heat. Stir well then bring up to the
   boil. The sauce will thicken up quite quickly due
   to the addition of the lemon juice.

2 Season to taste with salt and black pepper. This
   is best used immediately, or you can make 1 hour
   in advance and keep warm.

Nick says This is good with a handful of freshly chopped
herbs or some morel mushrooms.
John says For a touch of luxury, stir in a tablespoon of caviar.

fish cream

makes **about 150ml/5 fl oz**

ingredients
25 g/1 oz butter
2 medium shallots, peeled
  and finely chopped
4 button mushrooms, finely
  chopped
100 ml/3½ fl oz dry white
  wine
100 ml/3½ fl oz good fish
  stock (see p229)
100 ml/3½ fl oz double
  cream
freshly squeezed lemon juice
Maldon salt and freshly
  ground black pepper

method

1 Melt the butter in a medium saucepan, add
   the shallots and mushrooms and cook over
   a low/medium heat, stirring occasionally until
   softening but not colouring, about 6–8 minutes.

2 Add the wine, bring to the boil and cook hard
   until almost disappeared.

3 Quickly pour in the fish stock and again reduce
   until there is just a shiny glaze covering the
   bottom of the pan.

4 Stir in the cream, bring to the boil, then remove
   from the heat and season to taste with lemon
   juice, salt and pepper.

5 Strain into a clean pan and reheat to serve.

Nick says This won't freeze successfully but can be kept in
the fridge for up to 3 days. Always reheat gently or the sauce
may split.

basic dipping sauce

tomato salsa

makes **about 150 ml/5 fl oz**

makes **about 400 g/14 oz**

ingredients

1 garlic clove, peeled and finely chopped

3 tablespoons fresh lime juice

3 tablespoons Thai fish sauce (see p40)

1 tablespoon palm sugar (or golden caster sugar)

1 small red chilli, finely chopped, or 1 teaspoon chilli flakes

ingredients

250 g/9 oz cherry tomatoes, halved

½ small red onion, peeled and finely diced

1 garlic clove, peeled and finely diced

1 small red chilli, deseeded and sliced diagonally

2 tablespoons chopped fresh basil

1 tablespoon Chardonnay or white wine vinegar

3 tablespoons extra virgin olive oil

Maldon salt and freshly ground black pepper

basic recipes

method

1 Whisk all the ingredients together with 3 tablespoons water until the sugar is dissolved. Store in a sealed jar in the fridge for up to 1 week.

2 Other flavourings to try: ginger juice (see page 44), lime zest, very finely chopped carrot or courgette, and of course chopped fresh coriander and/or mint.

method

1 Simply toss all the ingredients together in a bowl until well-mixed. The salsa benefits from at least half an hour to let the flavours mingle, and will hold in the fridge for up to 3 hours.

Nick says For a very hot dipping sauce, add extra chilli flakes.
John says Coriander is good in this; coriander and mint is even better.
Alan says Add lime zest for an extra fresh fragrance.

mayonnaise

makes **600 ml/1 pint**

ingredients

3 egg yolks
freshly squeezed juice of ½ a lemon
1 heaped tablespoon Dijon mustard
500 ml/18 fl oz peanut (groundnut) or sunflower oil
a few drops of Tabasco sauce (optional)
Maldon salt and freshly ground black pepper

method

1 Put the egg yolks, lemon juice, mustard and a pinch of salt into a bowl and whisk together well. Now, very gradually, whisk in the oil until the finished mixture is thick and silky smooth; you may need to add some warm water if the mayo gets too thick.

2 Whisk in the Tabasco and a little more lemon juice to taste if you wish. Cover with clingfilm and chill until needed. This will keep for up to 7 days in the fridge.

3 For a lemon mayonnaise, add the zest of one lemon and a few more drops of lemon juice to the basic recipe.

Nick says Avoid using olive oil for making mayonnaise as it creates an overpowering flavour.

marie-rose sauce

makes **550 ml/19 fl oz**

ingredients

5 tablespoons homemade or Hellmann's mayonnaise
2 tablespoons Heinz tomato ketchup
1 teaspoon whisky or brandy
2 tablespoons crème fraîche
a dash or two of Tabasco or
a pinch of cayenne pepper
a good squeeze of lemon juice
Maldon sea salt and freshly ground black pepper

method

1 Mix together the mayo, ketchup, whisky or brandy and crème fraîche. Shake in a dash or two of Tabasco or a pinch of cayenne, a good squeeze of lemon juice, and some salt and pepper to taste and stir to combine. This is best made fresh, but should keep in the fridge for several days.

basic recipes

basic white sauce

makes **about 450 ml/16 fl oz**

ingredients
60 g/2¼ oz butter
30 g/1 oz plain flour
400 ml/14 fl oz milk
Maldon salt and freshly
  ground black pepper

basic recipes

method

1 Melt the butter in a small, heavy saucepan over a medium heat then add the flour, stirring vigorously, to make a mixture called a roux. Using a wooden spoon or heatproof spatula, stir the flour and butter over the heat for about 2–3 minutes, until it turns a very light sandy brown colour and smells of toast. This will cook out the starch in the flour and avoid the dreaded golf ball of dough that creates lumps when you add the liquid.

2 Leaving the pan on the heat, use a wire whisk to mix in the milk in two or three goes, whisking well until it thickens before adding the next splash.

3 When all the milk has been added, bring to the boil, whisking as the sauce thickens. Once boiling, remove from the heat and season to taste with salt and pepper.

4 Cover the surface with clingfilm to prevent a skin forming and keep warm until using it. If storing, cover and store in the fridge for 3–4 days. This will also freeze for up to three months.

5 To make a cheese sauce, stir in 30–50g/1–1¾ oz of strong grated Cheddar and 30–50g/1–1¾ oz of Parmesan once the sauce is thick. Don't freeze. Some recipes will require a thicker white sauce (e.g. macaroni cheese page 143); simply double the amount of flour.

Nick says I always use more butter than flour when making a roux, so that it melts over the base of the pan, frying the flour in the butter and helping it to cook out.

cumberland sauce

makes **about 350 ml/12 fl oz**

ingredients
500 g/1 lb 2 oz redcurrant
  jelly
250 ml/9 fl oz ruby port
finely grated zest and juice
  of 2 lemons
finely grated zest and juice
  of 2 oranges

2 teaspoons English mustard
pinch of ground cinnamon

method

1 Place all the ingredients in a saucepan and bring to the boil over a medium heat.

2 Skim away the froth and simmer slowly over a low heat for about 30 minutes to reduce by half.

3 Strain the sauce through a fine sieve and cool. When cold, it should have the consistency of runny honey. This will store in the fridge for up to 8 weeks.

Nick says I like to store this in an old tomato sauce dispenser (a squeezy bottle) so that it's easy to dribble around the outside of a plate.

pesto

makes **about 250 ml/9 fl oz**

ingredients

2 garlic cloves, peeled, crushed and chopped
6 tablespoons extra virgin olive oil
100 g/3½ oz fresh basil leaves
30 g/1 oz pine kernels/nuts
80 g/3 oz freshly grated Parmesan cheese
Maldon salt and freshly ground black pepper

method

1 Have a spatula handy to scrape down the sides of the food processor while you're making the pesto. You'll need to do this several times as you add the ingredients.
2 Place the garlic and oil in the food processor and blitz for a few seconds.
3 Add the basil and blitz for about 90 seconds until the mix resembles a syrupy paste.
4 Add the pine nuts and process for a few seconds more, depending on how much texture you want in the finished pesto.
5 Add the Parmesan and pulse twice to just combine, then pour and scrape the mix out into a bowl.
6 Taste and season with salt and pepper. Spoon into a clean Kilner or screwtop jar and cover with a layer of olive oil. This can be stored in the fridge for about 2 weeks. Pesto can also be frozen for up to 6 months.

tapenade

makes **about 350 g/12 oz**

ingredients

2 garlic cloves, peeled and finely chopped
100 g/3½ oz anchovy fillets (see p40)
100g/3½ oz salted capers, rinsed and drained
100g/3½ oz black olives (the crinkly ones), pitted and weighed *after* pitting
3 tablespoons extra virgin olive oil
a squeeze of lemon juice
Maldon salt and freshly ground black pepper

method

1 Put all the ingredients, except the olive oil, in a food processor and blitz until the mix forms a coarse paste.
2 Then add the olive oil and blitz again.
3 Add lemon juice to taste and scrape out into a jar, smooth down the surface and cover with a thin layer of olive oil. This will keep in the fridge for about 10 days, or tapenade can be frozen for up to 6 months.

John says Each time you use some, flatten the surface with a spoon and then splash on more olive oil before returning it to the fridge. This keeps it sealed and stops it darkening and losing its flavour.

thai red curry paste

makes **500 ml/18 fl oz**

ingredients

4 stalks of lemongrass
8 shallots, roughly chopped
10 fresh red chillies (to taste), deseeded and chopped
1 cm/$\frac{1}{2}$ in galangal or ginger root, thinly sliced
8-10 garlic cloves, peeled and roughly chopped

2 teaspoons shrimp paste or 2 tablespoons Thai fish sauce (see p40)
finely grated zest of 3 limes
juice of 1 lime
2 teaspoons peppercorns, ground in a mortar and pestle

method

1 Place all of the ingredients into the bowl of a food processor and blitz in short bursts, pushing the mixture down towards the blades with a spatula from time to time. You may need to add a little water to thin and get it moving initially, but don't add too much!
2 Blitz until you have a reasonably smooth paste.
3 Spoon into a Kilner or screwtop jar and cover with a layer of sunflower oil. It can be stored in the fridge for about 2 weeks or frozen for three to four months.

thai green curry paste

makes **500 ml/18 fl oz**

ingredients

$\frac{1}{2}$ teaspoon cumin seeds
1 teaspoon coriander seeds
8 green chillies, trimmed and deseeded
2 sticks of lemongrass
8 small shallots, sliced
4 garlic cloves, peeled and roughly chopped

2 cm/$\frac{3}{4}$ in galangal or ginger root, thinly sliced
6 kaffir lime leaves
1 teaspoon shrimp paste or 1 tablespoon Thai fish sauce (see p40)
75 g/2$\frac{3}{4}$ oz fresh coriander
zest of 2 limes
juice of 1 lime

method

1 Place the cumin and coriander seeds into a small dry pan and heat gently to release the oils and aroma of the spices. Take care not to overheat the pan and burn the spices. As soon as the spices start to give off an aroma, tip them into a mortar and grind with a pestle to a powder.
2 If you have long lemongrass stems, break off the bottom 10 cm/4 in of each stem and discard. If the stem is difficult to break, work a little further down the stem towards the bulbous end until the stem breaks easily. Chop the bulbous end roughly then add to the food processor with the ground spices, and all the remaining ingredients.
3 Blitz in short bursts, pushing the mixture down towards the blades from time to time with a spatula. You may need to add a little water to thin and get it moving initially, but don't add too much!
4 Blitz until you have a reasonably smooth paste. Spoon into a clean Kilner or screw-top jar, and cover with a layer of sunflower oil. This can be stored in the fridge for about 1 week. Or it can be frozen for up to 3 months.

basic recipes

Alan says For both of these pastes, each time you use some, flatten the surface with a spoon and then splash on more olive oil before returning it to the fridge. This keeps it sealed and stops it darkening and losing its flavour.

chilli oil

makes **about 1 litre/1¾ pint**

ingredients
225 g/8 oz red chillies
1 litre/1¾ pint sunflower oil

basic recipes

method
1 Slice the chillies in half lengthwise and place in a saucepan. Pour on the oil, and place on a medium heat. When hot, you should start to see a little steam rising from the surface of the oil (the steam is from the chillies, not the oil!)
2 Turn down the heat, and simmer gently for 5 minutes, remove from the heat and allow to cool (this takes approximately 2 hours).
3 Once cooled, transfer the chillies and oil to a sealed plastic container with a lid and store in a cool place for 2–3 weeks.
4 Then pour the oil through a sieve to remove the chillies. I usually keep chilli oil in an old olive oil bottle, but remember to label it well. A skull and crossbones will suffice! It will keep for 3 months.

Nick says Warning – this is seriously spicy stuff! Don't try frying with it, and take care not to get it in your eyes, or other sensitive parts of the body!

herb oil

makes **about 300 ml/10 fl oz**

ingredients
80 g/3 oz mixed fresh chives,
  parsley and tarragon
300 ml/10 fl oz extra virgin
  olive oil

method 1
1 Drop the herbs into a pan of heavily-salted boiling water for 10 seconds. This fixes the chlorophyll and keeps them green, giving the oil a lovely rich colour.
2 Drain and refresh under cold running water to stop the cooking process.
3 Wring them dry in a clean tea towel or kitchen paper and then chop roughly.
4 Put the herbs into a blender with the oil and blitz for 3 minutes until the oil is shiny and green. If the herbs are reluctant to give up their colour, tip the oil into a small saucepan and heat over a low heat: this should bring the colour out.
5 Cool immediately and store in a squeezy bottle in the fridge for up to 48 hours.

method 2
1 Best if your herbs are really fresh. Use a chef's knife to roughly chop the herbs (see page 65) then place into a blender with the oil and blitz together.
2 Pour into a small pan and heat very gently until the colour changes to vibrant green.
3 Pass through a fine sieve, cool and store in the fridge for up to 48 hours.

Nick says Chive oil retains its grassy colours better than any other herb, whilst the aroma of basil oil is unmistakable and guaranteed to lift your spirits!

shellfish oil

makes **about 350 g/12 oz**

ingredients

175 g/6 oz lobster shells,
  from the bodies and legs
350 ml/12 fl oz sunflower oil
1 star anise
3 black or white peppercorns
5 cm/2 in piece carrot,
  peeled and diced
2 shallots, peeled and diced

5 cm/2 in piece celery, diced
2 garlic cloves, peeled and
  sliced
15 g/½ oz mixed fresh herbs
  such as, parsley, thyme and
  tarragon
1 teaspoon tomato purée
50 ml/2 fl oz dry white wine

method

1 Crush the shells and drain away any liquid.
2 Heat 4 tablespoons of the oil in a large
   saucepan, add the shells, star anise and white
   peppercorns and fry over a medium heat for
   about 15 minutes, stirring every now and then.
3 Add all the remaining ingredients, except the oil,
   and cook until the wine has evaporated.
4 Add the rest of the oil, turn down the heat, and
   leave to simmer for 45 minutes.
5 Remove from the heat and leave to stand for
   24 hours.
6 Strain through a muslin-lined sieve, transfer to
   a bottle and seal. This will keep in the fridge for
   about 1 month.

gastric (gastrique)

makes **about 100 ml/3½ fl oz**

ingredients

50 g/1¾ oz granulated sugar
50 ml/2 fl oz good quality
  white wine vinegar

method

1 Place the sugar then the vinegar into a small
   saucepan and heat gently without boiling until
   the sugar dissolves.
2 Bring to a rolling boil then simmer for about
   10–15 minutes until syrupy, but not too thick
   as it will thicken up as it cools.
3 Pour into a squeezy bottle or jar and store in
   the fridge for up to 1 month.

245

basic recipes

Nick says You can use langoustine shells instead of lobster
shells in this recipe.

Alan says A useful thick sauce that benefits from the
addition of herbs or spices for extra flavour. Add it to
tomato soup recipes to balance the acidity of tomatoes.

vinaigrette

makes **about 500 ml/18 fl oz**

ingredients
1 teaspoon smooth Dijon
    mustard
100 ml/3½ fl oz white wine
    vinegar
400 ml/14 fl oz olive oil
Maldon salt and freshly
    ground black pepper

basic recipes

method
1 Place all the ingredients in a blender and blitz for
    30 seconds (or place in a sealable container and
    shake well).
2 Strain through a fine sieve into a jug, then pour
    the vinaigrette into a sealable container of your
    choosing (stoppered bottle, squeezy bottle,
    screw top jar) and store in the fridge.
3 The basic mix of mustard, vinegar and olive oil
    (with no herbs or garlic added) will keep for 3 to
    4 weeks, though it may separate. Give it a good
    shake to re-mix.

John says For variation, try adding a crushed clove of garlic
or chopped fresh herbs.

clarified butter

makes **about 200 ml/7 fl oz**

ingredients
250 g/9 oz unsalted butter,
    cubed

method
1 In a small saucepan, melt the butter over a low
    heat, being careful not to let it boil and burn.
2 Allow it to stand for a few minutes until all the oil
    rises to the top, and the milky solids sink to the
    bottom.
3 Skim or pour off the oil into a sealable plastic
    container and refrigerate for up to 2 months.

method 2
1 If you have a microwave, you can put the diced
    butter in a plastic jug, cover with a piece of
    kitchen paper to catch any splashes and
    microwave on 100% for about 2 minutes.
2 If it is not completely melted, heat again for a
    further 30 seconds, but do not allow it to boil.
3 Continue as above, discarding the buttermilk at
    the bottom.

Nick says I pour the melted butter into a tall jug and chill in
the fridge until set – you can then just lift off the crust of
clarified butter.
John says For the brave amongst you, it is possible to boil
and simmer the butter down until only the fat remains. But
be very careful if attempting this, as the butter is rather
likely to burn and may even catch fire.

duck fat

makes **about 300 ml/10 fl oz**

ingredients
3 whole ducks (see p28)
1 sprig of thyme
1 bay leaf
a few peppercorns
1 garlic bulb, halved across
   its equator

method
1 Remove the duck breasts and legs (keep them
   for cooking or freeze for later). Strip off the skin
   from the duck carcasses. Keep the carcasses
   for stock, or freeze.
2 Place all the duck skin in a medium-sized
   saucepan and add the thyme, bay leaf,
   peppercorns and garlic. Pour over just enough
   cold water to cover, put the pan on to the stove
   and bring to the boil.
3 Reduce the heat to very low and leave for
   2–3 hours, until all the water has boiled away and
   the fat has melted.
4 Strain the fat off through a fine sieve into a
   container and store in the fridge until needed.
   This will keep for 6 weeks.

Nick says The amount of fat rendered will depend on the
fattiness of the ducks. I once recovered 100g/3½ oz fat from
2 large duck breasts that had been trimmed right back.

pickled vegetables

makes **about 1.25 kg/2 lb 12 oz**

ingredients
3 large carrots
1 cauliflower
3 large onions, peeled and
   roughly diced
25 g/1 oz Maldon salt
900 ml/1½ pint white wine
   vinegar
350 g/12 oz caster sugar
1 teaspoon dried chilli flakes
Maldon salt and freshly
   ground black pepper

method
1 Peel the carrots and slice about 1.25 mm thick
   on the crinkle cutter blade of a mandoline. Cut
   the cauliflower into small florets.
2 Place all the veg in a large bowl, sprinkle with the
   salt and leave to stand for 24 hours to draw out
   the moisture. Rinse well in cold water and pat
   dry on kitchen paper.
3 Put the vinegar, sugar and chilli together in a
   large saucepan. Slowly bring to the boil over
   a low heat, stirring occasionally until the sugar
   is dissolved.
4 Dump in all the veg and bring back to the boil.
   When it comes to a rolling boil, stir once then
   turn off the heat and leave to cool completely
   without touching it.
5 The veggies are now ready to be ladled into clean
   Kilner jars, making sure that the vinegar syrup
   covers them completely. Refrigerate and leave
   for at least 1 week before eating. These will keep
   for up to 1 month.

basic recipes

rouille

makes **about 350 ml/12 fl oz**

ingredients

2 roasted red peppers (see left)

1 teaspoon tomato purée

3 garlic cloves, peeled and chopped

2 medium red chillies, deseeded and chopped

1-2 teaspoons ground coriander

1 thick slice stale white bread

1 large pinch saffron threads, soaked for 2 minutes in 2 tablespoons hot water

250 ml/9 fl oz homemade mayonnaise (see p239)

Maldon salt and freshly ground black pepper

method

1 Put the roasted red peppers, tomato purée, garlic, chillies and coriander into the food processor with plenty of salt and freshly ground black pepper. Blend until as smooth as possible. Tear the bread into bits and add to the processor (this will stabilise the sauce and stop it from splitting), sprinkling with the saffron and water. Blitz again until smooth. Beat this into the mayonnaise, taste and check the seasoning. This will store in the fridge for up to 1 week.

roast marinated peppers

makes **4 peppers**

ingredients

4 red peppers

extra virgin olive oil

2 garlic cloves, peeled and sliced

1 sprig fresh thyme

Maldon salt and freshly ground black pepper

method

1 Place the whole peppers on a roasting tray and sprinkle with a little olive oil and salt. Roast at 200°C/400°F/gas mark 6 for about 25 minutes or until soft and beginning to blacken on the outside. Remove from the oven, transfer to a container and cover tightly with clingfilm for 20 minutes. This will help loosen the skins.

2 When cool, uncover, then slip off the skins and pull off the green stems. Split the peppers open and remove the seeds. Slice into strips or cut into dice and toss with more olive oil and salt and the garlic, thyme, and freshly ground black pepper. Spoon into a Kilner jar and top up with more olive oil to cover. They will keep like this for up to 2 weeks.

Nick says If you just need one pepper, stick a fork in it and hold over a gas flame (or use a blow torch) until well-charred all over. Rub off the skin. The pepper will be firmer than oven-roasted.

John says Alternatively, you can grill them whole under a very hot grill for about 20 minutes, but remember to turn them every now and then.

Alan says The best roasted peppers are done on the barbie – they have that great smoky taste.

red onion marmalade

makes **about 500g/1 lb 2 oz**

ingredients

85 ml/3 fl oz olive oil
1.5 kg/3 lb 5 oz red onions, peeled and finely sliced
120 ml/4 fl oz best-quality sherry vinegar or, even better, Cabernet Sauvignon vinegar

75 g/2¾ oz redcurrant jelly
Maldon salt and freshly ground black pepper

basic recipes

method

1 Heat the oil in a large saucepan over a medium heat. Add the sliced onions, stir well to coat with the oil and then season with salt and pepper. Cook slowly, uncovered, stirring from time to time until the onions are very soft and the sugary juices have caramelised. This should take about 45 minutes and the onions should look thick, dark and sticky.

2 Add the vinegar and jelly and cook for another 10 minutes or so, until all the harsh vinegar has been boiled off and the marmalade has a glossy texture.

3 Leave to cool and then store in a clean Kilner or screw-top jar in the fridge. If you pour in a couple of tablespoons of olive oil to seal the top, it should keep for 6–8 weeks.

home-dried or mi cuit tomatoes

makes **24 tomatoes**

ingredients

12 large, really ripe plum tomatoes
50 ml/2 fl oz olive oil plus extra for preserving (approx. 200 ml/7 fl oz for a 600 ml/1 pint Kilner jar)

1 sprig of basil or thyme
1 garlic clove, peeled and crushed
Maldon salt and freshly ground black pepper

method

1 Preheat the oven to 110°C/225°F/gas mark ¼ – the lowest heat possible – you are trying to recreate the conditions of a sun-drenched Tuscan hillside!

2 Slice the tomatoes in half, through the growing eye at the top. Then remove the green eye. Lay the tomatoes on a baking sheet, cut-side up, and sprinkle lightly with crushed Maldon salt and freshly ground black pepper. Drizzle with olive oil.

3 Place the tomatoes in the oven (you may have to prop the oven door slightly open to keep the temperature down). Leave for 8 hours.

4 When you return, the tomatoes should be reduced to half their original size but not browned. Turn them over and leave for a further 4 hours or until they are nice and firm.

5 Remove from the oven and leave until cool. Then place them in a Kilner jar, add the sprig of fresh basil or thyme and the crushed garlic clove, then cover with olive oil.

6 These ultra-tasty beauties can now be stored in your fridge for up to 3 weeks.

Nick says Ripeness is everything for this dish, so find really good ripe plum tomatoes. The sweet, intense flavour means a little goes a long way.

café de paris butter

makes **about 250 g/9 oz**

ingredients
250 g/9 oz unsalted butter,
   softened
2 shallots
1 garlic clove, peeled
2 anchovy fillets, rinsed
2 teaspoons Dijon mustard
finely grated zest and juice
   of 1 lemon

a few drops of
   Worcestershire sauce
4 tablespoons fresh flat-
   leaf parsley, chopped
Maldon salt and freshly
   ground black pepper

method
1 Remove the butter from the fridge at least 30 minutes before using. Beat until very soft, pale and creamy.
2 Put the shallots, garlic, anchovy fillets, mustard, lemon zest and juice and Worcestershire sauce into a food processor and blitz, scraping down the sides occasionally, until well chopped. Scrape out of the bowl with a spatula and add to the butter with the parsley. Beat well to mix, then taste and season with salt and pepper and more Worcestershire sauce if you like.
3 Roll the butter into two logs between sheets of wet greaseproof paper, then wrap in clingfilm and place in the freezer. This can be frozen for up to 3 months.

Nick says For succulent, flavoursome fish, dot with Café de Paris butter and steam in a double-thickness parcel of tin foil (en papillot).

court bouillon

makes **about 1.2 litres/2 pints**

ingredients
1.2 litres/2 pints water
½ lemon, sliced
1 small onion, peeled and
   sliced (optional)
1 carrot, peeled and sliced
1 celery stick, sliced
1 fresh bay leaf
15 peppercorns

a handful of bruised parsley
   stalks (you can add other
   herb stalks, but too much
   can be overpowering)

method
1 Put all the ingredients for the court bouillon into a large saucepan and bring slowly to the boil over a low–medium heat.
2 Turn off the heat and allow it to cool.
3 Once cold, strain and use as needed. It will keep for up to 3 days in the fridge, or freeze for up to 3 months.

Nick says Water is obviously easier to use for poaching, but court bouillon adds a noticeably subtle flavour to whatever is cooked in it.

romesco sauce

perfect basmati rice

makes **about 500-600 ml/18 fl oz-1 pint**

ingredients

2 sun-dried peppers
1 red pepper
1 garlic clove, peeled and
  chopped
1 teaspoon sweet paprika
½ teaspoon chilli flakes
100 ml/3½ fl oz red wine
  vinegar

80 g/3 oz toasted flaked
  almonds
200-250 ml/7-9 fl oz extra
  virgin olive oil
1-2 tablespoons chopped
  fresh parsley or coriander
  (optional)
Maldon salt and freshly
  ground black pepper

method

1 Soak the sun-dried peppers in hot water for
  30 minutes then drain.
2 Roast the red pepper over an open gas flame
  until well-charred and wrap in clingfilm to cool.
  When cold, remove the skin, stalk and seeds.
3 Put both types of pepper, the garlic clove, sweet
  paprika, chilli flakes, red wine vinegar and
  toasted flaked almonds into the food processor.
  Season well with salt and pepper.
4 Blitz to a thick paste, scraping down the sides
  of the bowl with a spatula, then dribble in the
  oil with the motor running as if you were making
  mayonnaise, adding enough oil to make a thick
  but pourable consistency. If it is too thick add
  a little hot water.
5 Stir in the parsley or coriander. This will keep in
  the fridge for up to 4 days, or freeze for up to
  3 months.

serves **4**

ingredients

280 g/10 oz basmati rice
½ teaspoon salt (optional)

method

1 Select a pan large enough to give the rice grains
  space to move about, and make sure it has a
  tight-fitting lid. Fill with cold salted water and
  bring to the boil.
2 Wash the rice under cold running water until the
  water runs clear. This will show that you've got
  rid of most of the loose starch clinging to the
  grains, making them less likely to stick together.
3 When the water is boiling, toss in the rice, bring
  back to a rolling boil and stir once.
4 Turn down the heat and simmer for exactly
  8 minutes – check the rice, it should still have
  a slight crunch.
5 Drain well in a sieve then return the rice to the
  pan, cover with the lid and leave to steam in its
  own heat for 10 minutes in a warm (not hot) place.
6 Lift off the lid, use a fork to fluff up the grains
  and voila, perfect basmati! Rice is best served
  straight away, but if you must prepare it in
  advance, cool quickly by spreading the rice grains
  out onto a cold baking sheet, then place in an
  air-tight container, refrigerate and keep for up
  to 2 days.

Nick says The sauce may separate slightly when defrosted.
Blitz briefly in a blender to re-emulsify.

Nick says For variation, add chopped coriander, lime juice and
zest to the cooked rice, and leave out the salt.

mashed potatoes

serves **8**

ingredients

1.25 kg/2 lb 12 oz floury
potatoes (King Edwards,
Desiree, Red Rooster or
Maris Piper)
50–60 g/1¾–2¼ oz unsalted
butter, cubed
150 ml/5 fl oz double cream

Maldon salt and freshly
ground black pepper

method

1 Peel the potatoes and, if very large, cut into
even–sized pieces. Don't make the pieces too
small or they may absorb too much water and
start to break up.

2 Place in a pan of cold salted water, and bring to
a very gentle simmer, so that the water is barely
trembling. Cook gently until you can push in a
knife point without resistance, about 20 minutes,
but don't allow them to start disintegrating.

3 Once cooked, drain well, return to the pan and
place the pan back on a low heat for a minute to
dry them out. When they're dry, you'll see white
spots of starch appearing on the surface.

4 Pass the potatoes though a Mouli or potato ricer
into a clean bowl. This base can now be cooled
quickly and stored in the fridge for up to 3 days.

5 To serve immediately, return the potato to the
pan, add the cream and butter, season to taste
with salt and pepper and heat gently, stirring
well, until ready to serve.

6 To reheat the mash, place into a pan set over a
low heat and slowly stir in the butter and cream.
It will look lumpy to start with, but will eventually
come together and be smooth and silky. Season
to taste with salt and pepper.

7 The amount of butter and cream you add will
depend very much on the type of potato used
but these quantities are a rough guide.

Nick says Don't pack the potato into a container or it will
turn into a brick! Instead, mound it in loosely, and cover.

dauphinoise potatoes

serves **6–8**

ingredients

10 g/¼ oz unsalted butter
2 garlic cloves, peeled and
crushed
100 ml/3½ fl oz full cream
milk
300 ml/10 fl oz double cream

600 g/1 lb 5 oz floury
potatoes (Red Rooster
or Maris Piper)
Maldon salt and freshly
ground black pepper

method

1 Preheat the oven to 150°C/300°F/gas mark 2.

2 Use the butter to grease a large ovenproof dish
really well.

3 Put the milk, cream and crushed garlic in a large
saucepan and slowly bring to the boil over a
low–medium heat. Season to taste with salt and
pepper.

4 Peel and thinly slice the potatoes on a mandoline
(or in a food processor if your machine will
take a whole potato) – you really can't get them
thin enough slicing by hand. Do not rinse the
potato slices.

5 Add the potatoes to the pan a few at a time,
giving the pan a good shoogle (shake) and stir
to coat them evenly with the cream and milk,
as the slices often stick together.

6 Press the potatoes down on top making sure
they are *just* submerged. Bring back to the boil
and simmer on a low heat for about 15 minutes
until the potatoes are almost tender and the
potato starch has thickened the milk.

7 Turn the potatoes into the buttered dish, leaving
behind any that have burnt and are caught at
the bottom of the pan.

8 Bake in the oven for about 1 hour until nicely
browned on top. Serve immediately or leave to
cool overnight.

9 To reheat, cut the Dauphinoise into squares or
use a 6 cm/2½ in scone cutter to make rounds.
Lift them out of the cutter, place on a buttered
tray and pop into the oven at 140°C/275°F/gas
mark 1 for 45 minutes.

basic recipes

roasted potatoes

serves **4**

ingredients
8 medium-sized floury
   potatoes (Kerr's Pink or
   Duke of York)
6 tablespoons duck or goose
   fat (see p247) or clarified
   butter (see p246)

method
1 Heat the oven to 200°C/400°F/gas mark 6.
2 Peel and cut the potatoes in half, or if large cut
   into thirds – one cut across the end then cut the
   remaining portion in two – make sure all the
   pieces are about the same size so that they
   cook evenly.
3 Boil vigorously in salted water for 5–7 minutes
   then drain in a large wire sieve. You can use
   a colander for this, but a wire sieve is better.
   Give the potatoes a really good shake to remove
   as much of the water as possible and ruffle up
   the outsides. If you like, you can use a fork to
   create an extra-rough surface.
4 Put the duck or goose fat, or clarified butter
   in a roasting tin and place in the oven to heat.
   When hot, carefully add the potatoes and toss
   around until well coated.
5 Place in the oven and roast for about 15 minutes.
   Turn the potatoes over and continue roasting
   until crispy all over (about another 15–25 minutes).
6 When cooked, they can be left in a warm oven for
   15 minutes with the door ajar to let any steam
   escape. Serve immediately.

fondant potatoes

serves **4**

ingredients
20-24 even-sized new
   potatoes (Jersey Royals,
   Charlottes or Rattes)
175 g/6 oz unsalted butter
Maldon salt and freshly
   ground black pepper

method
1 Preheat the oven to 190°C/375°F/gas mark 5.
2 Use an ovenproof frying pan, preferably non-stick,
   which will hold all the potatoes in a single layer.
3 Slice the tops and bottoms off the potatoes,
   which should give you unpeeled cylinders around
   2.5 cm/1 in high. Cut the butter into cubes about
   5 mm/¼ in wide and line the base of the frying
   pan with them. Set the potatoes cut-side down
   on top of the butter to fill the pan. Season well.
4 Pour in enough cold water to come to the tops
   of the potatoes. Put the frying pan over a
   low–medium heat and keep an eye on it as the
   butter melts. It should just bubble gently but
   don't allow it to get too hot or you'll burn the
   bottoms of the potatoes and the water will
   evaporate without cooking them.
5 After about 20–35 minutes, they should be nicely
   browned underneath and all the water should
   have evaporated. If the potatoes are still a bit
   undercooked on top, turn them brown-side up and
   put the pan into the oven for 10–15 minutes more
   to finish cooking.
6 Remove from the oven and leave to stand in a
   warm place until you're ready to serve. They need
   about 5–10 minutes for the butter to be
   absorbed. To serve, lift out of the pan, turn them
   over and place on a plate with the richly coloured
   side up.
7 These will keep warm in a hot oven for up to
   1 hour, or can be cooled and kept at room
   temperature for up to 2 hours, then reheated
   in a hot oven.

basic recipes

stovies

serves **4**

ingredients

50 g/1¾ oz beef dripping,
  duck fat (see p247), or
  rendered bacon fat, or
  vegetable oil
2 large onions, peeled and
  thickly sliced
900 g/2 lb all-rounder
  potatoes (King Edward)
  cooked, cooled and cut into

5 cm/2 in pieces
225 ml/8 fl oz chicken or beef
  stock, or the gravy or meat
  jelly left over from a roast,
  diluted with a little water
2 tablespoons chopped fresh
  parsley
Maldon salt and freshly
  ground black pepper

method

1 Melt the dripping in a good heavy frying pan set
  over a medium heat, and add the onions. Stir
  them around a bit to coat with the dripping and
  cook for about 10 minutes until beginning to go
  soft and starting to colour around the edges.

2 Add the potatoes and give the whole lot a good
  stir. Season with salt and pepper and pour in
  the stock.

3 Bring to the boil, turn down the heat and simmer,
  half-covered, for 15–20 minutes. Give the potatoes
  a good stir once or twice during cooking, to help
  them break up a bit.

4 When cooked, the stovies should look lumpy with
  a thickened sauce of gravy and potatoes. Taste
  and adjust the seasoning, stir in the parsley and
  take the steaming pan to the table to serve.

crushed potatoes with olive oil, parmesan and basil

serves **4**

ingredients

450 g/1 lb new potatoes
  (Jersey Royals, Charlottes
  or Rattes)
75 ml/2½ fl oz extra virgin
  olive oil
25 g/1 oz freshly grated
  Parmesan cheese

3 tablespoons fresh basil
  leaves, roughly chopped
Maldon salt and freshly
  ground black pepper

method

1 Preheat the oven to 200°C/400°F/gas mark 6.

2 Place the potatoes into a large pan of salted,
  boiling water, turn down the heat and simmer
  until tender.

3 Drain and place in a large mixing bowl. Add the oil
  and using the back of a fork, gently crush each
  potato until it just splits.

4 Season with salt and pepper, then add the
  Parmesan and basil. Mix carefully until all the oil
  has been absorbed. Don't overwork it or you'll
  lose the texture.

5 Serve in nice big mounds, or use a mousse ring
  or 7.5 cm/3 in scone cutter to shape them into
  little cakes.

6 The mixture can also be made in advance, cooled
  and kept in the fridge overnight. When ready to
  serve, shape into potato cakes using a mousse
  ring, put them on an oiled baking sheet and bake
  in a moderate oven for 20 minutes, until golden
  brown on top.

chips

258

basic recipes

serves **4**

ingredients
900 g/2 lb floury potatoes
  (for dry, fluffy chips use
  Golden Wonder, Red Duke
  of York or Kerr's Pinks. For
  soft, moist chips, use King
  Edward or Maris Piper)
oil, for frying
Maldon salt

method
1 Heat the oil in an electric deep-fat fryer to
  160°C/325°F and heat your oven to its lowest
  setting.
2 While the oil is heating, cut the potatoes into
  chips roughly 5 x 1 cm/2 in x ½ in and place into
  a bowl of cold water until ready for cooking, but
  don't leave them any longer than 10 minutes.
3 Now get all your frying equipment together and
  line a colander with several layers of kitchen
  paper for draining the chips once fried.
4 Drain the potatoes in another colander and rinse
  them. Tip onto a clean tea towel and carefully pat
  them dry. Dry the colander, then return the chips.
  Tip half the chips into the basket of the deep
  fat fryer – too many will stick together. Fry for
  7–8 minutes until soft and on no account
  coloured. Lift out of the oil and drain on kitchen
  paper. Allow the oil to come back to temperature,
  fry the remaining chips, drain and set aside.
5 When almost ready to serve, reheat the oil to
  180°C/350°F (190°C/375°F for really puffy,
  souffléd chips). Fry the chips in 2 batches for
  2 minutes, or until light golden brown and crisp.
6 Drain the chips on kitchen paper and sprinkle
  with a little salt.
7 Do not cover the chips or they will lose their
  crispness – if keeping warm, spread them on a
  baking tray lined with kitchen paper and place in
  the pre-warmed oven, leaving the door slightly
  open (stick a wooden spoon in the door to keep
  it open!) to let any steam escape and keep them
  crisp. Serve as soon as possible, they won't keep!

potato rösti

serves **4**

ingredients
2 large floury potatoes,
  peeled (Golden Wonder or
  Kerr's Pinks)
4 tablespoons clarified
  butter (see p246) or duck
  fat (see p247)
4 tablespoons sunflower oil

Maldon salt and freshly
  ground black pepper

method
1 You will need 4 blini pans for this or one large
  frying pan.
2 Grate the potatoes coarsely into the centre of
  a clean tea towel. Fold the towel over the potato
  to form a ball and squeeze tightly to remove as
  much water as possible.
3 In a saucepan, melt the butter or duck fat and
  mix it with the oil. Heat four blini pans (or a large
  frying pan) over a medium heat and pour a little
  of the butter/fat and oil into each pan.
4 Open the cloth and season the potato with
  pepper only. Divide the potato mixture between
  the blini pans, or form into one large cake if
  using a single large pan.
5 Fry the röstis until golden brown, making sure
  that the fat bubbles up through the centre to
  cook the inside. Do not use too high a heat or
  the outside will burn before the centre cooks.
  Too little fat in the pan will result in a pale rösti,
  so if the pan appears dry add a little more oil
  around the outside.
6 When the first side is golden brown turn the
  rösti over, adding more oil as required. Cook until
  golden brown.
7 Season with salt, then lift the cakes out of the
  pans and drain on kitchen towel.
8 Serve immediately, cutting the large rösti into
  quarters if not using blini pans. If not serving
  straight away, transfer the cooked röstis to a
  baking tray and keep for up to 6 hours at room
  temperature. Reheat in a hot oven for about
  5 minutes.

potato, herb and olive oil stacks

serves **4**

ingredients
4 large all-rounder potatoes, (Maris Piper)
75 ml/2½ fl oz olive oil
2 tablespoons fresh rosemary, roughly chopped
1 tablespoon fresh thyme, roughly chopped
Maldon salt and freshly ground black pepper

method
1 Preheat the oven to 180°C/350°F/gas mark 4.
2 First thinly slice the potatoes, either by hand or on a mandoline (or in a food processor if your machine will take a whole potato).
3 Put the potatoes into a large bowl and add the olive oil and herbs. Toss well with your hands making sure the potatoes are evenly coated. Season with a little salt and pepper and toss again to mix.
4 Brush a heavy baking sheet with a little olive oil and start to build 8 stacks with the potato slices. Try to make them look random, and incorporate as many of the herbs as you can. Sprinkle any remaining herbs and olive oil left in the bowl around and over the potato stacks.
5 Bake in the oven for 35–45 minutes or until golden brown at the edges and tender all the way through. A good way to test is by inserting a thin skewer through the middle of a stack – it should slip through easily.
6 Serve immediately, or turn the oven to low and keep warm for up to 30 minutes. They can be cooled and left at room temperature for up to 1 hour. Reheat in a moderate oven.

wilted greens

serves **4**

ingredients
600 g/1 lb 5 oz mixed greens, such as spinach, bok choi, courgettes, Savoy cabbage and/or spring greens
2 tablespoons olive oil
3 tablespoons water
Maldon salt and freshly ground black pepper

method
1 Wash and then dry the greens in a salad spinner or on a clean tea towel. If using courgettes, slice thinly on a mandoline or cut into long shreds using a potato peeler. If using bok choi, split and remove the hard core. Roughly shred any leafy greens. It's important to cut everything to a similar size so that all the vegetables cook in the same time.
2 Heat a medium frying pan or wok until hot. Add the oil, swirl around the pan then toss in the greens.
3 Stir well and add the water. Stir-fry until the greens have wilted and all the water has evaporated. Remove from the heat, season with salt and pepper and serve immediately.

Nick says For an Asian-style flavour, add chopped garlic and chilli to the vegetables as well as a dash of soy sauce.

cabbage and carrots

serves **4**

ingredients
2 large carrots, peeled
1 small Savoy cabbage
25 g/1 oz unsalted butter
2-3 tablespoons water
Maldon salt and freshly
  ground black pepper

method

1 Cut the carrots into julienne strips using a
  potato peeler or a mandoline.
2 Halve the cabbage, cut out and discard the hard
  core and slice the remaining cabbage into
  1 cm/½ in-wide strips.
3 Melt the butter in a large pan set over a
  low–medium heat and add the carrots. Cover
  and allow to sweat down for 5 minutes.
4 Add the cabbage and the water, stir well then
  cover and leave to steam for 5 minutes. Season
  with salt and pepper and serve immediately, or
  keep warm for up to 15 minutes.
5 Alternatively, make this up in advance and cool
  quickly by spreading the carrot and cabbage out
  on a chilled baking sheet. Store in the fridge for
  up to 3 hours and reheat in a covered bowl in the
  microwave set on low, for about 2 minutes.

wilted spinach with garlic and lemon

serves **4**

ingredients
900 g/2 lb fresh spinach
1 tablespoon olive oil
25 g/1 oz butter
1 garlic clove, peeled and
  thinly sliced
freshly grated lemon zest,
  to taste
Maldon salt and freshly
  ground black pepper

method

1 Pick over the spinach and wash really well to
  remove all grit and sand. Spin it dry; there will
  still be a bit of water on it to help it steam while
  it cooks.
2 Take a wok or large frying pan, add the oil and
  place over a high heat.
3 Once the oil is hot, chuck in the butter, let it melt
  then add the garlic and fry for a few seconds.
4 Toss in the spinach and stir to coat in the butter
  and oil.
5 As it begins to wilt, add the lemon zest and
  seasoning and keep tossing and stirring so that
  the spinach cooks evenly. Serve immediately.

Nick says Adding lemon juice to this will turn it into khaki
slime, which is why we use zest here, which gives it the
perfume of lemons without the acid.

roasted root vegetables

serves 6-8

ingredients

2 tablespoons sunflower oil
40 g/1½ oz butter
¼ turnip (swede to
  non-Scots!), peeled
¼ celeriac, peeled
2 large carrots, peeled
1 large parsnip, peeled and
  cored

12 new potatoes
4 celery sticks, trimmed and
  cut into 5 cm pieces
2 garlic cloves, peeled and
  sliced
2 sprigs fresh thyme

method

1 Preheat the oven to 230°C/450°F/gas mark 8.
2 Cut any large potatoes in half.
3 Chop all the remaining root vegetables making
  sure you get all the pieces roughly the same size.
  Chop the celery.
4 Heat the oil and butter in a shallow cast-iron
  ovenproof dish or heavy roasting dish.
5 Add the turnip, celeriac, carrots, parsnips,
  potatoes and celery to the pan and fry for
  5–6 minutes over a high heat, until just beginning
  to colour.
6 Add the garlic and thyme, mix well then slam into
  the hot oven and cook for about 25 minutes,
  stirring only once at half-time.
7 This is best served immediately, or can be cooled
  and reheated in a hot oven up to 2 hours later.

cook school pizza dough

makes **two 10 inch pizza bases**

ingredients

25 g/1 oz fresh yeast
pinch of sugar
250 ml/9 fl oz warm
  (20°C/70°F) water
500 g/1 lb 2 oz Italian 00 or
  plain flour
2 tablespoons olive oil

1 teaspoon Maldon salt
fine semolina flour for
  rolling/dusting

method

1 Cream the yeast and the sugar together and
  slowly add the warm water, leave aside to
  activate – it should become frothy.
2 Sift the flour and salt into a large bowl and add
  the oil, then slowly add the yeast mixture to form
  a soft and pliable, but on no accounts sticky,
  dough.
3 Turn onto a lightly floured work-surface and
  knead for about 10 minutes or until smooth and
  elastic. Return to a lightly oiled bowl, cover with
  clingfilm and leave in a warm place until it
  doubles in volume. Meanwhile, preheat the oven
  to 220°C/425°F/gas mark 7.
4 When the dough is doubled in size, remove and
  knead back to the original size. Divide the
  mixture in two and shape into two smooth balls.
5 Dust a work surface with semolina flour then roll
  out the dough into thin pizza bases.
6 Top with your chosen topping, place onto a
  baking sheet and bake in the oven for about
  8–10 minutes.
7 Serve immediately. The raw dough will keep in
  the fridge for up to 12 hours, or frozen for up
  to 3 months.

basic recipes

cook school mighty white

makes **30 rolls or 4 loaves**

ingredients

500 g/1 lb 2 oz strong white
    flour
500 g/1 lb 2 oz wholemeal
    flour
20 g/¾ oz caster sugar
18 g/¾ oz Maldon salt
20 g/¾ oz dried milk powder
40 g/1½ oz fresh yeast

3 tablespoons extra virgin
    olive oil
a handful of sunflower seeds
    (optional)
a handful of pumpkin seeds
    (optional)
about 500 ml/18 fl oz warm
    (35°C) water

method

1 Put both flours, the sugar and salt into a table-top food mixer fitted with a dough hook, and start mixing. Add the milk powder, crumbled fresh yeast and olive oil and mix until combined. Now add the sunflower and pumpkin seeds to the mix, if using.

2 Slowly add the warm water and mix to form a soft and pliable dough. If the dough looks too dry, add a splash more water. If it looks sticky, add a little more flour.

3 Then continue mixing for a further 4 minutes. Remove from the mixer and knead by hand into a smooth round ball.

4 Lightly wipe out a large bowl with a little more olive oil, place the dough in the bottom and cover with clingfilm. Leave in a warm (not hot) place until the dough has trebled in volume.

5 Punch down the risen dough with your fist to knock out most of the air. Turn the dough out onto a lightly floured board and knead thoroughly until back to its original size. This process is called 'knocking back'.

6 If making rolls, cut the dough into 5 equal pieces, and knead each piece into a smooth ball. Roll each ball into a sausage, then cut the sausages into about 6 equal pieces (30 in total, roughly 40 g/1½ oz each) to form the rolls.

7 Place the rolls onto a lightly-floured baking tray, quite tightly together, so that when the rolls rise again (the proving stage), they are touching each other. Cover with a tea towel or make a tent out of a bin bag (place the tray in a bin bag and tuck the open end under the tray trapping as much air inside as possible) and leave in a warm place to prove until doubled in size. Meanwhile, preheat the oven to 200°C/400°F/gas mark 6.

8 When risen, bake the rolls for about 15 minutes. Remove from the oven and leave to cool slightly then serve.

9 For loaves, cut the dough into 4 equal-sized pieces after knocking back. Form into four loaves and leave to prove, as above. When doubled in size, cut deep scores over the top to allow the bread to expand during baking. Dust lightly with flour and bake at around 200°C/400°F/gas mark 6 until golden brown and crispy, about 30–35 minutes. To check if they're done, tap the bottom of the bread; it should sound hollow. Leave to cool.

10 These will keep in a bread bin for 2 days, or can be frozen for 2–4 months.

pasta dough

ingredients
200 g/7 oz plain flour, plus
  extra as needed
2 whole eggs
fine semolina flour for
  rolling/dusting

basic recipes

method

1 Follow the step by step technique for making pasta on page 86.
2 Tip out the dough onto a clean work surface and form into a ball shape.
4 Knead briskly for 1 minute. Wrap in clingfilm and rest for 1 hour before using (or up to 3–4 hours).
5 Cut the dough into 2 pieces. Dust your work surface with semolina flour, then flatten each piece of dough with a rolling pin to 5 mm/¼ in thickness.
6 Once cut, the pasta can be frozen. Alternatively, blanch in small amounts in boiling salted water for 20–30 seconds, drain, and refresh in cold water.
7 Drain well, toss in olive oil, cover and keep in the fridge for up to 48 hours.
8 To serve, plunge into boiling salted water for about 2–2½ minutes, drain and serve as required.

breadcrumbs

ingredients
4 or 5 slices stale white
  bread

method

1 For fresh crumbs, cut the crusts off the bread and discard. Rip the remaining bread into chunks and toss into a food processor. Pulse for a few seconds, then blitz until they are broken down into breadcrumbs.
2 For dry crumbs, cut the crusts off the bread and discard. Dry the bread in a low oven or leave in a warm place until hard then blitz in batches in a food processor.
3 If storing breadcrumbs, place in zip lock bags and freeze for up to 4 months.

Nick says Use dried breadcrumbs when you want a fine crust on something and fresh ones when a thicker crust is required.

shortcrust pastry

makes **enough for one 25 cm/10 in flan/tart**

ingredients
110 g/4 oz butter
280 g/10 oz plain flour
large pinch of salt
1½ large eggs, beaten

method

1 To make the pastry, rub the butter, flour and salt together in a mixing bowl until the mixture has the consistency of fine breadcrumbs. Add the egg and bring it all together into a dough. Knead this lightly 3 or 4 times with floured hands.
2 Cover in clingfilm and refrigerate for an hour before use.
3 Preheat the oven to 200°C/400°F/gas mark 6. See page 88 for our step-by-step guide to blind baking.
4 Use immediately, or store in an air-tight container in the fridge for up to 48 hours. Alternatively, these can be frozen for 3–6 months.

yorkshire pudding batter

makes **12**

ingredients
120 g/4 oz plain white flour
4 large eggs (210 g/7½ oz)
110 ml/3¾ fl oz milk
110 ml/3¾ fl oz water
about 300 ml/10 fl oz beef dripping or duck fat (see p247)

Maldon salt and freshly ground black pepper

method

1 See the technique for making batter on page 90. Sift the flour and salt into a large bowl and add the eggs. Beat really well until the mix hangs from the whisk in long elastic strings with no sign of any lumps. Mix the milk and water together and gradually add to the mix, whisking until smooth. Cover and leave in a cool place for at least 15 minutes, or up to 6 hours. Refrigerate if keeping longer than half an hour, bring back to room temperature before using, and whisk well.
2 Preheat the oven to 220°C/425°F/gas mark 7.
3 To cook the puds, use either beef dripping or duck fat. Add 2 tablespoons of fat to each segment of a twelve-hole deep bun tin. Place the tin on the top shelf of the oven and heat for a couple of minutes until the fat is smoking hot – this is very important.
4 Put on oven gloves and remove the tin carefully from the oven. It will be scorching hot by now. Working quickly, use a jug or small ladle to pour the batter into the bun tins, filling each segment to the top. The batter will immediately cling to the sides and start rising. If it doesn't, your fat isn't hot enough so stop, tip out the batter and reheat the tin and fat until smoking hot.
5 Return the tin to the oven and cook for about 20 minutes until well risen. Turn the oven down to 150°C/300°F/gas mark 2. Turn the Yorkies upside down in their bun tin, or tip out into a roasting tin and return to the oven to cook for another 10–12 minutes, allowing them to dry out and firm up.
6 These are best eaten immediately, or keep at room temperature for up to 2 hours and reheat.

basic recipes

scotch pancakes

makes **about 12 pancakes**

ingredients
75 g/2¾ self-raising flour
1 teaspoon baking powder
50 g/1¾ oz granulated sugar
1 egg, whisked
150 ml/5 fl oz milk

basic recipes

method
1 Sift the flour and baking powder into a bowl and stir in the sugar. Whisk the egg and stir it into the dry ingredients – it is very important that you don't beat it in.
2 Now whisk in enough milk to give a batter the same consistency as thick double cream.
3 Heat a smooth, cast iron griddle (*girdle* in Scotland), or heavy frying pan over a medium–high heat. Test the heat by sprinkling the griddle with a little flour. If it browns straight away it is too hot. If it takes a few seconds before it browns then it's perfect.
4 Drop 3 large tablespoons of batter spaced a little apart, onto the griddle. When bubbles appear over the tops of the pancakes and they are golden brown underneath (about 2 minutes), flip them over using a palette knife and cook for another 2 minutes until golden brown on the other side.
5 Lift them onto a plate and cover with a clean tea towel or napkin and keep warm while you cook the rest. Best eaten fresh, these can be cooled and stored in an air-tight container for up to 3 days or frozen for up to 1 month.

muffin mix

makes **12 small or 6 large muffins**

ingredients
10 g/¼ oz unsalted butter, for greasing
250 g/9 oz plain flour
125 g/4½ oz caster sugar
1 tablespoon baking powder
½ teaspoon Maldon salt
1 egg
125 ml/4 fl oz milk, plus a little extra
50 ml/2 fl oz sunflower oil

method
1 Preheat the oven to 180°C/350°F/gas mark 4.
2 Grease a twelve-cup muffin tin with butter or place a paper case in each muffin cup.
3 Sift together the dry ingredients – flour, sugar, baking powder and salt, into a large bowl (or prepare the mix the day before and store in a plastic bag).
4 Whisk the egg in another large bowl and whisk in the milk and oil. Add the dry ingredients and stir just to blend. The mixture should look very rough and lumpy, but with no floury pockets.
5 Spoon into the prepared muffin cups, filling them ¾ full.
6 Bake for about 20 minutes or until well-risen and golden brown.
7 Remove from the oven and turn the tray upside down onto a cooling rack. Leave for 2 minutes for the steam to loosen the muffins.
8 Lift off the tray and turn the muffins the right way up.
9 Serve warm, or cool and store in an air-tight container for up to 3 days. They'll also freeze for up to 1 month.

Nick says This is a basic muffin mix. If you are looking to add flavourings, fold them in at the end of stage 4.

sweet shortcrust pastry

makes **enough for 1 x 25 cm/10 in flan/tart**

ingredients
125 g/4½ oz unsalted butter
50 g/1¾ oz caster sugar
pinch of Maldon salt
250 g/9 oz plain flour
1 medium egg yolk

method

1 Cream the butter, sugar and salt at a medium speed in a table top food mixer. When light and fluffy, add 50 g/1¾ oz flour. With the mixer on a lower speed, add the egg yolk and the remaining flour a tablespoon at a time. When the flour is fully incorporated, add 1 tablespoon of cold water and mix for a further 15 seconds.

2 Remove the bowl from the mixer, tip the dough onto a floured worktop and, with floured hands, gently knead it 3 or 4 times until it comes together. Wrap it in clingfilm and let it rest in the fridge for at least 3 hours before you roll it out.

3 Preheat the oven to 200°C/400°F/gas mark 6.

4 See page 88 for our step-by-step guide to blind baking. Use immediately, or store in an air-tight container in the fridge for up to 48 hours. Alternatively, these can be frozen for 3–6 months.

tuile biscuits

makes **8-10 biscuits/cones/cups**

ingredients
50 g/1¾ oz caster sugar
50 g/1¾ oz plain flour
2 egg whites
50 g/1¾ oz melted butter,
  plus extra for greasing

method

1 Preheat the oven to 180°C/350°F/gas mark 4.

2 Put the caster sugar, flour and egg white into a bowl and beat together to a smooth paste. Beat in the melted butter and then cover and chill in the fridge for 20 minutes.

3 To make shapes, drop about 4 teaspoons of the mixture spaced well apart on a lightly greased Silpat (see page 52) or directly on to a lightly greased non-stick baking tray.

4 Spread the mixture very thinly into circles approximately 13 cm/5 in round. Put the Silpat, if using, on a baking tray and bake for 6–8 minutes until lightly coloured in the centre with a rich golden edge.

5 Remove from the oven and leave to cool for a few seconds. Then, working as quickly as you can, lift each one off the baking sheet with a palette knife and roll into your preferred shape, I find cones, cups and cigar shapes work well. Leave to cool and harden.

6 Any extra ones can be kept in an air-tight container in the fridge for up to 1 week or can be frozen for up to 2 months.

Nick says If you're making these for the first time, bake two at a time until you become more confident at shaping them.

brandy snaps

ingredients
125 g/4½ oz unsalted butter,
   softened
200 g/7 oz icing sugar, sifted
100 g/3½ oz golden syrup
100 g/3½ oz plain white flour

basic recipes

method
1 Cream the butter and sugar together until pale
  and creamy, beat in the syrup then fold in the
  flour. Cover and rest in the fridge for 24 hours.
2 Preheat the oven to 200°C/400°F/gas mark 6.
3 When ready to bake, pinch off walnut sized
  pieces and shape/roll into small balls. Place these
  on a baking tray, spacing them well apart and
  flatten with the palm of your hand.
4 Bake until golden brown, remove the tray from
  the oven, cool slightly until they will happily be
  lifted off the tray without falling to bits – test
  with the tip of a palette knife. Form as required
  by draping over an oiled rolling pin to form tuiles,
  roll gently to form cigars or drape over an
  upturned cup to form baskets.
5 If the biscuits start to harden before you've
  shaped them, pop back into the oven for a
  minute until they soften up a bit.
6 These are best served as soon as possible, as
  they're difficult to store and can go soft very
  quickly if left out in the damp.

Nick says Here too, if you're making these for the first time,
bake two at a time until you become more confident at
shaping them.

vanilla ice cream base

makes **about 700 ml/1¼ pint**

ingredients
300 ml/10 fl oz full fat milk
300 ml/10 fl oz double cream
1 vanilla pod, split, seeds
   scraped out and reserved
30 g/1 oz liquid glucose
5 egg yolks
about 90 g/3¼ oz caster
   sugar

method
1 Put the milk, cream and vanilla pod into a
  saucepan and bring to the boil. (Leave out the
  vanilla at this stage if you are planning to flavour
  the ice cream with anything else.)
2 Remove from the heat, stir in the glucose and
  cover the pan. Leave to infuse for 15 minutes.
  In a stainless steel bowl, beat the egg yolks and
  sugar together with a balloon whisk until the
  mixture becomes thick, fluffy and pale.
3 Reheat the milk and cream mix until boiling, and
  add the hot mix to the eggs. Then follow steps
  4–7 of the technique given for making custard
  (see page 95).
4 When strained into a clean bowl, cover the
  mixture and cool. To cool quickly, place the bowl
  in an ice bath or in cold water and stir until cold.
5 Pour into an ice cream machine and churn until
  frozen, then transfer to a suitable chilled
  container and store in the freezer until needed.
  This is best if eaten within 3 days, but will keep
  for up to 1 month.

John says If you partially defrost ice cream then re-freeze it,
you're increasing the risk of cross contamination by bacteria,
so only take enough out the freezer for immediate use and
don't attempt to re-freeze melted ice cream.

stock syrup

makes **1.25 litres/2¼ pints**

ingredients
1 kg/2 lb 4 oz granulated
   sugar
1 litre/1¾ pint water

method
1 Put the sugar and water in a medium-size
   saucepan, place on a medium heat and slowly
   bring to the boil, stirring from time to time.
2 Once all the sugar is dissolved, simmer for
   5 minutes before skimming off any impurities
   that may have risen to the surface.
3 Stir in any flavourings, such as vanilla, lemon zest
   and juice, orange zest and juice etc, and leave
   to cool.

Nick says This keeps for 8 weeks in the fridge, so you can
make it well in advance and always have it handy. Stock syrups
are used in many desserts (and cocktails), for example added
to a caramel to create a light caramel.

cook school custard

serves **8**

ingredients
150 ml/5 fl oz full fat milk
150 ml/5 fl oz double cream
1 vanilla pod, split, seeds
   scraped out and reserved
3 egg yolks
30 g/1 oz caster sugar

method
1 See the technique for this on page 94. Place the
   milk, cream and vanilla pod and seeds into a heavy-
   based pan and place on a high heat until boiling. In
   a stainless steel bowl, beat the egg yolks and
   sugar together with a balloon whisk until the
   mixture becomes thick, fluffy and pale.
2 Add the hot mix to the eggs. When stirring make
   sure that you cover the whole pan by stirring in a
   figure of eight rather than round and round.
3 The mixture should begin to thicken within about
   2 minutes. You're looking for a temperature of
   82°C/180°F, and a thermometer will prove
   invaluable. If you don't have a probe, watch for
   little puffs of steam escaping from the side
   of the pan. These are a warning sign that the
   custard is getting too hot, so take the pan off
   the heat and continue stirring.
4 When the mix has thickened enough to coat the
   back of the spatula, take off the heat and strain
   immediately through a fine sieve to remove any
   small lumps which may have formed.
5 Serve immediately, or store for up to 3 hours in a
   vacuum flask that's been preheated with boiling
   water. To cool, pour into a clean bowl, cover with
   clingfilm (touching the surface to avoid a skin
   forming) and chill in an ice bath. Keep in the fridge
   and use as soon as possible. Do not reheat.

Nick says This recipe makes quite a large quantity of
custard, but it's awkward to make it in smaller amounts.

basic recipes

caramel sauce

makes **about 700 ml/1¼ pints**

ingredients
375 g/13 oz caster sugar
500 ml/18 fl oz double cream

basic recipes

method
1 Before attempting this recipe for the first time, read through the step-by-step technique on page 96. Then when you're ready to go ahead, put some rubber gloves on, as boiling sugar can give a nasty burn and is almost impossible to remove if it drips onto the skin.
2 Heat a heavy-based pan (about 18–20 cm/7–8 in diameter) over a medium heat, allowing it to warm for 3–4 minutes.
3 Add the sugar to the pan and follow the instructions in the step by step guide until you have a pale caramel. When it's ready, the sugar will give off a distinctive smell of caramel.
4 Keep on the heat and carefully begin to stir in the cream. It's important to stir the pan as you do this to release the superheated steam, but be very careful as the pan will start to bubble and splutter the moment you add liquid. Add the cream in splashes of about 50 ml/2 fl oz. If you add too much at once, you'll get lumps of caramel. Too little and the mix may start to burn.
5 When ready, the sauce can be served hot or cold, but if kept warm, be careful not to let the sauce become too thick (a little water can be added if needed) otherwise you may end up serving toffee! Or for convenience, cool and pour into a squeezy sauce bottle, reheating if required, in the microwave or in a bowl of hot water. Caramel sauce will keep for up to a week in the fridge, and can also be frozen for up to three months.

passion fruit sauce

serves **4-6**

ingredients
24 fresh ripe passion fruit
50 g/1¾ oz caster sugar

method
1 Cut the passion fruit in half and scoop out all the pulp and seeds into a sieve placed over a medium-sized pan.
2 Press the pulp and juice through the sieve into the pan and add the sugar. Rinse the seeds left behind and set aside. Stir the juice over a medium heat until all the sugar has dissolved.
3 Carefully bring the mixture to the boil – it will thicken up quite a bit due to the amount of pectin in the fruit. Add the reserved seeds back into the sauce and stir through.
4 Cool, cover and chill until needed. This will keep in the fridge for up to 7 days or freeze and keep for up to 3 months.

Nick says This is fab with Pavlova or ice cream.

mango sauce

serves **6-8**

ingredients

1 large fresh ripe mango
3-4 tablespoons stock syrup
  (see p271)
finely grated zest and juice
  of 1 lime

or

425 g/15 oz tin sliced
  mangoes in syrup
  (Alphonso are best)
finely grated zest and juice
  of 1 lime

basic recipes

method

1 Place the mango on a chopping board and cut a
  thin slice off the top and bottom to allow it to
  sit up on the board.
2 Use a sharp knife to peel away the skin or, if it's
  not too ripe, you can use a peeler. You will now
  have a skinless mango.
3 Cut down vertically on either side of the stone,
  which runs lengthways, and then pare away the
  remaining mango left clinging to the stone.
4 Cut into cubes and blitz in a blender with the
  stock syrup until smooth. Add the lime zest and
  juice, to taste.
5 Thin with extra syrup if required. This will keep
  in the fridge for 3 days, or freeze for up to
  3 months.

method 2

1 Drain the tin of sliced mangoes and reserve the
  syrup.
2 Place the mangoes in a blender and blitz to a
  purée with 3–4 tablespoons of the reserved
  syrup.
3 Transfer to a bowl and stir in the lime zest and
  juice to taste. This will keep for up to 3 days in
  the fridge, or will freeze for up to 3 months.

Nick says The lime juice will help to bring out the full flavour
of the mango. You could also make this sauce with paw paw
instead of mango.

raspberry sauce

makes **about 200 ml/½ pint**

ingredients

350 g/12 oz fresh or frozen
  raspberries
25 g/1 oz icing sugar, or
  more to taste
1 tablespoon freshly
  squeezed lemon juice

method

1 Place the raspberries, icing sugar and lemon
  juice into a blender and whizz for 45 seconds.
2 Pour this through a fine sieve into a bowl, cover
  and refrigerate before using. This will keep for
  up to 3 days in the fridge, or 3 months in the
  freezer.
3 An alternative method is to pour the sugar over
  the raspberries and lemon juice and leave for
  20 minutes before forcing the mix through a fine
  sieve. This avoids splitting the raspberry seeds,
  which can make the sauce bitter.

John says Heating the raspberries just until the juices start
to flow gives the sauce extra vibrancy and flavour.

bitter chocolate sauce

makes **about 150 ml/5 fl oz**

ingredients
6 tablespoons double cream
4 tablespoons cocoa powder,
  sifted
4 tablespoons caster sugar
2 tablespoons mild honey or
  golden syrup

method
1 Whisk all the ingredients together in a saucepan
  and warm through, stirring constantly to create
  a smooth dark sauce.
2 Serve immediately, or chill quickly. This will keep in
  the fridge for up to 1 week.

quick and easy chocolate sauce

makes **about 200 ml/7 fl oz**

ingredients
100 ml/3½ fl oz whole milk
125 g/4½ oz dark chocolate
  (60% cocoa solids, see
  p41), grated

method
1 Heat the milk and chocolate together gently in
  a saucepan, stirring until the chocolate has
  melted. Do not allow the milk to boil. Serve
  immediately, this won't keep!

rich and glossy chocolate sauce

makes **about 250 ml/9 fl oz**

ingredients
1½ tablespoons mild runny
  honey
130 ml/4½ fl oz water
175 g/6 oz dark chocolate
  (60% cocoa solids see p41),
  grated
45 g/1½ oz unsalted butter
75 ml/2½ fl oz double cream

method
1 Put the honey in a medium saucepan with the
  water, chocolate, butter and double cream.
2 Heat gently, stirring every now and then until the
  chocolate is smooth and melted, but do not boil.
3 Keep warm and serve. Or chill quickly and
  refrigerate for up to 1 week.

glossary

al dente – literally 'to the tooth'. When cooking pasta, the term describes a yielding yet still slightly chewy texture.

bake – cook in an oven with no liquid.

bain-marie – a double boiler, usually a small pan sitting inside a larger pan of water. Traditionally used to keep food warm, but now mainly used for gentle cooking and melting chocolate.

baste – pour or spoon hot liquid over an ingredient, usually roasting meat, to keep it succulent while cooking.

blanch – place food in boiling water or oil for a set time before removing and cooling quickly (see also refresh).

blind baking – bake pastry, especially tart cases, before adding the filling.

boil – bring a liquid to the point where bubbles appear on the surface and evaporation begins. In an ordinary saucepan, water boils at 100°C/212°F and you won't get it hotter than that without using a pressure cooker. It's a waste of energy trying to heat it further.

braise – slow cook in a sealed pan with a small amount of liquid.

brown – cook foods until they begin to caramelise and change colour.

caramelise – term used by chefs to describe the process by which high temperatures cause the breakdown of complex sugars in food into new flavours and aromas, such as in the browning of meat or vegetables or melting sugar to create a caramel.

clarify – make something like a stock or butter clear, usually through heating and skimming. Classically, mixtures like broths were clarified by whisking in a protein, especially egg whites, which would attract small particles and then settle in a sort of crust on the surface.

concassé – a method of preparing vegetables, particularly tomatoes, by peeling, deseeding and dicing.

confit – French term to describe foods that have been preserved, most commonly used to describe meats slow cooked in their own fat, like duck legs.

creaming – process by which dry ingredients are thoroughly mixed with eggs or butter to create a smooth result and incorporate air.

cure – process by which foods are preserved through the addition of salt and often sugar, either with a wet cure (brine) or a dry cure.

Curing is commonly carried out before smoking or air drying, eg with salmon or bacon.

curdle – separation into liquid and solids (lumps) that occurs particularly with dairy products, like milk, and sauces such as custard (see also split).

dariole mould – small metal container used to prepare desserts etc.

deglaze – process by which liquids such as wine are added to a cooking pan (e.g. a frying pan after cooking a steak) and then scraped or mixed around to dissolve all the caramelised solids left in the pan, usually for the creation of a sauce or gravy.

dice – cut into cubes or cuboids of various sizes.

dropping consistency – the consistency at which a liquid mix (e.g. batter) clings to a spoon but will drop off with a gentle shake.

eggwash – mix of egg and either water or milk, brushed onto bread or pastry before baking to produce a shiny or brown crust.

emulsion – sauce etc produced by distributing tiny droplets of fat (invisible to the naked eye) throughout another liquid and fixing them so that it feels silky in the mouth, mayonnaise being the most famous example (see also split).

flake – break up food (especially fish) into small pieces.

fold – mixing technique using a metal spoon or spoonula to add a light ingredient to a heavy one. Wooden spoons have a blunt edge which tends to knock air out of the mix.

glaze – a shiny coating on sweet or savoury food. A glaze can either be added or built up during cooking, often by basting.

glaze consistency – used to describe a reduced sauce that has had all the liquid evaporated, leaving a sauce with an almost honey-like consistency.

infuse – steep something in a liquid, most often hot or boiling, to draw out the flavour.

julienne – cut ingredients, most commonly vegetables, into long strips.

jus – thickened and enriched stock.

knead – process by which doughs are worked before cooking to improve the texture.

lardons – little cubes of pancetta or bacon. Also, strips of bacon fat.

let down – thin, particularly a sauce.

macerate – to soften an ingredient, especially fruit, by soaking in liquid. The liquid is usually sweet, and may be flavoured.

marinate – process of soaking an ingredient in a liquid, which often includes wine or vinegar, oil and spices. The liquid is called a marinade. The purpose of marinating is to impart flavour, but the acid in the wine or vinegar also has a tenderising effect on ingredients such as meat.

mise en place – literally 'set in place', the organisation and pre-preparation that chefs carry out before cooking a dish.

parcook – partially cook an ingredient or dish. The cooking process is usually finished just before serving. If parboiling (partially cooking in boiling water), remove from the water when desired and refresh immediately to stop the cooking process.

pass – purée by forcing a sauce etc through a fine sieve, usually a chinois, using the back of a ladle, spoon or a spatula.

poach – process of cooking food in hot, but not simmering, water or stock.

purée – turning solid foods to smooth paste or liquid through chopping, mashing or grinding.

reduce – evaporate off liquid in a sauce, gravy or stock through boiling, usually to intensify the flavour. The resulting liquid is sometimes called a reduction.

refresh – plunge freshly cooked produce, often vegetables, into cold or iced water to stop the cooking process. Or freshen limp salad leaves etc in iced water.

relax – allowing meat, dough, pastry and other dishes to stand after or before cooking.

roast – usually refers to an ingredient cooked in an oven with oil.

rolling boil – when water or another liquid reaches a constant vigorous boil, with lots of bubbles rising up to the surface.

roux – mix of flour and butter used as a base for white sauce.

sauté – cook food in a little fat, over a high heat, for a short period of time. Generally the food is kept moving and the wide, shallow pan used called a sauté. Sautés often have sauces created from the juices left in the pan.

season (1) – enhance the flavour of a dish, commonly by adding salt and pepper, but also sometimes with hot, sweet, salty and sour flavourings such as chilli, honey, Thai fish sauce, and lemon juice.

season (2) – the process of preparing a pan for first use. Wash well, then heat gently on the hob. Add vegetable oil and carefully rub it over the inside of the pan with paper towel. Repeat this process until the paper towel comes away clean. Don't scrub a pan that's been seasoned, wash with plain water only.

shuck – remove shellfish meat such as scallops or oysters from their shells.

simmer – heat a liquid so that it's just boiling. Bubbles will appear on the surface, but these will be disrupted if you stir the pan.

skim – remove unwanted substances, often fat, from the top of a liquid using a spoon or ladle.

split – when the tiny fat droplets in an emulsion come out of suspension and join back together, making the sauce greasy. It will look oily on the surface instead of glossy.

steep – see infuse.

stock syrup – usually a mix of equal parts of water and sugar, e.g. 1 kg sugar to 1 litre of water.
sugar syrup – see stock syrup.

weat – soften an ingredient, often vegetables, without colour, in a lidded pan over a low heat with a little oil or butter. This releases the sugars but doesn't allow caramelisation.

top and tail – slice off a small segment from the top and bottom of ingredients, such as vegetables.

unmould – take something (particularly a dessert) out of its mould.

zest – the skin of citrus fruits, notably oranges, lemons and limes. Grated finely, it can be added for flavour.

index

287

index

acknowledgements

This book just would not have happened without the totally invaluable input and help from the wonderfully talented team here at the Cook School. So, firstly a huge thanks to John Webber and Alan Mathieson for their support, enthusiasm and knowledge. Also to Alan for the cracking food styling – top work mate! Next up thanks to Jenny for translating my ramblings into print. To Nadine, our General Manager for rescuing us all from meltdown and my PA Julia for her good humour and organisation. Maxine Clark, my long time friend and collaborator for always being at the end of the phone. Outside of the school, huge thanks go the Francesca Yorke for her understanding and most of all her truly stunning photography. Last but not least Laura Price for having faith, not to mention her truly extraordinary patience and dedication to the project, and Jo Wilson at Cassell Illustrated for pulling everything together at the end.

suppliers

Nick Nairn Cook School
Port of Menteith, Stirling
FK8 3JZ, 01877 389900
www.nicknairncookschool.com

Meat, Game and Poultry
Caleyco
tel: 01573 227 310
www.caleyco.com

The Aberfoyle Butcher
2 Main St, Aberfoyle FK8 3UQ,
tel: 01877 382473
www.aberfoylebutcher.co.uk

Burnside Farm Foods
Kelso, Scottish Borders, TD5 8NR,
tel: 01573 229890

Charles McLeod
Ropework Park, Stornoway, Isle
of Lewis HS1 2LB,
tel: 01851 702445
www.charlesmacleod.co.uk

Crombies Butcher
97 Broughton Street, Edinburgh
EH1 3RZ
tel: 0131 557 0111
www.sausages.co.uk

Fletchers of Auchtermuchty
Reediehill Deer Farm,
Auchtermuchty, Fife KY14 7HS,
tel: 01337 828 369
www.seriouslygoodvenison.co.uk

Macsweens of Edinburgh
Dryden Road, Bilston Glen,
Loanhead Edinburgh, EH20 9LZ
tel: 0131 440 2555,
www.macsween.co.uk
Simply the best haggis around.

Ramsay of Carluke
22 Mount Stewart Street,
Carluke, Lanarkshire ML8 5ED
tel: 01555 772277
www.ramsayofcarluke.co.uk

Puddledub Pork & Fifeshire Bacon
Co.Ltd
Clentrie Farmhouse, Auchtertool,
Kirkcaldy, Fife, KY2 5XG
www.puddledub.co.uk

Rannoch Smokery
Kinloch Rannoch, Pitlochry Tayside
PH16 5QD
tel: 01882 632344
www.rannochsmokery.co.uk

Fish and shellfish
Keltic Seafare (Scotland),
Unit 6 Strathpeffer Industrial
Estate, Dingwall IV15 9SP
tel: 01349 864087
www.kelticseafere.com

Salar
The Pier, Lochcarnan, South Uist,
Outer Hebrides, HS8 5PD
tel: 01870 610324
www.salar.co.uk

R. R. Spink and Sons,
33-35 Seagate, Arbroath, Tayside
DD1 1BJ
tel: 01241 872023
www.rrspink.com

Griggs of Hythe
The Fisherman's Landing Beach,
Range Rd, Hythe, Kent CT21 6HG.
www.griggsofhythe.com

Cheeses
I J Mellis
492 Great Western Road,
Glasgow G12 8EN
tel: 0141 339 8998
and stores in Glasgow, Edinburgh
and St Andrews.
www.ijmellischeesemonger.com